IT'S NOT RAINING, DADDY, IT'S HAPPY

Benjamin Brooks-Dutton

IT'S NOT RAINING, DADDY, IT'S HAPPY

HODDER &
STOUGHTON

First published in Great Britain in 2014 by
Hodder & Stoughton
An Hachette UK company

1

At the time of going to press, no decision had yet been taken on whether the driver of the car that hit Desreen, or anyone else, should face any criminal charges in connection with the incident.

Permission for Appendix kindly granted by © Care for the Family. Care for the Family is one of the UK's leading family-issues charities and provides seminars, training courses, resources and support networks to strengthen family life and support those facing family difficulties. Find out more at: www.careforthefamily.org.uk

Man and Boy, Tony Parsons (HarperCollins, 1999). Copyright © Tony Parsons, 1999

A CIP catalogue record for this title is available from the British Library

Hardback ISBN 978 1 444 75477 3
Trade paperback ISBN 978 1 444 79539 4
Ebook ISBN 978 1 444 75476 6

Typeset in Sabon MT by Palimpsest Book Production Limited, Falkirk, Stirlingshire

Printed and bound by Clays Ltd, St Ives plc

Hodder & Stoughton policy is to use papers that are natural, renewable and recyclable products and made from wood grown in sustainable forests. The logging and manufacturing processes are expected to conform to the environmental regulations of the country of origin.

Hodder & Stoughton Ltd
338 Euston Road
London NW1 3BH

www.hodder.co.uk

DEDICATION

I wrote this book to honour the memory of my beautiful wife's past and I dedicate it to my beloved son's future.

Jackson, although you were only two years old when your mum was taken from you, I will never let you forget what an incredible woman she was. One day I hope this book will help you to understand what a profound impact you had on me throughout the darkest days of my life.

Sometimes we are only aware of how happy we are when the moment has passed. But now and again, if we are very lucky, we are aware of happiness when it is actually happening.

Tony Parsons, *Man and Boy*

INTRODUCTION

On 10 November 2012 my life changed forever. Just after 8.00p.m. I left my friends' house a happily married thirty-three-year-old father. By 9.17p.m. I was sitting in an ambulance on their street, a widower in shock. I only remember the time because I noticed that the hands on the clock were in the same position as when our son was born two years and three weeks before.

My son and I managed to narrowly dodge the car that killed the woman I'd loved for the last eight years. The woman I'd married just the year before. It killed a wife; a daughter; a sister; a friend treasured by so many. But perhaps worst of all, it killed a toddler's beautiful and devoted mummy.

How do you even begin to pick up the pieces after such a tragic loss? This question plagued me. I found myself wanting to share my experiences and find answers from people just like me, widowed young and caring for grieving children. My search for those people seemed fruitless. It just made me feel even more isolated.

'I'm thinking about starting a blog about losing Dessie,' I told a friend. 'It worries me that I'm finding so little out there to help men left alone raising kids.'

'Just do it!' he responded, immediately understanding my intentions.

So on 7 January 2013, two months after the death of my wife, Desreen Brooks, I published my first blog post. Within a week the *Guardian* asked me to write a feature, for its Family supplement, about my experience in helping my two-year-old son understand what had happened to his mum. I was also interviewed on *BBC Breakfast* and ITV's *This Morning* on the same subject. Within four months the blog generated widespread media coverage, amassed a devoted UK and international audience, received in excess of half a million views and won a blogging award for making people sit up and pay attention to an issue that could, ultimately, touch any parent.

My original intention was to try to encourage other men to open up, to challenge perceptions of male grief and to attempt to force a reappraisal of the stiff upper lip being a badge of honour when it comes to loss. The blog, however, attracted people from different walks of life united in their own immediate loss, or by their care and concern for grieving loved ones.

All sorts of people started to get in touch: women and not just men; old not just young; people who had lost their husbands or wives within a week of my son and me losing Desreen; parents who had lost children; partners who had not yet started grieving because their terminally ill husbands or wives were still finding the strength to hang on; teachers who had found some suggestions for how to deal with children who had lost or were facing loss; and people wanting to understand how to help their own loved ones suffering the pain of bereavement.

My aim is to give a real insight into raw and live grief. I've documented everything as it happened. I decided I needed to start writing soon after my wife died because of an analogy that one day popped into my head: if women could remember every ache and pain of labour, perhaps none would have more than one child. Human beings' capacity to forget pain is enormous, and in many ways that is a good and necessary thing. Morbid as it may sound, though, it filled me with dread to imagine that I would ever forget the agony of my loss. I was even more worried that I might not be able to explain it to my son when he was old enough to start asking serious questions.

This book is about the journey that my son and I have been on. I've seen the world of grief through the eyes of both adults and children. We've gained invaluable insights into heartbreak, parenting and living with loss, and we've picked up priceless lessons along the way. I've learned more from a small child, my son Jackson, than any grown-up has ever been able to teach me.

I truly hope that in opening up about our experiences, we can help other people who are either suffering the pain of loss or attempting to help their friends and family through it.

WINTER

THAT NIGHT

Desreen was taken from us without any warning.

We had just spent the most perfect day with our son, Jackson, and two of our closest friends, Zac and Laura. I've never been one to rose-tint the past because some of my favourite times with Desreen had their imperfections, but this day really did hold everything she loved. In fact, she'd even commented on how happy she was in the company of her husband, child and friends.

She'd spent time doing what she called 'being creative' at an arts café, joyfully painting mugs and pencil pots for her new office, which she'd thrown herself into refurbishing. We'd all laughed at how determined Jackson was to throw paint at her 'art' rather than concentrate on his own little project. He wanted to steal her attention away from her piece of pottery, because he adored her and hated to share her. Later, she had let the rest of us cook while she, as always, sat looking on, chatting and drinking Prosecco, because kitchens bored her. She'd taught Jackson to dance to Bill Hayley's 'Rock Around the Clock' and she'd told Zac, whom she knew from university and whose home we were visiting, that although she didn't call him that much anymore, she wanted him to know how much she loved him.

Other friends joined us for dinner and after eating, we said our goodbyes and made our way up the stairs out of the basement flat and onto the pavement of West End Lane in West Hampstead. At just two years old, Jackson was a feisty little boy who never got into his pushchair without causing a fuss. Once Desreen and I finally managed to strap down our convulsing toddler, we both looked at each other and laughed. Beaten again, but not without putting up a decent fight.

'I don't mind,' she said. 'He's been so good today, so much fun. I'm so proud of him.' And those were the last words she ever spoke.

I took the pushchair and began to walk down the street towards the train station as my wife followed just a couple of steps behind. I remember reaching for my phone in the inside pocket of my jacket to check for messages then thinking, Leave it, wait until you get on the train. Thank God for small mercies because just as that thought passed through my mind I saw a car come speeding round the corner, the fastest I'd ever seen a car able to manoeuvre through the typically sluggish streets of London. I remember thinking it must be a police chase. Drugs, I mused. I also recall feeling quite detached from it all, as though in a few seconds my wife and I would be talking about how we had never seen anything like it and that we would be cursing the driver's lack of regard for the safety of other human beings.

But then suddenly the car was on the curb. Its lights were right upon us and I had a flash-forward to the car hitting my son, spinning his pushchair into the air and leaving him dead on the road. There's a scene in the film *Speed*, starring Keanu Reeves and Sandra Bullock, where her character is driving a bus that will detonate a bomb if it drops below fifty miles per hour. Horrified, she hits a pram, which she can't avoid. Fortunately in the movie it was just full of cans. I suddenly saw that scene in my head, but in real life it wouldn't be groceries that hit the street – it would be our son. I imagined our screams as we raced to reach him. I imagined our lives being over with his even if we still lived. In my mind, in these crazy few seconds that allowed my brain to process so many thoughts, Desreen and I were never really at risk.

So I reacted on sheer impulse; I found a gap. Fortunately a narrow gate was open and I launched my son's pushchair into the space. In doing so the momentum also forced me out of the car's path, but apparently only just.

As I spun around to check on Desreen I saw she'd been hit and I screamed for help. I let out this noise at a volume I didn't know I had in me. I was like an animal.

'Help me! Help us!' I screamed down the street.

There seemed to be people everywhere but I could only see them staring, immobile.

'Why are you not doing anything?' I roared. 'Why the fuck is no one helping us?'

Doubtless dozens of emergency calls were made immediately. But I was suddenly in a bubble where all I could hear was my own voice and all I could see were blurred faces, street lights and my wife lying on the floor – her eyes open but lifeless-looking.

Otherwise she looked perfect. She'd been hit by a car but she looked exactly the same, no scratches, no visible breakages, she was just lying there still on the pavement. It was her eyes and mouth that scared me, though. They were both open but they weren't looking at me or talking to me. They weren't scared or in pain or peaceful. They were just open.

Within seconds an ambulance turned the corner. It hadn't been called to the scene; it just happened to be passing and pulled straight over. I threw myself at it begging for help. In my fear-induced short-sightedness I didn't know that another girl had been struck and also desperately needed help or that the driver of the car had crashed into a wall and needed attention, too. All I knew was that my wife, my son's mother, was lying motionless on the pavement in the cold – in the dark.

'Someone please help us!' I screamed again.

Then, suddenly, a young woman was by her side.

'Don't move her,' I shouted, convinced by watching so many medical dramas that moving her might leave her paralysed. But this woman was a doctor in the right place at the right time. Before I knew it there were more besides.

By this time the street was full. My son was still in his pushchair, facing away from the carnage. I couldn't let him see me because he would know something was really wrong. I knew he would be scared at the sight of a face so familiar but also so immediately changed, so contorted in distress. I asked the people around me to check if he was okay.

'He's fine, he's fine,' female voices with no faces reassured me.

I ran to our friends, who by now were out on the street, and asked them to take Jackson inside. The look on Zac's face crushed me. He looked as if he knew she was going to die, when I was too shocked and confused to know anything.

Laura provided the voice of reassurance. 'It's okay, it's okay, she's going to be fine,' she told us both.

The paramedics and passing doctors were performing CPR on Desreen, which is never a sign that someone is *fine*.

I squeezed my head in my hands, pulled at my hair, rubbed my eyes fiercely and screamed and screamed, stamping my feet like a toddler who hasn't yet got the vocabulary to express himself.

The ambulance that just happened to be passing didn't have all of the equipment that the paramedics needed and I could hear the medics chatting quietly about what was missing.

'Tell me what you need and I'll get it,' I wailed, frustrated as hell that it all seemed so casual, like just another day in the office. They needed some kind of pump to empty her stomach so I ran to one of the other ambulances and screamed for help.

'There are other people who need help here too, sir,' one paramedic said to me.

'Yes, but the other people aren't my wife and they don't have a toddler sitting inside that house while his mum is dying in the street. Just give me a fucking pump,' I shouted at him. I ran back with it and handed it to the people trying to save Desreen, who set it to work straight away.

I don't know the timings. I've no idea how long they worked on her but I do remember the most unexpected thoughts passing through my head, my brain totally fucked up from what my eyes were witnessing.

She'll be fucking livid they cut that sweater off her, I thought, as the paramedics tried anything to stop her from dying.

She'll be so cross when she finds out that she was practically naked in the street with so many people around.

This is why you always have to leave the house in nice underwear, just in case.

Well, I can't imagine I'll make that meeting on Monday.

Thoughts I would eventually feel ashamed of thinking but that I had no control over at the time.

'She's going to be fine,' Laura said again. 'They're putting her on a stretcher to take her to the hospital.'

I felt relief pour over me as I saw the stretcher on the street. But then they came: the words that I didn't think people actually ever said; words that should just be lines you hear on TV.

'There's nothing more we can do for your wife. We did everything we would have done at the hospital.'

A howl erupted out of me. I can't even spell the noise I made and it would look ridiculous on the page if I tried, but it was described as beyond distressing by witnesses. As she was pronounced dead I cried the kind of tears that I'd never cried before, completely unaware of the people looking on.

Somewhere far away I heard Laura, whose dad had been killed in a car crash years before, calmly ask, 'How can this be happening again?' I've never seen a person more composed in such tragic circumstances. Somehow she really had to be there the night my life was torn to pieces. Both Zac and I needed her to help pick us up because we were literally on the floor screaming, praying that we hadn't just heard that Desreen was dead.

Then, suddenly, Laura's sense of composure somehow took hold of me and I straightened up. I started making jokes. I told Zac that there was no excuse for an adult man to have such a disgusting runny nose and passed him a tissue from inside the ambulance that sat useless in the street. Now it was just a place to keep warm rather than a miniature hospital with the potential to save my wife.

I apologised to the police for the fleece blanket someone had draped over me, knowing that my wife would have wanted me in Welsh lambswool. I started making plans. I asked Zac to draw up a list of things that needed to get sorted at the office on Monday because, as well as being close friends, we worked together. I went over to Desreen's body and I told her things were going to be okay and that I'd look after our son. I was in intense shock and I told myself to *be strong.*

The police took my initial statement and then we sat drinking tea in Zac and Laura's flat for what seemed like hours. I needed to be taken home, but I didn't want to go anywhere until I knew that the local Hampshire police had told Desreen's parents about her death. I wouldn't forgive myself if they found out over the phone or if they jumped straight into a car and put themselves at risk by racing to London late at night. The process was delayed because the officer who took the original call was a family friend – a young woman who had known Desreen for years – and she just couldn't face being the one to break the news of her death to her mum, a woman she knew as Auntie Bev. In any case, we couldn't go anywhere until London's Met police located a child car seat so that we could get Jackson home safely.

That night I discovered that when you suffer a trauma and go into shock your body can completely change in an instant. I had to interrupt the brief statement several times to go to the toilet. This lasted for weeks, as did my overwhelming body heat. While others wrapped up warm in November and December, I prayed for colder winter days so I could go out in a T-shirt and cool off.

Once the child seat arrived I had to wake my son from a strange bed to put him into what should have been the car of his dreams, a car that says *Nee nor!* Except he didn't look excited, he looked confused and exhausted. He was usually a chatty little fellow but he simply sat with his head tilted towards mine, holding my hand while I told him that I loved him and that we would be okay. I was high on shock at the time, so what the hell did I know about how we would be?

Imagining that night from a two-year-old boy's point of view, the simple fact is this: when we left our house that day he was with both his parents; when he returned home that night, there was just Daddy. At some point during the evening Mummy had left without saying goodbye.

I know it was past midnight by the time we pulled away from West Hampstead because the label on the transparent plastic bag that contained her belongings reads 23:59. I remember hearing a young couple, returning home arm-in-arm from a night out, tell two officers that they would need to pass the police line to gain access to their house. 'No one's been hurt by the looks of it,' the man reassured his wife or girlfriend.

As we crawled slowly through the streets of London, for some reason I felt the need to chat to the two policemen who drove us home. I couldn't handle the silence that filled the car. I forget the name of the guy in the passenger seat but the officer driving was called Barrington. He'd taken care of me when it was time to say goodbye to Desreen and had hugged me really tightly as I walked away from her body. He reminded me a bit of one of her uncles and judging by the emotion in his face, I couldn't help but wonder if Desreen reminded him of a niece. When I told him my address in East Dulwich he said he knew the area well and so I struck up a conversation by asking him how. It turned out it was his old stomping ground in the Seventies, which made me smile and shake my head a little at the same time. I realised that being married to a black woman had made me no better at identifying the age of a black man – I always pitched them at least ten years younger than they ever turned out to be.

Once home, the police officers helped me into our flat and waited in the hall as I tried to settle Jackson into his bed. I thanked them for everything they had done as I waved them off.

Jackson was restless but I couldn't face lying in bed with him unable to sleep and with my mind racing, so I took him into the living room and comforted him on the sofa. I had asked Zac and Laura to come back and keep us company.

As if it's not confusing enough for a toddler to be driven home one parent down, after midnight, our living room grew fuller the later it became. Desreen's best friends – the self-titled Spice Girls – came over soon after the police dropped us home, which was sometime after 1.00a.m. Marianne was Baby Spice because of the striking resemblance to Emma Bunton, Caroline was Sporty Spice because she was the most active in the group, Anna was Posh Spice simply because she had brown hair and Desreen was Scary Spice for no other reason than the fact they both had dark skin. I never actually met the group's own Ginger Spice but I'm told she left Hampshire's answer to the band around the same time Geri Halliwell decided to go solo. And now they were another member down.

I'm not sure why we all got together that night. It was already so late by the time Desreen's parents found out that she'd been killed but I think her mum, Bev, must have called Caroline's mum, Ethna, to tell her what had happened. Ethna called Caroline and then Caroline was the first person to call me, as Jackson and I were sitting in the back of the police car. I picked up the phone with one hand and spoke quietly while holding Jackson's little hand in the other. He was staring out of the window. Despite the time, I told Caroline that she and the others were welcome to come over if they wanted to be together. It wasn't as though any of us would sleep anyway, and we all lived so close to each other that it felt like the right thing to do.

As they rang the intercom to open the gate that led to our block of flats, I decided to walk downstairs to meet them rather than buzzing them in. It would give me a moment to talk to them without disturbing or confusing Jackson any further. Zac and Laura were taking care of him in the living room. I led everyone up the two flights of stairs to our second-floor flat, and saw a neighbour smoking on her balcony.

'Hi babe,' she said perkily. She'd been out, it was late and it must have seemed as though we were all crawling home from a daylong session that had left us looking like shit. 'Are you okay?' she asked.

I couldn't say the words. My jaw moved and I shook my head

but nothing came out; I couldn't speak. She must have thought I was either out of my head drunk or just damn rude as I closed the door without answering her question.

I guided everyone into Jackson's empty bedroom to finish explaining what had happened. Until that night I'd never seen any of the girls really upset. Marianne usually finishes her sentences with a joke and a cackle and Desreen, Marianne's best friend and number-one fan, was usually in the room laughing along. I was used to hearing Caroline creating some sort of mischief with Des, while she and Anna would compare notes about their vast array of often unlikely anxieties, from pigeons getting stuck in their hair to suicide bombers attacking them in the cinema.

That night Marianne sobbed and asked how this could be happening and the others sat almost in silence. Anna's husband Paul was there too. None of us knew what to say. I offered people drinks: water, tea and Hennessy was all I had. I opted for the cognac because I thought that was what people did at a time like this. My son ate yoghurt and played with his trains, but he did both crossly.

I've no idea how long everyone stayed. Having spent most of our late twenties together at parties or on group holidays to Spain and Ibiza, we had got used to being up until the early hours of the morning. More recently, however, most of us had kids who needed looking after in the mornings. Marianne had given birth to her second daughter, Lucia, only a week before; Desreen met her just once. Marianne's first daughter, Annalise, and Caroline's son, Arlo – two of Jackson's best friends – were left at home with their dads, Olly and Lee.

As they all left I handed Marianne a little hand-knitted woollen dress, which Desreen had bought for Lucia earlier that day. It was the last gift she ever bought. Just a few hours later

Caroline and Lee would find out that they were expecting again, this time twins, who Desreen would neither meet nor even know about.

Eventually I took Jackson to bed, hoping that we'd both wake up relieved that we had just eaten a bit too much cheese the day before. Exhausted, I slept for about an hour before going back downstairs.

I'd asked Zac and Laura to stay and they heard me sobbing on the sofa, so we all got up to face the situation, to tell our family and friends the devastating news and to embark on the first day of our new lives. The lives for which we could never have planned. The lives we would have given anything to avoid.

CHANCE ENCOUNTERS

'You'll never get in tonight,' I explained, 'but we'll be in that bar over there if you want to join us.' They were the first words I spoke to my future wife when we met by chance in the queue for a London nightclub on 17 December 2004.

I had been pretty hacked off just before I laid eyes on her. Having queued for over an hour, Martin, one of the friends I was with that night, decided he'd had enough. He would sweet-talk the guy on the door and get us straight in. Only, the guy in question, who had struck a deal with Martin, promptly disappeared and we were facing the frustration of rejoining a queue that was now half a mile long. 'No way!' I exclaimed, seething that he had messed up our night.

Looking back, something tells me that I wasn't meant to walk though the doors of Fabric that night. I'd had an amazing day already. I'd been at a client Christmas party and I'd won myself and my team thirty bottles of wine and champagne via the tiebreaker in a pub quiz. I'd been on a roll with the answers so I got nominated to represent my group in a single head-to-head pop music question. All I had to do was be the first person to name the song from the lyrics alone.

'In France . . .' the quizmaster began.

'"Sign o' the Times". Prince!' I shouted immediately.

'Fix!' everyone shouted back, dismayed that I could name that tune in just two words.

I began to recite the whole song word for word and said I'd be happy to continue performing it if there was any further doubt. My team and I revelled in our glory. The combination of winning, Prince – who I love – and spending the day eating and drinking on someone else's tab made a twenty-five-year-old guy without much money in his pocket think that things couldn't get any better. Then I thought of the line-up of DJs due to play at Fabric later that night and started to wonder if maybe the fun had only just begun. And now, here we were being turned away.

With hindsight it was as though the distractions were gradually being removed, preparing me for meeting Desreen. One by one, the friends I had gone out with started to peel off and make their way home. I got crosser and crosser as they left.

As Martin and I walked away, crestfallen and in search of another place to spend the last Friday night before Christmas, I spotted a colleague, Jenny, standing in the queue with some friends. I explained what had happened and said we were going elsewhere. The queue was so long and they were so far back that it didn't look like they would have any luck, either. I suggested that they should join us in a neighbouring bar.

Only I wasn't really speaking to my workmate. I was speaking to her friend. I was speaking to my new world. I was speaking to the beautiful young woman who would become the mother of our adorable child five years and ten months (to the day) later. I was speaking to my future best friend who would become my wife six and a half years later. I was speaking to a girl then so full of life, whose death would prompt the owners of the club we never got into that night to send my son and me flowers eight years later, when they read in the newspapers about her death.

'Do you think they'll come?' I asked Martin, glancing back at the queue as we moved off. But it didn't really matter. We were young, free and very single back then. I'd say I was going through a dry spell but the truth is neither my friends nor I were particularly interested in meeting anyone. We were all around twenty-five and only cared about having fun. Relationships could wait.

At least, that's what I thought. They say love has a habit of finding you when you're not looking for it, and I was busy hiding from it at house parties, nightclubs, festivals and on holidays with my friends. The thought of being tied down, of not being able to do exactly what I wanted when I wanted, petrified me.

But then suddenly, I saw these beautiful big brown eyes; and they saw me, too. And they *really* saw me. They saw me like I hadn't been seen in a long time. They never stopped seeing me, either. They followed me round the bar we spent the first part of that night in and then they followed me round her friend Alice's flat, where we ended up.

'I think I fancy that boy,' Desreen told Alice that night.

Martin was apparently less aware of the liaison that was unfolding in front of everyone's eyes. '*You've* got a date with *her*?' he exclaimed two weeks later. 'Weird. I thought she fancied me.'

In Martin's defence, perhaps his mistake was down to the fact that Desreen and I spent that entire first evening quarrelling about everything: what music to play, what to drink, where to go, when to leave, whether to leave – you name it, we argued about it. I think we were both a bit confused about what suddenly began to happen. Two loud, obnoxious twenty-five-year-old party animals left their homes for a night of unadulterated festive fun and flirtation with no strings attached, but ended up quietly tied up.

The flat was full of people although it was as if there was no one else but us there. Martin was in the kitchen making a new best friend because his old one had ditched him for a girl, and Desreen was curled up on the sofa flirting with me. I can barely remember what we spoke about because it was all such drunken nonsense but she was just so funny and so beautiful. But *so* beautiful that I didn't think the flirtation would come to anything at all. I can switch on confidence when I need to, but really it's all just an act. I'm shy and I've always needed a girl to make the first move.

Martin and I left at the same time as Desreen. She was heading home to east London and we headed west. We walked each other to our taxis in the small hours of the morning and Desreen and I found ourselves simultaneously reaching for each other's hand. We didn't kiss because she didn't make her move and because my friend was still in tow; we just walked down the street like a couple of innocent children, hand in hand. And my free hand chivalrously reached for her bags. A retail-therapy addict to the end, only Desreen could have had her shopping with her on a night out.

We went our separate ways without remembering to exchange numbers, but fate wasn't going to wait for us to do its work. The very next day, on the last Saturday before Christmas, she spotted me on Oxford Street while she was out buying presents with her mum. I didn't see her, but this second chance encounter apparently gave her the opportunity to 'check out the goods' from the night before in the cold light of day.

Thankfully she still approved enough to make the next move. Back at work on Monday, my colleague Jenny, who had been with Desreen in the queue at Fabric that night, shot across the office with news. She'd had a message from Des asking for my details. Shortly after, an email dropped into my inbox; and that's how it all began.

The first night of our lives together took me totally by surprise. It came completely out of nowhere. Our relationship started just as Desreen's life would stop: randomly and without warning. Two perfect days that ended in a way that I will never forget. One with joy, the other with despair.

BEING STRONG

It's incredible to think how scared I was to call people the morning after Desreen was killed. I had just gone through the most harrowing experience of my life and yet I found myself putting off telephoning friends and family out of fear. Perhaps forcing my mouth to speak the words *she's dead* was going to make it all too real.

I decided to delay a little longer and take a shower. The water burned my face. My eyes were on fire from the tears shed the night before; tears that screamed and streamed down my face. Tears that were somehow more saline than any others I'd ever cried before. Tears that actually hurt my skin.

As I stared in the mirror, exhausted, haggard and grey, I heard the front door open. It was Desreen's parents.

Feeling heavy with dread, I opened the bathroom door. Her mum, Bev, yelled out and threw her arms around me.

'I'm so sorry. I'm so, so sorry,' I sobbed.

She immediately recoiled and steeled her grip as if to reprimand rather than comfort me. 'What are *you* apologising for? You didn't do this!' she exclaimed. 'Now, you listen to me. We have to be strong for Jackson.'

I wept and nodded. I had told myself to *be strong* the night before and so I tried to pull myself together. I took a seat and I told them everything, desperate to be able to put things right but completely powerless to do a thing.

As I looked at them, both usually stoic towers of strength but suddenly ruins bowing in grief's storm, I felt the most hurtful of emotions. I felt guilty to be alive. *Why their daughter, why not my parents' son?* I began to ask myself. *Could I have done more?*

Desreen's dad, Kelson, seemed broken. Usually chatty and upbeat, he seemed to sink silently into the armchair he always sat in when he came to visit. The shock would give us both physiological problems to contend with: indigestion, acid reflux and diuresis. For the first time the man whom I sometimes trained with in the gym, who at sixty-one still had a six-pack, seemed old. But then so did his thirty-three-year-old son-in-law, as I saw every time I caught my reflection in the mirror.

In her typical style, Bev took charge of the house. She would try to cook and clean away her grief and focus her attention on her grandson. Even then, before Bev and I had discussed any formal arrangements for Jackson's care, I suppose we both knew how it was going to be. We both knew we would need to take time off work to deal with the shock and to look after Jackson. The rest we would figure out in due course.

When I eventually summoned the courage to make some calls I dialled my parents' home number first. I was calling early enough for them to know that something was wrong. My voice was usually met with a cheerful tone but instead I heard my mum's tired 'hello'. I can't remember my exact words but they came fast and direct – something along the lines of 'Desreen's been killed. She's dead.'

I could picture the scene. I could see them in the bed they had shared in the house we had lived in as a family in Southport since I was seven. It was as if I had sent lightning down the line to shock them out of their sleep. Worry has kept my mum awake at night for years but I suspect this was something that had never crossed her mind. I know her immediate thought was that something was wrong with Jackson. Desreen's own mother even told me that she never worried about her daughter's safety because Des was always so careful.

I gave my parents a little more detail and then suggested that they try to get their heads round what I'd just told them, compose themselves and call me back.

Then I called my best friends. It was still only around 7.00a.m. so I started with Lee because he had a four-year-old son and I knew he would be awake. Since having Jackson I'd loved the fact that I could chat to Lee no matter how early in the day because we were both in the same boat.

His wife, Olive, answered with a cheerful 'Hi dude!' I couldn't reflect her tone and so, again, I just came out with it. All I remember is hearing Lee say, 'We're coming now.' They live in Leeds but it felt as if they were in London within the hour.

My parents weren't far behind but they'd had to wait until a more sociable hour so they could first visit my grandma and her husband, to break the news in person. They were too fragile to hear that they had lost a granddaughter-in-law over the phone.

Lee was one of the two best men at my wedding. The other, Woody, wouldn't be awake yet. He was still in a position to make the most of his Saturday nights but I knew that Lee would call him repeatedly until he got an answer.

When my mum and dad arrived I felt the beginnings of a new dynamic in our relationship, something that would take me until eleven months later to work out. I suppose they needed to feel that they could take care of me the way they had when I was a little boy. I imagine they wanted to take the pain away and fix things as they might once have dealt with a graze or a bruise. Nothing like this had ever happened to us before though and we were the typical 'that kind of thing doesn't happen to families like ours' family. Except now it *had* happened and none of us had any experience in how to handle it.

I understood immediately this but still their concern and worry felt uncomfortable and unfamiliar and it made me feel irrationally angry towards them. All I knew then was that I didn't want to be mothered or smothered. I felt I had already lost everything and so I needed to hold onto the feeling of being in control. I couldn't allow people to take over – that would feel to me as if I were accepting that being widowed had left me useless and incompetent. Even being asked if I wanted a drink in my own home made me feel so mad.

But the person I was most afraid to see was Desreen's big brother, Anthony. I just couldn't get my head around how huge an impact Desreen's death would have on him. He had been so protective towards her for her entire thirty-three years on Earth. I remember their mum telling me how he had once gone for a playgroup teacher when they were both tiny because he misread her body language as aggression towards his little sister. How was he going to feel about the driver whose car had killed her?

When I opened the door to Anthony he sort of fell into the hall, almost hyperventilating. He's a big lad, he towers over me and I would never be able to prop him up if we found ourselves drunk together in a bar, but suddenly I had the strength. Like me, it was as though he was on another planet. We spoke nonsense at each other like two guys who had taken the wrong medication.

When Jackson woke late on the morning after his mum was killed he was cross and confused having slept so little the night before. He didn't seem at all happy to see any of the people who usually thrilled him standing in the living room. His three favourite things in the world had gone missing during the chaos: his mother, his scooter and Thomas the Tank Engine. While I set about recovering the two things that could be replaced, some other things showed up: grown-ups, lots of them.

Our little flat bulged with people: grandparents, uncles, godparents, friends and neighbours. Bev and I played hostess and host to visitors from near and far. A kind of sombre carnival took hold, with a melancholy conga running through my front door, into all the rooms, back down the stairs to the flat and straight to the pub over the road, which acted as an overspill facility for the hordes of guests. We'd celebrated Jackson's second birthday there just three weeks before. Now it became our second home – a place of consolation rather than celebration.

Jackson had spent the last hour of his birthday party sulking, overwhelmed by all the attention. That same look was back on his face. Everyone he knew well was in the room except for his mum. *How could we be having a party again so soon, but this time without her? Why was everyone crying? Where was the cake?*

While I could see the questions in his big brown doe-like eyes, which he inherited from his strikingly beautiful mum, he didn't ask any questions for weeks. He was used to Desreen and me going away for work or with friends for a couple of days at a time and, after all, we were having what he must have thought was a party almost every day for a month. The house was always full so there were plenty of people and presents to distract a little boy arguably too young to know for sure whether it had been a day or a fortnight since he last saw his mummy.

It was comforting to have everyone together but no amount of comfort or condolence could mask the gravity of the situation. I could feel in my heart and see on my son's beautiful little face that life would never be the same again. And that was never more apparent than when the police arrived the day after Desreen died, to talk us through the night before.

'Can I ask you something?' I pleaded as the two female detectives finished describing the events surrounding the incident. 'How close did the car get to my son?'

They looked at one another as if they knew more than they were letting on.

'We've watched the CCTV footage,' one replied, 'and I can honestly say that it's a miracle that you and your son are alive.'

I don't imagine detectives, whose jobs are based on finding concrete evidence, often turn to acts of God for their answers. But the look in their eyes told me that they had no idea how the two of us had got away without so much as a scratch. Of course, wounds aren't always of the flesh. We may have escaped physical injury but inside I was entirely broken and still at a loss to know what damage my child had sustained.

Three days after Desreen was killed, her family and I were invited to the coroner's office in London's King's Cross. Heading there I felt completely displaced. I was about to talk to the police about the death of my wife, see her body and witness the look on her parents' and brother's faces when they finally saw that this was for real. That it was their beautiful girl who had been killed and not a case of mistaken identity.

But why there? Anywhere but there. This previously secret corner of central London used to be home to the city's best nightlife: clubs that the tourists couldn't find; venues where we forgot the week gone by and thought, To hell with the week ahead. We were in the prime of our lives; nothing could stop us. All we ever wanted to do was to have fun. And now, as I walked down a once derelict street that had been completely redeveloped and that had sprung to life with shops, restaurants, offices and flats, all I was facing was her death. The happy times of our lives were officially buried in the past.

I believed this would be the last time I ever saw her. She lay in the chapel of rest in the grounds of the coroner's office behind a glass wall, with only her face showing. Desreen's parents, her brother and I went in one by one and my parents followed us. She looked peaceful, almost as though she was just sleeping. I clung to the screen and wept. 'How can this be happening? How can you be dead?' I wailed at her before stopping myself.

Ridiculous things came into my head when I was out of my mind with shock and grief and I suppose I just couldn't imagine her being dead enough to not be able to hear me yet. So I echoed what I had told her the night that she was killed: that there was nothing to worry about and that everything was going to be okay, that I loved her and I promised to take care of our son.

This was the day when the madness really started. My madness. I was as high as a kite. This cocktail of emotional drugs was turning me into a man I had never met before. While everyone around me was crying, pensive, desperately trying to get their heads around what had happened, once I had emerged from seeing Desreen I was efficiency defined. No more tears, because I had work to do. I had to *be strong* because that was what everyone was telling me to be. And if you have never gone through anything like this before, I guess you'll take commands and advice from anyone that offers.

Sadly, I know now that some of the people around me were getting it wrong. Looking back I feel genuinely ashamed for the steeliness I showed following the death of the wife I so adored. 'What's wrong, mate? You seem really down,' I callously asked one of Desreen's oldest friends, Olly, in the pub just a couple of days after she died. When people asked, rhetorically, 'But why you?' I would bark, 'Why *not* me? It hasn't happened to me anyway, has it? It has happened to Des.'

'Well, her life was short but at least she enjoyed it.' What sort of man says that about his wife when she was taken just five weeks after her thirty-third birthday and three weeks after her son's second? The sort of man who doesn't know his own mind. The sort of man so desperately in shock that he doesn't know where to turn. The sort of man overinfluenced by the innocent, well-intentioned, but often ridiculous platitudes offered to the bereaved by people who are just trying to show they care.

You have to be strong. It could have been worse. At least she went quickly. She's in a better place now. She's still with you. I know how you feel.

Most were just trite but well-meant remarks. But one was directional; one was an instruction. You *have* to be strong. So I manned up. I'm just 5ft 7ins tall, but I felt the need to be a big man for the first time in my life. And when the papers started calling our friend Zac three days after Desreen was killed outside his house, I realised that I needed to take control. I hadn't expected that our personal tragedy would make the news, but it did. I read a piece in the *Evening Standard* that upset me, because Desreen was referenced as an 'unnamed mother' and I was just 'this guy'. I understood that the paper was missing the details it needed to report a full account of what happened, but it made the tragedy that had hit our lives feel hollow and vague.

I had worked in public relations for twelve years so I knew how to tell a journalist when they were stepping over the line, or when I was talking to someone with little experience. The impossible insensitivity of a young news-desk trainee is something to behold. It's not what they ask; it's how they ask it. I was actually laughing when I got off the phone from one journalist, astounded not so much by the lack of aptitude for an interview but by their inability to show any sense of humanity.

Nonetheless, I had to handle them myself. If the facts weren't straight, I knew that someone would make them up. I don't mean maliciously, but I saw the process of how Chinese whispers start the moment I walked into the coroner's office. 'I must warn you, there is a rumour Desreen was pregnant,' the family liaison officer told me, 'but I can confirm she was not.'

I can see how these things happen. The story begins: 'Oh my God, a woman has just been killed down the road,' then spirals rapidly from 'She was a mother,' 'She had a child,' to 'She was having a child.' The story ends: 'Oh my God, a pregnant woman has just been killed down the road.'

But I didn't want the story to be any more painful for Desreen's family and friends or for our son in the future. So as the others recovered from the frightful experience of seeing her lying dead at the coroner's office, over coffee at St Pancras International I paced the freezing cold concourse, taking and returning calls, giving quotes and rolling my eyes at the lack of sensitivity shown by one or two junior reporters.

It was just like being back at work but this time I was the client and my life was the story. As it developed my adrenaline diminished. Over the next few days my face seemed to be everywhere. My life was all over the papers for everyone to see. I knew that taking control was the right thing to do but I wasn't prepared for how it would feel to be *that poor guy* who people pointed at and whispered about in the street – the man who made a stranger cry over her pizza just by walking through the door of a pub. So I started trying to hide myself with sunglasses, hats and a beard that I didn't trim for weeks. I thought that all eyes were on me, even if they weren't. And I hated it.

This period immediately after Desreen's death is now difficult to pull apart in my mind – the first three weeks felt more like one long sleepless day. Having previously neither kept a diary nor written anything other than a dissertation at university and press releases at work, for some reason I began to write down how each day felt. But I felt stupid when I found myself looking back over lazy lists of adjectives that couldn't do justice to the pain I was in. I imagine there may have been a subconscious need for me to capture my emotions, perhaps even a naïve hope that I would be able to find some peace in whatever progress I might appear to be making over the days and weeks ahead.

On 19 November I wrote the following words in my diary: 'Helpless. Breathless. Insecure. Hopeless. Scared. Empty. Frustrated. Anxious. Hollow.'

The next day I wrote just one word: 'Emotionless'. I can't remember now, but I can only think that that must have been the time I first took Valium – a drug that helps take away some of the pain but that also steals away the natural process of grief. A process that I've come to believe a bereaved person really must go through.

BECOMING TWINS

After that first meeting, three and a half weeks passed before Desreen and I saw each other again. I'm from Merseyside and she was from Hampshire, and we were both spending Christmas at our respective family homes, so we didn't have our first proper date planned until 3 January 2005, when we would be back in London. We would get through Christmas, hang out with our friends at New Year and then see what happened.

Around Boxing Day, however, she'd got bored at home and the text messages started to come thick and fast. *Oi! Were you planning on getting in touch, or what?* That was her opening gambit. I always knew I would end up with a girl who wore the trousers; I was quite low on self-esteem at the time. She made me laugh immediately without even physically being there.

I could come now if I got the train, but it'd take me about seven hours, I replied.

No thanks, she typed back without delay, *I'm brushing my hair.*

I was floored; she was the one chasing me but suddenly she was too busy. And she wasn't *washing* her hair, she was brushing it. Was she really using a variation on that ancient line? I imagined she had quite a job on her hands if it were true. Her long black curly hair was one of the first things I noticed about her, second only to her breathtaking big brown eyes. It wasn't just me who was bowled over by those eyes; since she died I've had a number of messages from people she went to school with, some of whom I've never met, telling me that she could make those pretty eyes cry on command to get her own way with teachers. I would soon come to witness that few could resist her charms, which I'm sure remained as impish in adulthood as they were when she was a child.

Worth staying in all night, her final message of the evening began. *I've just found a pound coin!* I would go on to learn that brushing her hair was no euphemism with Desreen: it really did take her the best part of a day to wash, brush and dry it.

And that disproportionate elation in the pound coin was totally authentic, too. She asked me for 'gold coins' all the time, like a child asking easily persuaded relatives for sweets. In the beginning I just couldn't say no; it was worth a quid to be the subject of her hilariously childish manipulations. As things grew more serious, however, I would try to explain that I was the one trying to save the deposit for a flat and that every coin counted.

'Where did you get that money from?' I would often ask. 'You never carry cash.'

'Oh, I stole it from you, Benji,' she would reply. 'You shouldn't leave it lying around if you don't want me to take it.'

'Right, do you do that often?'

'I haven't paid for my own lunch in months!' she admitted proudly, before exploding into a fit of laughter so intense that she wept over her own joke. Like I said, she was impish, but irresistible.

When 3 January came around, I called Martin. We'd been out together on New Year's Eve and I hadn't really put the party to bed until after my flatmate Michael's birthday on 2 January.

'When are you seeing that bird that fancies me?' he asked.

'Tomorrow night, mate,' I replied, glancing at the date on my watch as I did so. 'Oh fuck! It's *today*! I've missed it.' In the party fuddle, I'd lost a day.

Fortunately she had, too. She'd been with Marianne and some of her other friends for days and I heard nothing but relief and empathy on the other end of the phone when I called to apologise for not having been in touch. We agreed to meet the following Sunday. We would keep it casual and go out to a gig with some of the friends that we had been with the night we met. I decided to go alone because I didn't want to babysit a friend; I just wanted to get to know her better.

I was excited and nervous; I hadn't been on a proper date in ages. I had butterflies, not because I was scared that it wouldn't go well but because I still wasn't sure how to pronounce her name. I'd been calling her Des'ree, like the singer, for three weeks. It turned out that she didn't like that. Given I hadn't even heard her tell me her name properly, I grew anxious about not being able to understand much else of what she said. I'm northern and she was southern and on the night we met I had only managed to catch every few words. It didn't really matter on that occasion because we had all been so drunk that if Desreen had been speaking Dutch I probably wouldn't have noticed.

But as we stood at the bar trying to speak over the band playing behind us, I realised that it wasn't actually her accent that confused me – in fact she was well spoken – it was the manner in which she spoke. Often her conversation was a verbal stream of consciousness, total nonsense, frequently about nothing and usually without direction, that only made sense to her. She didn't make eye contact when she was nervous, either, and I was so puzzled by our exchange that I found myself checking whether she was speaking to me or trying to order a drink from the bar.

Little did I know that one day I would become bilingual; that I'd be fluent in both English and *Desreen*. In the end there was no better interpreter than me. When people looked as perplexed by her dialogue as I must have that night, I would step in and tell them exactly what she was trying to say. And I would often be met by a look of even more intense bewilderment, as the person in question marvelled that someone was able to make sense of such a muddled selection of words so rapidly.

That night though, I just smiled when she smiled and laughed when she laughed, like any other guy out on a date with a beautiful girl he couldn't quite hear or fully understand.

'Is it really forward if I ask him back to my place tonight?' Desreen asked Alice, the friend whose flat we had gone back to the night we met.

For what it's worth, I might have thought it was pretty forward, but I was definitely cool with being asked back to a gorgeous girl's flat on the first date.

'The only problem is, it's Sunday,' I blundered. 'I've got work tomorrow and I've got no change of clothes. I wear contact lenses, too, and I haven't got any with me.'

'Well, first things first, what's your prescription?' she asked without hesitation.

'I'm basically blind,' I replied.

'Me too, so that's that sorted. You can wear some of mine,' she insisted. 'Now, who do you live with? Can they send you some clothes in a taxi?'

And that was Desreen all over. There was a solution to every problem. She liked to get the result she wanted without being outwardly pushy, and she hated negativity.

So we went home together and by Monday morning we were in a relationship. No messing around. We just hit it off immediately and we really liked each other, so we didn't waste time skirting round the issue. We were boyfriend and girlfriend and, before we knew it, we were in love.

I spoke about her all the time. I carried a passport picture of her in my wallet to prove to my friends, most of whom hadn't met her yet, that she was real (Facebook barely existed back then) and that she was really beautiful, too.

No one had ever made me laugh as much as she did. She wasn't a person who told jokes, in fact she was more likely to be the one who didn't get them, but she was just naturally hilarious. Immature; mischievous; naughty but so sweet she never got the blame; no inhibitions; slapstick humour; favourite film, *The Man With Two Brains*; favourite TV show, *The Fresh Prince of Bel Air*; no control over the volume of her laughter if someone tripped over in the street. She was the kind of girl you'd have a good time with if you were sharing a table at a wedding where you didn't know anyone else. She was the one who would take care of you all night and who you would laugh about for months later.

'Which party are you voting for tomorrow, Brooksie?' Michael asked Desreen in the kitchen of the flat he and I shared, on the night before the 2005 general election.

'None of them, mate,' she replied before jumping into the air wearing the rubber gloves she had put on to wash the dishes from dinner. 'I'm starting my own party: the *Party* Party!'

Before too long we were inseparable. She would even tell people who'd never met us before that we were twins. Without exception they would laugh, sometimes nervously, because all they could see was a black girl and a white guy who looked nothing alike.

'What's funny?' she would ask, poker-faced. 'We look exactly the same. Anyone can see that.'

We may not have looked the same but we certainly got along

like twins, 'especially when there was trouble to be had,' as Desreen's cousin Jerome put it after she died. And like twins, Des and I loved each other unconditionally; we bickered just as we did the first night we met; we always shared a seat – even if there was a room full of others to choose from – and we could fit into each other's jeans. Going on our first holiday together, we arrived at Heathrow's departures hall unintentionally dressed identically: white Converse trainers, skinny blue jeans, black and white striped Breton T-shirts, grey marl hoodies and the exact same backpacks, crammed full of enough clothes to see us through two weeks in Brazil. We were both so embarrassed by the stares we received that I stripped off at check-in and fumbled through my bag for a change of clothes.

Before too long we moved in together. We spent our wages on having fun and taking amazing holidays to destinations in Europe, South-East Asia, India and North America. We would treat each other to little trips to places like Île de Ré, Paris and Rome for each other's birthdays. Sometimes we even stayed at hotels in London, just because we loved the city so much and would feel cheated if we never got a chance to indulge in its finest rooms.

For my thirtieth birthday Desreen sent a taxi to pick me up from work and take me to a place the driver had sworn to keep secret. Winding through the streets of Mayfair we finally pulled up outside Claridge's, the art deco five-star hotel where she knew I had always wanted to spend the night. She offered to take me to one of the hotel's restaurants but I already had everything I wanted right there in our suite so we ordered room service: something fancy for me and posh fish fingers and chips for her. She loved few things more than a fish finger, which she referred to as 'sushi' to help make her sound more refined in her tastes.

And that's how we were. We indulged, we lived it up and we enjoyed every minute we had together. And I have to thank God that we did. Sometimes I can still hear my cautious voice telling Des that she couldn't have that gold coin, that we couldn't afford something she wanted or that we should try harder to cut back, but in the end she always got her own way. And looking back now I'm so glad she did because her time on Earth was way too brief to live within limits.

COLD COMFORT

Naturally, loved ones feel the need to be there when tragedy strikes, but when they arrive it must be impossible for them to know what to do. I imagine everyone who came to visit me felt useless. And the truth is that most people were. All anyone seemed to want to do was put things right or take away my pain, and those things just aren't possible when you lose someone you love. Sometimes I would find myself almost rolling my eyes at hearing the same ultimately useless comments time and time again. In trying to help people not to irritate me – and perhaps give them something to do to help them feel better about themselves – I would respond to comments like, 'I just wish there was something I could do' with suggestions such as, 'There is. You can clean the bathroom.'

I'm not sure I'll ever know how people saw me in those first few days but I'm pretty positive I wasn't acting the way they expected. Hardly surprising, given that I wasn't acting the way *I* would have expected, either. If I had been able to foretell my fate and had known that my wife would be dead just a year after we'd married, I would have pictured myself as a man devastated to the point of insanity, completely unable to function, struck down by shock. And I *was* in shock, but shock turned out to be different from what I might have imagined. It made me appear strong; perhaps it even *made* me strong. I suppose that's what people thought, and that was the reason they kept telling me to be so. After all, it made me easier to deal with than if I had appeared to be a broken man.

But at this point the intensity of my emotional problems hadn't even kicked in. Shock produces chemicals to prevent a person who has witnessed the unthinkable from growing hysterical. As with any drug, however, they wear off. For a short while I seemed extraordinarily calm and others took this at face value. We all do it: we decide how people are based on a fleeting impression. So I suppose I was labelled accordingly: *He's doing unbelievably well. He's so strong. He's been a rock.* It was as though I was characterised in headlines but few bothered to interrogate the copy underneath. While others could condense my behaviour into two or three words, I was going to need a bigger diary to list the adjectives that applied to what was going on inside my head and my heart.

I became almost a host for everyone's grief. I curated three weeks of mourning before Desreen's funeral finally came around. I spent my time trying to make sure that everyone else was okay.

I suppose part of my motivation stemmed from a feeling of guilt. I knew just how easily it could have been me who was killed rather than Desreen, and that made me want to overcompensate in how much support I offered her friends and family. And I imagine some people picked up on that and inadvertently came to me to receive support rather than to offer it.

I took to making cute videos of Jackson when we woke up in the middle of the night, which I would send to friends and family to try to cheer them up; maybe even to try to show how well we were both coping. His speech was still developing so he made funny and charming mistakes when addressing people, such as calling Marianne 'Auntie Mouse' instead of Auntie Maz. I also called people regularly to check that they were all okay, and when I had received more flowers than I could fit in our flat, I would drop them round to friends. Perhaps I thought that being kind would make the pain less intense than if I was angry and bitter.

But this feeling wore off with the shock. Four days after Desreen was killed my two older brothers both came to London. My eldest brother, Matthew, arrived first from his home in Southport, Nicholas later that same day from Hebden Bridge in Yorkshire. Both are married, each with two children, whose ages ranged from sixteen to four. Before they could come to London to see Jackson and me, they had to explain the situation to their own kids and help them with their own grief. Mat had to tell his daughters, Sophie, then sixteen, and Lucy, then fourteen, that the woman they had come to love as a friend rather than an auntie was the first significant person they had ever lost. Nick's task would be to try to explain to his children, Reuben, then six, and Willow, four, that they would never see their Auntie Desreen again.

I knew that my nieces and nephew, who each adored her, would be deeply affected by her untimely death. It didn't matter where Desreen went socially, she always focussed on the young ones first. She would empathise with sulky teenagers skulking in the corner at family parties and pull the shy girl who knew no one at a wedding from her chair and onto the dance floor. By the end of the evening that quiet young girl, who at first had lacked the confidence to mingle, would be the life and soul of the party and would believe she could be anything she wanted in life because Desreen was going to help her to get there. It didn't matter that they had never met before.

I grew up in a house with my two brothers – Mat seven years and Nick two-and-a-half years my senior – and a cousin, Graham, who is twelve years older than me. As the youngest in the house, I suppose I've always been seen as the baby of the family. And once you've been the baby it can be hard for your family to see you any other way. Subconsciously this has probably made me fight hard to be taken seriously. I remember once hearing my brothers say that 'Little Benji' would probably never leave home. I did though, and moved to Leeds (with a stint in Malaga) to attend university at eighteen before making my way to London at twenty-one.

When Mat arrived I could tell that he just wanted do something, anything, to help. I've always looked up to him and we've spent our whole lives laughing at the same jokes and finishing each other's sentences despite the seven-year age gap. But there were no gags now and I was suddenly the grown-up in the relationship. Witnessing my wife die had made me grow up fast. While he felt useless I was doing everything that needs to be done when a person dies. And as the guilt continued to envelop me, I was more focussed on Desreen's friends and family than my own.

Mat offered to pick up the bill for a wicker basket I decided I needed, to deal with all the shoes that were making a mess of my hall as the visitor count continued to increase. I could hear that the kind, empathetic tone, which I used on those closest to Desreen, disappeared in front of those closest to me. 'I'm fucking sick of all the fucking shoes,' I barked at Mat in the shop down the road from my flat.

Basket in hand, the two of us stopped in at a pub on the way back. I knew Jackson was asleep at home with all four of his grandparents there to look after him, so we opted for a change of scenery. It wasn't long before we had company. Some of my friends came to see me every day after Des died and not a day passed when I didn't see the Spice Girls and their partners. My parents came to join us too, because Nick wasn't too far behind and they wanted to get the family together.

When Nick arrived I was trying to comfort Olly, one of Desreen's oldest friends and husband to her best friend, Marianne. Nick stood alone at the bar, sobbing, and I could sense my mum's eyes were trying to catch mine. I glanced over and she gave me a look, which silently told me to get up and go to my brother. My whole family was there and yet it was my job to take care of him, even while I had someone else crying on my shoulder. I was the one who had lost his wife. *Who's going to comfort me?* I suddenly thought, as I went to Nick.

But the contradictory truth of the matter was that a big part of me didn't want to be comforted. I didn't want to be hugged, mothered or smothered. I became a husband focussed on comforting those closest to his wife, and a father focussed on comforting his son. I ceased to be a son who wanted to be taken care of by his parents or a baby brother wanting to be looked after by the bigger boys. I can only imagine how difficult it must have been for the four of them to feel so powerless to make things better for the boy they used to affectionately call 'Boof'. But as a son and a brother who needed to feel like he was able to be a man, being treated like a child no longer seemed an option.

I began to resent much of the support that was offered – and from all directions. It felt more like pressure than provision. My phone never stopped ringing. 'How are you?' I was asked several times a day by the same people, as if they were hoping I would have made progress. I felt conflicted because I wanted to be left alone but I also knew that I needed help, not so much for my own sake but for Jackson's. But I found this feeling of pressure overwhelming: pressure to feel better, to look better, to act better, to be better. The woman I'd hoped to spend the rest of my life with had been taken in an instant and I sensed that people wanted me to try to get over it so that they didn't have to see me in so much pain. I know now that was only because they cared, but it made me resentful and angry. And the more people willed me better the more irritated I got by them.

The people who were hurting most at the sight of my agony were my parents. As I have so painfully learned, it's hard to see your own child suffer. Yet there's a tension in the child-parent dynamic. The unwritten rule of the relationship is that the parent offers the child love and support without condition. The child, no matter their age, can, and often will, push the boundaries. Before Desreen died I was often treated as our son's emotional punchbag – he would smack and bite me out of frustration just seconds after kissing and cuddling his mum. For a short time after she died I would become the focus of his once maternal affections before eventually becoming the target of his grievances again. As the child in our relationship, I suppose that's what he needed – an outlet for his anger and confusion – and he trusted me, his father, enough to know that I would forgive his sometimes volatile behaviour. And that's what I also did as my parents' son. I grew frustrated with them. I pushed them away. I asked them to give me space. I looked forward to their visits but when they arrived I didn't always want to talk to them.

I'm a person who likes my own space at the best of times. I don't like constant conversation and I'm comfortable around silence. That's one thing that Desreen and I had in common from the start. Some days Des wouldn't say a word and it wouldn't occur to me to mind. But in their concern for me, my parents would come and stay for days at a time. My head felt too busy with its own thoughts to engage my mouth, but if I didn't speak I would feel as if I was being rude and dismissive. The more time I spent with people, the more I wanted to be alone.

Before too long I realised that this antisocial response to

Desreen's death was not just directed at those closest to me. Surprisingly, in a world where so much communication is now by social media, it took quite some time for the news of my wife's death to filter through to all my 'friends'. I use inverted commas not because I have anything against these people; I'm referring to the large group of old friends, ex-friends, colleagues and acquaintances that make up a person's extended networks these days.

Eventually, the majority of the collective grief and condolences for Desreen unfolded online but initially I decided not to mention her death on Facebook or Twitter. This would probably have stunned her because she always rolled her eyes at how much time I spent on both. 'Why don't you just *watch* the programme rather than talking about it online?' she would ask.

'You just don't get it, do you?' I would reply with a smile. 'It's much more fun to critique a programme with friends online than it is to watch it.'

Now I asked everyone to actually *talk* to one another and not say it online. I just couldn't bear the thought of anyone casually sharing some embarrassing post-weekend pictures on Facebook and then suddenly finding out that their old friend had died – and that it might hurt them even more to think that they were the last to know.

It was when the news coverage started to appear that the social media outpouring really began. My brother-in-law, Anthony, asked me if he could share an interview with me that the *Evening Standard* had published. I agreed. I think he had an embargo in mind, like he'd say his piece, thank well-wishers for their kind words and then refrain from talking about the death of his sister online again.

It seems slightly strange to me now, to think that I kept quiet, given how much I've embraced the internet since. But I know why I initially kept away from social media: exhaustion. Nothing could have prepared me for the barrage of contact that followed the news coverage and subsequent social media posts.

Suddenly it felt as if everyone I had ever known was all over me: the visitors, letters, cards, emails, texts, calls, flowers and gifts seemed never-ending. Follow-up versions of each form of communication from people saying that they were worried they hadn't heard back from me. Follow-up versions of each of those forms of communication from people saying that they were amazed that they had. Others actually chasing me because they didn't think I had replied to them within an appropriate timescale, despite having not spoken to many of them in years. Some pressing me to meet up when, to be frank, I couldn't even put faces to their names. One particularly insensitive person sent an email of condolence that also doubled up, rather creatively, as a job application for the firm where I was, at the time, the managing director.

Before long I was drowning in contact and although I resented the suffocation, I couldn't stop throwing myself back into the pool. The violent contradictions of grief were exposed: *Why can't everyone just fuck off and leave me alone? I can't believe X hasn't been in touch.*

I was so tired from the kindness that people were showing me and yet I would stay awake all night and stare at the chat function on Facebook to see who was online and think, They can see I'm here. Are they really not going to say anything? Then as soon as they did I would ignore them, grasp my head in my hands and mutter, 'What the hell do you want from me?'

It wasn't until much later that I realised what was wrong. I was urging my phone to ring. I was desperate to hear the ping of a message or the swoosh of a tweet but I felt no satisfaction or solace when I did. I wasn't willing friends to get in touch. I was waiting for a message that was never going to come. I was waiting for Desreen.

THE PILGRIMAGE

In the immediate aftermath of Desreen's death there was so much to contend with – from telling people what had happened to the police investigation, calls from the media to dealing with work – that Bev and I made the decision to keep Jackson in nursery, at least for a few hours each day. There were endless upsetting practical things to attend to and the idea of taking him to view her at the chapel of rest or to sit through the proceedings at the coroner's office felt unbearable.

We needed time to start to process what had happened and think about how we were going to deal with the enormity of telling a two-year-old that his mummy was gone forever. We needed time to think about how we planned to raise him without her.

For the first few days after Desreen died, Jackson often watched the front door to check if his mummy was coming in from work, but he didn't ask where she'd gone (he didn't for weeks). It hurt me to think that he hadn't yet fully registered her absence, but it also allowed me to bide my time and think about how I was going to address this once unimaginable situation.

But something started to feel wrong as I sat in the pub that first week, brooding with friends and family. On the Wednesday or Thursday after Des was killed on the previous Saturday, I decided to pick Jackson up early from nursery and bring him back to see everyone. As we sat around talking I took a look at him playing with a train on the floor. He didn't return my smile. It suddenly occurred to me that although he asked me to 'play trains' all the time, he'd never once asked if he could accompany me to the pub to watch me drink red wine. I put my coat on, picked him up and walked out, telling everyone it was time for me to focus more on him and less on me. It was as though I could hear Desreen telling me that I ought to be ashamed of myself. I imagined that, if the roles had been reversed, she would have handled the whole thing with a *Jackson first, me later* approach and it was time for me to try to do the same.

The first decision Bev and I made after that moment of realisation was that, as of the following week, we would reduce the number of days that Jackson attended nursery. We couldn't see ourselves back at work anytime soon but we didn't want to stunt his progress, so he would go in on Mondays and Tuesdays and spend the rest of the week with us. It felt only fair to ensure that happy and playful company surrounded him at least some of the time. And it also felt important to face the fact that I was going to need some time to be an openly grieving husband and not just a sole parent doing his best to hide his pain from his son. This compromise felt better, more attuned to Jackson's needs while acknowledging mine, and Bev's. I imagined Desreen's approval.

Des adored our little boy from the moment he was born and she made an incredibly natural mother. For her, motherhood was the supreme form of love, even before Jackson came along. When she and I first fell for one another her love for me was addictive and all-consuming. It meant that she could say the weirdest things. 'I want to get back inside your tummy again!' she once told me as we cuddled up.

'What on earth are you talking about, Dessie? You've never been inside my stomach,' I replied.

'I have! You gave birth to me. You must have done for me to love you this much.'

Strange, but there's a beautiful sentiment in there somewhere.

Later, she expressed her love for me and her desire to have a child in similar terms. 'Benji, I want us to have a baby *right now.* I've decided I want another little Benji – one I can take everywhere with me and who can't run off to work or on nights out with his friends.'

Ironically, she also used to tell me she was afraid that something might happen to me and she would be left 'Benji-less'. But then Jackson came along and that all changed. She still loved me as much as before but I was no longer her number one.

'Dessie, you haven't said any of those things you used to say to me recently. I'm beginning to think you love Jackson more than me.'

'Don't be ridiculous, Ben. Of course I love Jackson more than you,' she replied. Then she laughed, not at her own comment but mine. 'He's my baby. You used to be and now you're my husband.'

I always thought what a lucky boy he was to receive that sort of love, having been its main recipient for so long. I'd play-sulk but I couldn't have been happier that our little creation was so cherished.

Jackson was the wriggliest of unborn babies. Desreen would get cross about how much he seemed to want to break out, especially as the ferocious kicking would usually start just around bedtime. He was no better when he was born, either. He wouldn't be swaddled, he hated his Moses basket and he eventually loathed his cot. Just like his mum, he was not a person who liked to be shackled, restricted or told what to do. So he took to our bed and he had no problems there. Right until the day his mummy died he was fighting his departure from our room. He just didn't want to leave her. So fierce was his adoration that I would often wake up in the night to find him sleeping on her head. Despite having been so desperate to get out from inside her it seemed he missed being quite so close after all.

Now, all I can think is how grateful I am that they had that time together. Once he was born, Jackson became Desreen's world.

'I know how much I love him by the ridiculous things I put myself through now,' she told me one day.

Rhyme Time was one such activity: a mother and baby sing-along session held in our local library, where new mums sat in a circle singing with babies so young they could barely gurgle. 'I just sit back and think of Net-A-Porter,' she told me, referring to the online fashion store that she used to log on to about six times a day.

She always put him first. As his obsession with Thomas the Tank Engine developed, she indulged him with toys, tracks and DVDs. The very night before she died I had gone shopping at Hamley's to buy Jackson a couple of new trains, including a glow-in-the-dark Thomas to help encourage him to take to his own bed. 'Benji, please don't give him his presents until I get home from work. I really want to see his face,' she said during what would become our final telephone conversation.

The last text message she ever sent to her mum was a picture of Jackson playing with his new toy. Bev later told me how she'd commented on just how happy Desreen seemed that week and that day. And as I know from the last words she ever spoke, she died loving and living for her son.

Just weeks before she was killed she had decided it was time for us to take Jackson to Thomas Land – the sort of place that she would normally consider hell but which is guaranteed to delight a young child with an obsession for irritating, class-obsessed, talking locomotives. We were both thoroughly sick of Thomas and all his annoying little steamy friends, but we also knew it would make our son incredibly happy.

It was a trip that Desreen would never make. The tickets were booked for Saturday 17 November, exactly a week after she was killed. There I was, a shell of a man, and yet I knew we still had to go. In just seven days the simple 100-mile journey from Euston to Tamworth had become much more than a trip to a theme park. It was now a pilgrimage. I knew in my head that we could cancel and go another time, but in my heart I understood that I would never get back the date that she had chosen.

It was one of the worst experiences of my whole life. That Saturday wasn't just another day at Thomas Land; it was the opening day of *Christmas* Thomas Land. Happy families frolicked in fake snow. Festive hits and Christmas carols poured from the speakers. The Fat Controller (I can't believe it's still acceptable to call him that) and his period-costumed friends performed a song and dance routine on the balcony of Knapford Station. And meanwhile Jackson slept.

He had a habit of staying awake when you wanted him to sleep and sleeping when you wanted him awake. His eyes began to roll in the taxi that transported us from the train station to the park. To make things worse, the driver wouldn't shut up.

'Alright, mate? You were in my cab last week, weren't you?'

'No, it wasn't me,' I replied curtly.

'Yeah, it was. I remember you.'

'No, mate, it definitely wasn't me. I've never been here before.'

He fell quiet for the briefest moment but took several looks at me in his rear-view mirror. 'Are you off the telly?' he went on.

'No, I'm not.'

'Then how do I know you?'

I couldn't bear it any longer. I just wanted him to stop talking. 'Have you read the papers this week?'

'Yeah, mate. Every day,' he replied.

'Well, then you've probably seen my picture. My wife died last Saturday and her death was covered in most of them. I'm taking my son to Thomas Land because she booked the tickets and it's what she would have wanted.'

'Er, right. I don't really know what to say.'

Well then shut the fuck up, I thought but just about had the courtesy not to say.

Jackson slept for an hour and a half. Eventually I decided I could take no more. I positioned him in front of the giant head of his favourite train at the time (Percy for the record) and gave him a nudge. He pulled a grumpy face and slowly opened one eye. In a split second both were wide open and he leapt from his pushchair, elated. I liked the idea that he might have thought he was still dreaming; that the magic of Christmas had entered his little soul. He suddenly had the smile on his face that his mummy had wanted to see.

I also put on mine for the pictures that I took, but inside I was in pieces. I realised then that it was time to stop trying to be a hero and face up to the reality of the devastation that had shattered our lives.

BEING DESREEN

We didn't bury Desreen for twenty days. I'm not sure how anyone would go about organising a funeral any quicker. But then I guess some deaths come with more notice. The intensity of the shock we all felt left us reeling for days and weeks. I was in no rush to accept what had happened, either, so when Desreen's dad, Kelson, reminded me that his sister was getting married on 24 November, we agreed to wait until the week that followed to hold Desreen's service.

Although Jackson still didn't know what had happened to his mum, he grew increasingly irritable about certain things that concerned her. One day, as I packed to leave for Desreen's parents' house in Havant, I starting throwing things into one of her holdalls, just because it was the closest thing to hand.

'Don't touch it, Daddy!' he yelled. 'It Mummy's!'

He repeated the same sentiment to Bev when she tried to dress him in one of his tops that must have reminded him of one of Desreen's.

Of course he knew something was wrong, how could he not? He hadn't seen his mother for two weeks and everyone around him was behaving oddly, no matter how much they tried to hide it. And yet, with so much to think about for the funeral, we decided to wait until afterwards, and for a moment when we felt it was the right time to explain. I suppose a big part of me

– maybe a weak and scared part – could have waited forever. I'm still not sure I can think of anything worse than having to tell a child that he'll never see his mother again.

The date of the funeral was set for Friday 30 November. Desreen's body would be buried just a short walk away from her parents' home and we arranged for the vicar who married us to hold the service outside of his own parish, in the church where she would be laid to rest.

The day before her funeral was the last time I ever saw her. Her body lay in the chapel of rest, this time in the premises of the funeral directors who had helped us with all the arrangements. I don't wish that I hadn't seen her, but equally it's not something I'm pleased I did. She wasn't like Desreen anymore, just an entirely lifeless shell. It was a completely different experience from the time before. This last visit was more serene and dignified than it had been at the coroner's office – the lights were dim, candles burned and she was dressed in her own clothes and jewellery – but she was in a coffin and all the softness of her features had long since gone. I repeated the sentiment I had last left her with, telling her that I loved her and promising to take good care of our son.

I had ambitiously set about organising the best funeral that had ever been held. I later realised that this was a contradiction in terms and that I must have been on another planet to be worried about the credibility of the occasion and the efficiency of the event. But then, as a public relations professional, event management was part of my job. Had I been a man of the cloth, I imagine I would have wanted to ensure the religious ceremony really delivered, too.

Our actual man of the cloth is a very special man indeed. John had married us just fifteen months earlier. A while before our wedding day we'd been to visit him in his home to ask for his permission to marry in one of his eight parish churches. We fell for his charms immediately.

'Desreen. Desreen,' he repeated several times after she introduced herself, looking into her big brown eyes. 'What a beautiful name.

'And it's Kevin, isn't it?' he said to me, his eyes still on her.

'No, it's actually Ben,' I replied. 'Don't worry though, I know that Desreen is a much easier name to remember. It happens all the time.'

'And Desreen,' he continued, refocusing his attention on my fiancée, 'you work in the fashion industry, don't you? That must be very exciting. Tell me all about it.'

Her profession was difficult enough to describe at the best of times so I wasn't quite sure how she was going to explain it to a vicar who, by his own admission, knew very little about couture. Essentially she would shape and manage the careers of stylists and hair and makeup artists in the fashion industry. It was her job to find her artists the right kind of work and keep them in the right kind of work. She acted as the bridge between her artists and the fashion brands and media outlets they worked for, negotiating jobs and contracts, and managing the subsequent workload for the talent she represented. She never quite found a concise way of explaining it though, but John nodded along enthusiastically and looked as though he could have listened to her all day. Once she'd finished he turned back to me and said, 'And you're a builder, aren't you?' I suspect if he'd paid a little more attention to the soft typing hand that shook his on the way through the vicarage door, he'd have known that I had barely changed a light bulb in the previous thirty years.

We talked at length about our families. John had served in the British Navy, like Desreen's dad, and by a huge twist of fate, had taken a job that Kelson also considered just before he repatriated his family from Saudi Arabia to the UK. John was also a northerner by birth and so took an interest in my family's Lancastrian roots. His interests, however, generally leaned more towards Desreen.

'Do you think we should tell him about Jackson?' I whispered to her as the vicar turned his back to rummage through a pile of papers.

'Are you mad?' she murmured back incredulously.

Jackson was just a few weeks old at this point and Desreen was afraid John wouldn't approve of his birth out of wedlock. The next time we met, once the vicar had agreed to marry us, she dropped his name into the conversation.

'Oh, you've got a child?' he asked. 'This is new.'

'No, no,' Desreen replied, knowing exactly what he'd meant, 'he's four months old now.'

'No, I mean you didn't mention it last time I met you.'

'Oh, I'm sure I did,' she responded, poker-faced.

'Well, now this is interesting,' he continued.

I thought we'd scuppered our chances but what he was about to tell me taught me never to judge a book by its cover. His first child was also born out of wedlock. He felt no compulsion to marry beforehand because, at the time, he was an atheist – and quite a fierce one by all accounts. He found God later on in life and more children followed.

'Jackson! Jackson!' he repeated, with the same enthusiasm he had spoken Desreen's name the time before. 'Well then, he must play a key role in the wedding.'

We loved him; he made our wedding day so special. The congregation were in fits of laughter and, for once in my life, someone made me look tall.

'John,' I said after the service, 'I've brought that glass of water you asked for but you appear to be holding a glass of Pimm's.'

'Well you see, I did ask for water but Jesus has a habit of turning water into wonderful things at weddings.'

It was these kind of comments and his evident joy for life that meant there was only ever one person who could conduct a ceremony to celebrate my wife's life. John and I spoke over the phone, then we met and I sent him a long biography of Desreen's entirely too short existence, which I pieced together with the help of her friends and family.

Kelson and I also visited the vicarage soon after she died, to talk about her death. What touched me most was that he spoke to us as a parent and a man and not a person of religion.

'I can't know how either of you feel,' he said softly, 'because I've never lost a wife and I've never lost a child.'

No platitudes, just a comforting tone, hot tea and ears ready to listen.

'I'm just so sad that I didn't get the chance to say goodbye,' Kelson explained.

'But you did,' I interrupted. 'You saw her the day before she died, you had a wonderful time together and she told you that she loved you. She even told you the password to her laptop and she would never have told *me* that.'

Since then I've have had the opportunity to actually say goodbye to someone before they died, in the full knowledge that it would probably be the last time we would see each other. My maternal grandmother lost her fight with a lung disease almost nine months after Desreen's death. Looking back at what I said to Kelson at the vicarage that day, I felt stupid and naïve. I had told people that I would have hated to see Desreen ill, that she would have hated it herself, and that I didn't regret the fact that I had no chance to tell her how I felt because I told her every day. But when I was given the chance to sit and talk with my grandma two weeks before she died, I knew that I'd got all that wrong. We had a wonderful conversation, we shared stories and we spoke of our love for one another. Now I know that I'd rather have the chance to say farewell, every time.

But I was in a very different state of mind back then. My wife's death brought out a drive in me that I had only really seen once before. And even then it wasn't something I'd seen in myself. I suddenly took on the energy and dynamism with which Desreen had planned our fantastic wedding day. I decided that the funeral had to be perfect, everything from the songs to the flowers, from the coffin to the seating plan in the church. Never again would I have an opportunity like this to show her just how much I cared.

The service was beautiful. People spilled from the church and into the graveyard. I had suspected they might so I'd ordered a PA system so that guests could still hear the ceremony from outside. Fortunately the sun was shining brightly after what had been twenty days of darkest cold and rain.

I was still telling myself to *be strong* and I was still being told to do so every day. I didn't yet know that there was any other way. To fuel my vigour, however, I decided that I could be excused for taking Valium before I arrived at the church and a hip flask full of rum for once I was inside. There are those who might think both are in bad taste, but then I would have to ask if they have ever had to stand in front of two or three hundred people and conduct a eulogy for their thirty-three-year-old wife while their two-year-old son looked on. I guess we just do what we need to do to get through.

My role that day was clear. I would honour my wife and I would do everything in my power to alleviate the suffering of her friends and family by helping to create a service that was a true celebration of her life.

John, the vicar, set the tone beautifully. He delivered his sermon as a friend. He talked of the treasures that Desreen had bestowed on each and every one of us. He even brought the Spice Girls and Ibiza into the proceedings, which broke up the tears with laughter. And then it was my turn.

I'd been drafting notes for over two weeks. It had occurred to me that everyone I spoke to was making nonspecific offers of help – 'let me know if there's anything I can do' – and I had few ideas about what tasks I was supposed to dish out. But then suddenly it came to me. I would invite everyone to try to be more like Desreen. That, for me, would make the world a more loving, kind and entertaining place to live.

As I stood at the pulpit I looked out at a blurred sea of faces. Every so often I would catch a glimpse of someone that I was surprised to see, from old friends I hadn't seen in years to ex-colleagues I never expected to attend. I saw people smiling at me the way close friends might but when I looked back I just couldn't place them. My memory was shot by the confusion of the situation.

I decided to focus on the front few rows; I took a deep breath and drank a sip of water. My mind was so shattered by grief and shock that after I put my bottle down I cracked an entirely inappropriate joke about how I was acting like Mariah Carey at the 2005 Live 8 concert held in Hyde Park (she behaved like a diva, complaining about needing water at the globally televised music event that was held to help fight extreme world poverty). I composed myself and then somehow managed to deliver Desreen's eulogy without shedding a tear.

It struck me just the other day that one of my greatest fears since Desreen's death was that I will age while she stays eternally young, making us feel even further apart than we already are. But what seems to be getting me through is being able to hear what she would say in reply to my thoughts. And to that one she would say, 'Oh come on babe, let's face it, you were always going to age badly compared to me with all of that white skin.'

So I can't make this talk sad or laboured because I can hear her saying, 'Benji, I'm getting a bit bored.'

That's not to say that you won't cry – God knows I probably will – but if you want to laugh, then laugh and if you want to smile, then smile.

First of all I'd like to thank you so much for coming, and thanks to all of the people who brought Desreen's floral vision to life. Hundreds of people have been in touch – friends, family and even strangers moved by what's happened – asking what they can do to help. Many of you have contributed to the flowers, others have brought food and friendship and there have been countless additions to Jackson's rapidly growing selection of Thomas the Tank Engines.

While I'm sure this pain has only just started and that we will call on all of you for support way into the future, right now I can only think of one thing you can do to help.

And that is to keep my beautiful wife's memory alive by trying, in your own individual ways, to be more like her.

Here's the guidebook to being Desreen.

Be strong. Be quietly determined. Be remarkable. Be fun-loving and hedonistic. Talk nonsense that somehow makes total sense. Wind people up. Laugh hysterically when people fall over.

Be there for your friends and be unconditionally supportive of them. Love your family but keep them on their toes. Go round to your parents' house, have them wait on you hand and foot but give them feedback on how they could have done better. Buy your brother Amazon vouchers to fuel his gadget addiction. Own a sewing machine, but get your mum to do all your sewing.

Listen more than you talk. Give more than you receive. Put your children first. Make candles for friends. Believe so strongly that you'll have a little girl one day that you already have her full name in the back of your diary. Read *The Secret* and hang on its every word.

Fall asleep on the bus even if you are only travelling one stop. Buy flowers and enjoy them. Love your wardrobe. Relaunch yourself regularly. Get every single niggle checked by the doctor. Self-diagnose and expect the worst. Take the remote control to work instead of your mobile phone sometimes.

Buy pretty things, and, if you find that they aren't as pretty as you hoped they'd be, give them to charity and buy prettier things. Say, 'Oh wow, cheaper than I thought' when the label on a T-shirt says £400. Yell at me to 'Just go for it' when an umbrella costs £150. Never class hot chocolate as chocolate.

Take the *Desperate Housewives* box set to hospital when you go into labour and after three days and two epidurals, be positive enough to say you're having a really nice day. If you ever have a

Caesarean, make your first post-operation question 'Can I have a lemonade now please?'

Talk about your extreme detox with friends with a ciggy in one hand and a glass of prosecco in the other. Write to the vicar who married you because you're sad you haven't seen him for a while. Send thank-you cards. Drink olive oil before you go to bed to keep yourself regular. Re-carpet the rental property you're living at because you've got friends coming to stay. Play music and be joyous enough in life to dance alone. Tell Norman Jay to get an earlier flight home from Ibiza because he's annoying you. Light up a room. Ask waitresses completely inappropriate questions about the chicken you're eating.

Jump from sleeping to leaping in a split second when an incredible, articulate, intelligent mixed-raced man becomes President. Support Jamaica if they're winning, support your favourite holiday destination when they're not, but stop supporting England – it's never going to happen.

Have a different treatment every week on maternity leave and take your baby with you while you have a facial. Brush your skin. Tell yourself you look pretty today. Blame cow's milk for mucus, not cigarettes. Eat a whole punnet of plums in ten minutes and then blame the pain on a dodgy heart. Believe yourself to be fabulous but don't be arrogant enough to think there isn't room – and money to be spent – on self-improvement.

Love all creatures great and small, apart from most creatures great and small. Say 'byeee' when you leave a room. Call your auntie 'auntieeeeeee'.

Dress well. Go to Paris and tell people it looks like Net-A-Porter in 3D. Own a Marc Jacobs nappy bag. If you can't afford the price, simply ask the sales assistant for 70 per cent off, stating no other reason than 'I really want it and haven't got the money.'

Be truly kind. Have presence. Help people through grief. Excel at your job. Never compromise and never let your standards slip. Don't buy anything cheap when it could be expensive, knowing that if you buy cheap you buy twice. Think you have money and you always will.

Be brilliant. Inspire people. Never give up and don't tolerate mediocrity. Speak your mind because life's too short to mince your words. Support businesses that inspire you. Exercise and never give up on looking as beautiful as you can. Wear colour. Fill a room with personality. Plan good times with amazing friends.

Be creative. Nurture creative talent and make other people's success your goal. Believe in people and guide them. Be a mentor. Give shops feedback that they aren't trying hard enough with their stock. Make a beautiful home. Plan to be buried at Liberty.

Be mischievous. Be headstrong and brave, but be childlike too. Record your life intentions; have a plan. Look at old photos and laugh – take lots of new ones. Sign up to the goop.com newsletter and cleanse your system. Meditate. List your achievements – not just your goals – in your diary and be kind enough to let your husband know that you credited a 'great balanced marriage' amongst the best. Set out to achieve good health not just for yourself but for your children and family. Plan to spend a month in Ibiza in August and volunteer to be the one to *tell* not *ask* your husband's boss.

Be positive because negativity is too draining. Keep a clean house. Have a bit of class. Be confident but never boast. Never leave anyone uncertain about how you feel. Don't put off until tomorrow what you can do today. Be vivacious, organised, passionate, warm, intense, kind, considerate, gorgeous, funny, interesting, quirky and high maintenance. Make your children laugh by being daft. Be there for them. Buy your kids clothes for when they are a year older so other children won't be wearing them. Buy the carers at your kids' nursery Christmas presents. Come home from honeymoon a day early because you miss your child. Go home early from hen weekends so you can spend more time with your husband and son. Play with the kids at parties rather than just getting hammered with all the adults.

Teach me how to be a better father. Spoil me: take me to Paris for Valentine's Day, take me to Morocco for my birthday and take me to the Olympics on my wedding anniversary. Tell me off for getting in at 3.30a.m. even though I got home at 11.00p.m. and fell asleep on the sofa. Forgive me, even though I did nothing wrong, then put me back in the doghouse for the same non-event when it suits you. Tell me you're going to cook for me every Saturday but only do it once. Embarrass me in a busy restaurant by having the waiter bring over a diamond ring and ask me to marry you, when we're already engaged. Send me a lesbian Valentine's card. Tell me that my point of view is interesting but that yours is right. Love my grandma. If your bum is small enough, always share a seat with me. Turn up late to meet my parents because you got so drunk before leaving work that you found yourself at Heathrow on the Piccadilly line. Never let me win an argument: tell me I can't prove something, even if I already have. Tell me you're having a weekend off sugar and then blame Jackson when three of the four scones we bought have disappeared. If I ever leave you at home without food, have a bottle of wine for dinner.

Make sure you tell someone the password to your computer the day before you die. Make sure you tell someone how much you love them and how proud you are of them the minute before you die. Be the most wonderful person you can be. Love me, love Jackson, love both of our families and I promise we will do her proud.

Dessie, I promise to take good care of our son. I know I'll never get over you. I know I'll never get over the fact you picked me to be the love of your life. I know I'll never forget how happy we made each other over the last eight years. And I know that Jackson and I will love you forever.

After the service the vicar and I walked arm in arm to the cemetery behind the church and together we committed Desreen's body to the ground. I had woken early that day to write her a letter, which included a rare picture of her, Jackson and me together. I have little recollection of the words but they were full of love and disbelief.

As others scattered earth on her coffin, I threw in the letter and a single rose I'd pulled from her beautiful spray. Bright winter sun shone down, and I stared up at the sky in sheer astonishment at what was going on. Tears fell down my cheeks as I looked across to my family and friends, who stood on the opposite side of her unfilled grave. And then I walked away alone. My wife's life wasn't with me in that field anymore – only her death.

BEING WEAK

The fact that the day after Desreen's funeral, 1 December, was the beginning of the festive party season was not lost on me. I woke up with a worse head and stomach than I've ever experienced from any office Christmas party.

Over the years I seemed to have developed an always-regrettable taste for neat whisky at a funeral. It started at Christmas 2009 when one of my two best men, Lee, lost his dad, and continued when the other, Woody, lost his mum two Christmases later. As each other's best friends we had now all been forced to prop one another up at the most devastating of events. I even remember making a gallows humour comment to our other mates about not spending too much time with the three of us during the Christmas that followed Desreen's death, just in case we were cursed. A stupid comment, but one that was made when I was still crazily high on grief and shock.

Desreen's funeral proved no exception to my whisky habit. I started the day with dignity, fortitude and resilience and then gradually fell apart. Lee ended up walking me back from the pub in tears to Desreen's family home nearby, where he sat with me at their table. As soon as more whisky appeared I took myself off to bed. I'd already drunk enough for the sight of it to make me sick.

The next morning I woke up in pieces. Reality had finally

kicked in. I had the sort of blues – if wildly more tragic and intense – that many people get soon after their wedding day. The event that's taken so long to plan is over and although you're away on honeymoon together, you kind of miss being surrounded by the people you love.

I was sick to the stomach and worried and confused about the future. *How was I going to live my life without Desreen? How was I ever going to care enough about life again to keep living? How was I going to look after Jackson alone? Would I ever feel anything but sadness again?* I was lying in the bed that my wife slept in as a child and when I looked out of her window I faced the direction of the cemetery where we had buried her the day before.

I needed to get out of my in-laws' house as soon as possible, so I called my wife's great friend Caroline to ask if she wanted to go for a drive. We decided to visit the place where Desreen and I had got married just fifteen months before. Woody and his girlfriend, Katy, arrived with Lee and his wife, Olive, and our friend David who had flown over from New York to attend the funeral.

It didn't seem possible that we could be standing in the same spot where the wedding had happened a few short months before. And yet we shared jokes about how much money Desreen had spent on filling the marquee with flowers, only to tell Lee that he would need to drive her back to the wholesale florist to buy more.

'Dessie, I think you're buying too many flowers. Benji's going to get really cross when he finds out how much money you've spent,' Lee advised my soon-to-be bride.

'You're right,' she replied, as she picked out just one stem and asked the girl at the check out if she would be kind enough to return it to its original display.

On our wedding day I was pacing my room by 5.00a.m., unable to sleep from nerves, when I heard the swoosh sound of an email dropping into my inbox on my iPad. It was the final balance for the wedding. Desreen had thought that I wouldn't check my messages before the ceremony but also didn't want to tell me afterwards in case it ruined the honeymoon. I decided not to reply. I didn't want to get cross with her on the morning of our special day – so I waited until the afternoon.

'You look amazing, darling,' I whispered to her as she met me at the altar forty-five minutes late, 'and thanks for your email.'

She pulled her usual mischievous hand-hidden laugh. One that started in her eyes, expressing her recognition that she was in trouble but ended on her lips, telling you that she thought her own misbehaviour was hilarious. I've never met anyone else who could make themselves laugh so hard.

As the six of us wandered the grounds of our wedding venue, I slipped off by myself to sit on a bench in front of the very beautiful Stansted House, the backdrop to our nuptials. Then we huddled, cuddled and cried together. I had lost my wife but they had lost a great friend and all of us were shocked and heartbroken.

My true heartbreak, I was soon to discover, had barely begun. The day after Desreen's funeral was the beginning of my descent into a new phase of grief. As my hangover kicked in the shock began to wear off. As the adrenaline that had seemed to keep me strong for the last three weeks dissipated I was physically sick. When the shock-induced strength began to fade I felt disgusted at the person I'd been for most of the time since Des died. I hated that I'd got through my wife's funeral with hardly a tear. I was repulsed by some of the insensitive things I had said. I was ashamed that I'd been able to function so well when

I had lost the woman I love. I felt it was time to stop seeing strength as some sort of badge of honour when my wife had just died. I wondered why I wasn't allowed to be weak when the worst thing that I could have imagined had just come along and ruined my life. And I wondered what sort of role model I was going to be for my son if I acted as though nothing had happened when his mother had been taken from him just weeks after his second birthday.

TELLING JACKSON

Jackson was at his mother's funeral but I don't think he had any idea what was going on. In fact he spent most of it playing outside with a family friend. By this time I'd learned from a child bereavement charity called Winston's Wish that a twenty-five-month-old child can't grasp the concept of death. His sense of loss didn't seem to set in for quite some time. Since Desreen's death he had been surrounded by friends and family. Gifts, affection and attention all came pouring through our door.

I'm sure that he did notice her absence from one day to the next because he would often squeal with excitement when he heard a key in the door, and yet it wasn't until after the funeral that he really started to show any noticeable signs of missing his mum.

Our kitchen window overlooked the front door and often Desreen would arrive home from work as I was feeding Jackson his dinner in his high chair. She would never just let herself in without first trying to make him laugh: she'd pull faces; she'd play peekaboo; or she'd walk down imaginary stairs, disappear out of view and then pretend to walk back up. Jackson would howl with laughter and scream with joy until his mummy came in and kissed him all over his face. They were just so in love.

After she was killed, Jackson walked my dad to our front door and pointed at a light shining through the frosted glass.

'It's Mummy,' he told his granddad. And I suppose we all wanted it to be so – that her spirit had come to visit her son – but really I think that it was business as usual in my son's little head and he genuinely expected her to come home as night fell.

His apparent lack of heartbreak over the extended absence of his mum crushed me. Our home had been full of people calling her Desreen and not Mummy. So he joined in; within a matter of days he'd gone from calling her Mummy to Desreen too. It was like a dagger through my heart because I thought he was forgetting her.

Then something happened that brought me back to my senses. I put on a DVD, something like *Ben & Holly's Little Kingdom*, a show he hadn't watched in weeks, whatever it was, and he recited all the characters' names. I realised then that he couldn't have forgotten the person he idolised the most; he was just copying the big people.

Even so, it took about a month for Jackson to actually *ask* for Mummy in my company. Waiting so long for him to start to question her absence was the single most painful thing I ever felt as a bereaved husband, and the pain was for my wife rather than for myself. I felt as if she was being cheated. As if all the time and love she had invested in him had disappeared in an instant. Sure, he'd stood at the front door and shouted her name when he thought she was coming in from work, but he hadn't yet asked, *Where's Mummy?*

When he finally did, he probably couldn't have chosen a worse time. I was begging for it to happen. It wasn't going to make me feel pain; it was going to bring relief. But he did it in front of Desreen's father, Kelson; brother, Anthony; and one of my two best men, Woody. That evening I learned that the unprepared male doesn't tend to be too great at this kind of thing.

'Where's Mummy? Where's Mummy? Where's Mummy gone?

Where's Mummy gone? Want Mummy. Want Mummy. Want Muuuuuummmmmmyyyyyy!' he cried over and over again.

He had been storing it up and now he was using it all in one go, and the men present unanimously did that thing where you think if you can tense your shoulders hard enough, you won't be in the room anymore. A kind of cross between an ostrich with its head in the sand and the nose wiggle from the US comedy *Bewitched* that made the characters disappear.

The weight lifted off my shoulders and was transferred straight on to theirs. For me it meant that it wouldn't be long before I could finally tell him the truth about what had happened instead of continuing to put off the inevitable; for them it meant they were sitting in the middle of the one situation that they had dreaded most and didn't know how to deal with. Who the hell does?

As Jackson sobbed, I took him from the living room to his bedroom. I switched off the lights and we looked out of his window. The home we lived in at the time was a third-storey flat on top of a hill in East Dulwich. It had a view overlooking Canary Wharf with the O_2 Arena in the distance. There were lots of bright lights and I had discovered that looking at them from his dark room calmed him.

I understood two things in that moment: firstly, that I wasn't going to talk to Jackson about Desreen's death while he was clearly already so upset; secondly, that I wasn't going to use the darkness of the night sky as an opportunity to tell him she was up in the stars. Although he had now started to ask questions, that night would not be the moment he was told he'd never see his mummy again. He was already too distressed.

The right time came soon before Christmas. I'd taken Jackson up north to see my parents and family in Southport. I'd decided to spend Christmas Day itself with Desreen's parents as that was what Desreen had planned. Any other decision felt disrespectful and inappropriate.

I should never have gone home, though. It was much too soon. I knew I'd made the wrong decision when an acquaintance offered to buy me a shot in a pub I visited with Woody to mark the anniversary of his mum's death – she had died the year before. I was taken aback by the thought that tequila could be a gesture of respect. But worse still, I realised that this guy had never met my wife. I'd known him for twenty years and it somehow made it feel like my relationship and life with Desreen had never happened. I was suddenly just Ben; Ben and Desreen never was and never would be again.

The change of scenery brought out a different side in Jackson. He was more playful and seemed happier than he had been during the past few weeks. I, on the other hand, was sinking into a deeper and deeper abyss. I felt guilty that I had to keep shifting him from one place to another when he must already have been so confused. I felt bad that we had no sense of routine and that I needed to keep leaving him in the care of family to be able to handle all the pressures that had fallen on me since Desreen's death: work, nursery, media, funeral directors, the police, solicitors, financial advisors, child bereavement advisors, doctors and therapists. I felt wretched; I wasn't eating well. I was constantly tearful, often snappy and usually unappreciative of the help, love or support that those close to me tried to offer. I was drinking every day; not much, because I couldn't really stomach it, but enough to leave me with too little energy to be fun company for a little boy. As if I could have been fun anyway. I was partially drugged on sleeping pills to help me drift off at night, high on caffeine to keep me awake in the day and attempting to maintain some sense of balance with over-the-counter tablets designed to bring about calm.

I had tried Valium a couple of times to help stop my mind from racing. A friend gave me the leftovers of an old prescription when my doctor failed to offer support. I visited him three or four times after Desreen was killed, but decided that was it when he asked me, 'Are you that guy whose wife died?' in front of both my son and my mother-in-law. I'm sure that if I had gone in with a severed limb he would have done nothing other than ask if I'd considered counselling.

The night after we arrived in Southport, I took Jackson to bed while he was happy and calm. I lay with him, read him a story and told him how much I loved him. He cuddled up to me softly. I realised that the time was right to start trying to explain what I knew was going to take some time to sink in.

As soon as my son had started asking where she had gone, I made a decision about how to handle it. I decided to tell him the truth. Somehow the illustrated books I'd been given by well-meaning friends, which explained to a badger that his elderly rabbit friend had gone to the stars, were not going to help my child understand why his mother would never be back.

So that night, the week before Christmas, I showed him a picture of Desreen on my phone and invited him to kiss it.

'Jackson,' I began, 'Mummy's gone away and she can't ever come back.'

Our vicar's wife had given me some literature that she had dug out about child bereavement, something she had studied as part of a Master's degree years before. This had pointed me in the right direction of charities including Winston's Wish, Grief Encounter and Child Bereavement UK, who explained that Jackson was too young to understand the meaning of *dead* or *killed*. In fact, I'd learned that children don't even know what *ever* or *never* are until they are around five or six. But still, I felt that a consistent narrative would be important to maintain over the years.

'She didn't want to go,' I continued. 'She would never have left you out of choice because she loved you more than anyone or anything in the world. But Daddy's still here and I'm going to look after you now. And I know how to look after you because Mummy taught me.'

Jackson didn't get upset; he simply cuddled up close, nodded and repeated some of my words back. There was no way he had taken in what I'd said but I knew I needed to start somewhere.

We lay together until he drifted off. Once he was asleep I gently peeled him off my chest, tucked him into bed and went back downstairs to tell my mum what I'd told my son. I asked her and everyone who cared for him to use exactly the same words as I had, to try to minimise his confusion. I banned expressions such *gone to a better place* because I worried that he might want to go there too or, perhaps worse, think she'd chosen that mysterious place over him. And I chose not to talk about heaven because, at that time, he didn't know the geographical difference between paradise and the local park.

I suppose in my heart I knew that it was going to take months, perhaps even years for the message to sink in and to be truly understood. The maddening thing about bereaved toddlers, or rather, any toddlers, is that you can tell them something one day but they may well have forgotten the next. Even if they say they understand, you can often find ways to prove that actually they don't.

Jackson used to do this thing that I loved. When I took him to bed and he snuggled up to my chest, I could ask him anything and he would agree with a silent nod. At two years old this was the only time when he was actually quiet because he would talk, sing and giggle all day long and often even in his sleep. It was also the only time he wasn't contrary, because he was going through the phase of saying 'No!' and 'Not!' to almost everything anyone said.

'Jackson, do you want some milk?' Silent nod.

'Jackson, do you want a dummy?' Silent nod.

'Jackson, could you do a better job at fixing the economy than the current coalition government?' Silent nod.

No end of fun for me. Fun aside, however, it meant that when I asked him if he understood what had happened to Mummy at the one time of day when we really got to talk as man and boy, undisturbed, he would simply *silent nod*. I would go to sleep more or less peacefully, thinking that he had started to take it in, but the next day I really couldn't be sure if he was going to ask where she'd gone, again and again.

The fascinating thing, though, is that he never really asked 'Where's Mummy?' after that night. The question quickly turned to the statement 'Want Mummy.' His question had been answered and he proved to me that he had absorbed the information when Caroline's three-year-old child asked the same question just four months later.

'Where's Jackson's mummy?'

Caroline and I froze and gawped at one another as her son, Arlo, asked the question that we'd all come to dread. But Jackson, a child thirty-one years our junior, casually looked up and replied, 'She's gone away in the sky, far away. She can't come back.' Then he continued to play with his trains before moving on to a spot of colouring with crayons and inks.

Although I felt sad that he had to explain why his mum was no longer with us, I was also so proud of everyone who'd had a role in delivering a consistent message to him. Sure, heaven came into the equation for some people, 'the sky' slipped in when it wasn't quite the message I'd originally briefed, but the important thing was that my son, who was not yet even two-and-a-half, could answer for himself. He didn't follow a question with another question. Although my heart broke for both of us in that moment, I just couldn't imagine how much worse it would have been for him if he were still asking all the questions about his mum himself.

But questions weren't the only thing that hurt; sometimes Daddy just wasn't enough. When Jackson fell over he would call 'Mummy!' Whenever he felt sad he did the same. It's beyond painful to hear your child cry for something, for someone, you cannot provide. Yet over time the mentions of her name would become a great comfort to me. Yes, Jackson would be distressed when he called for my wife and perhaps it sounds strange that I could draw any solace from his suffering. But to me it meant she was still there in his head or his heart; that his reflexes immediately responded with a desire to be with Desreen.

I was told by someone who worked at the bereavement charity Winston's Wish, 'He might forget the memories but he'll never forget the love.' What a wonderful thought to hang on to when a child loses a parent too soon.

MERRY CHRISTMAS

The run-up to Christmas was a difficult time to lose my wife. Casual friends and acquaintances seemed to go back to their normal lives even more quickly than they might otherwise have done, because it was such a busy time of year. And, if anything, my wife's death appeared to have encouraged people to seize the day.

It's hard work watching the party season unfold before your eyes on the street, on the television or online when you are in pieces. That Christmas I got close to understanding how it must feel to be alone at that time of year: in bed without my wife but unable to sleep as partygoers sang drunken songs outside my window; seeing everyone having fun via their Facebook posts. It's not that I actually was alone. Friends and family came to visit or stay; and yet I'd never felt more left out or more isolated.

Having bought me tickets for the athletics at the London 2012 Olympics to celebrate our first, and ultimately only, wedding anniversary on 6 August, six days later Desreen handed me the tickets for a birthday trip to Marrakech. We were meant to fly on 5 December but instead I found myself emailing the owners of the riad where we had planned to stay to tell them that the person who booked the room was now dead. A big part of me wanted to honour her gift, but the trip just a few miles north to Thomas Land caused me enough heartache to know that flying to another continent to be alone in a bustling and unfamiliar city would be a pilgrimage too far.

I couldn't really distinguish the month that followed, save Christmas Day and New Year's Eve. The days and weeks had become a blur of sleeplessness, alcohol and Valium. My amazing friends, who never faltered in their support, visited regularly but I was incapable of behaving like my old self. I would fall asleep mid-conversation. I would have to leave the restaurant they had taken me to because I needed to rest but then I'd lie awake in bed all night thinking about Desreen and worrying about Jackson. I would go through pictures of the two of them on my iPhone and laptop and I'd torture myself for having shot video footage too tightly focussed on my son to clearly see his mum. I would read all the comments that people had left about my wife on Facebook, think about how much she seemed to have been loved by people some of whom I didn't even know, and that would make me miss her even more.

I also spent a lot of time on the internet in the middle of the night trying to find other men roughly the same age as me who had been widowed and were now left caring for children alone. I wanted to speak to someone to whom I could relate in the (perhaps naïve) hope that they might tell me that it was all going to be okay. My search was in vain and the hours I spent hoping to find empathy and support from other young widowers only served to make me feel more alone.

I can't remember a time during the weeks that followed the funeral when I wasn't in tears. My eyes constantly felt like they were on fire; Olive bought me silk handkerchiefs to stop me from irritating them further with tissue and Laura gave me cream that she thought might soothe the skin around them. I may have damaged or blocked a tear duct from sobbing so much because even when I stopped crying, one of my eyes still watered. I would feel tears running down my face even when Valium temporarily robbed me of my true emotions.

Life being what it is, even this time wasn't without its funny moments. Lee and Woody took me to the same local restaurant on two separate occasions within a week. Both times I asked the waiter if we could have a quiet corner because we needed to talk privately. I guess I meant I wanted to *cry* privately. The tears inevitably came and, each time, both friends reached out across the table to take my hand and comfort me.

'Lee, please don't touch me,' I begged. 'It's bad enough that I've just lost my wife, but now it looks like I'm being dumped in public by a man.'

'Woody, put your hand away,' I found myself repeating a few days later. 'Lee was all over me in here the other night and I was crying. It's going to look like I can't keep a woman *or* a man.'

But dark humour was little comfort for the tortuous pain. I wept uncontrollably to my dad about what a terrible father I thought I'd become. I didn't even have the energy to play with my little boy because of what was going on in my head at night and what I was doing to my body all day. Dad tried to comfort me by telling me that I must never think or say that, which just made me cross. I didn't want to be told to stop feeling the way I felt. I later realised that he was right; I was the one who was making myself feel so bad about how I had responded to the grief. In that moment I knew that I was the only person who could really affect my own feelings. But that moment of realisation was a way off.

So I struggled through Christmas, put on a brave face and put up a tree. It was as though Desreen had decorated it herself. I discovered beautiful purple bags from Liberty, Dessie's favourite shop in the whole world, filled with new baubles and trinkets to accompany those she'd overspent on the year before.

I also discovered that the things one might expect to hurt don't always trigger pain. I knew *The Holiday* – a schmaltzy festive film in which Jude Law's character reveals he's a widowed father with two beautiful little girls – was on television the night I put up the tree. Desreen loved that film and she knew how much the widower scene always pulled at my heartstrings, but this time, I was completely unmoved. Suddenly it was just an actor playing a part. It had happened to me for real. Somehow this fictitious scene no longer warranted my tears.

Everybody around me was trying so hard to help while grieving their own loss, too. Yet I felt ungrateful, angry, irritated and as though I were the one responsible for making everyone feel better by allowing them to ease *my* pain. Immediately after Desreen died I told myself that kindness would get me through, allowing it in and passing it on, but a devil pushed that angel from my shoulder and whispered in my ear that it was time to be honest, to be direct and to just tell it as it was.

I was still inundated by a barrage of correspondence, most of it ending with the line, *Let me know if there's anything I can do to help*. I was unsure why I so detested that offer until I spoke to someone at a charity called Care for the Family. They pointed me in the direction of some guidelines they had published online, which would eventually help me to help others to help me. The document – entitled 'How you can help me – things I wish you knew', which I've included at the back of the book – was designed to give friends and family an insight into how they might best support widows and widowers.

One of the tips included: *Give practical support. I'm not able to cope with routines at the moment so providing meals; help at home and with my children is vital.* Another read: *Remember my children! They can sometimes be neglected, as they may not be so willing to talk.*

Finally I had something practical I could forward to people to take the pressure off me. And something that didn't involve *me* coming up with ideas. You see, I was in shock, overwhelmed and overtaken by grief; I was caring for my two-year-old child; I was trying to find the appetite to eat and summon the thirst to drink; I was willing myself to have the stomach to keep both food and water down; and I was hosting dozens of people through the suddenly revolving doors of my tiny flat and getting absolutely no sleep. I had no energy left to try to think up ideas for how people could help me. I had spent my entire career coming up with solutions to save others the bother and suddenly I resented it. People offering to help me was just making my to-do list seem even longer, and so I stopped and wrote the following email to my closest friends and family.

I wanted to share something with you that a charity supporting Jackson and me provided me with today. It basically sums up the *What can I do to help?* conundrum.

If I'm honest it's a question that I'm coming to dread. It's like having the longest ever to-do list, no time or energy to do any of the work on it and then being asked to do something else by everyone you've ever known. It means that the person being asked has to think of something when that person can barely decide what to have for breakfast or whether to even bother. That might sound bloody ungrateful but I'm learning that honesty is really important at the moment.

I've spoken to some of you more than others over the last couple of weeks, but I thought I'd just let you know that I am turning to a number of charities, resources and lots of literature to try to understand the grief process and what to expect from it. Especially when it comes to Jackson. As things arise that I believe are worth sharing, I will.

I know we're all in it together so I think it's important to share and be as open as possible. Feel free to pass the attachment on for any of our sakes.

Love, Ben & Jackson xx

I felt a positive impact from circulating this note almost immediately. My friends and family stopped saying 'Let me know if I can help' and instead offered practical support without being asked. Anna (Posh Spice) left a bag full of homemade food on my doorstep and sent me a text later to let me know it was there. I remember how much I appreciated not having to play host in return because I was already so busy taking care of Jackson and tidying up after the constant stream of visitors. When Jackson and I went away to be with family for a couple of days Marianne let herself into my flat, with a key I'd given her for emergencies, to drop off some groceries for when we got back. But the thing I wanted people to do more than anything was to focus their attention on Jackson when they came over to visit. I knew that he could sense all the sadness around him and the last thing I wanted was for him to be left alone in the corner with his trains as the grown-ups talked about his mother's death. Thanks to the suggestions that I'd shared, friends and family started to come over to play and not just to talk.

As things started to improve with the people close to me, I

think the anger that I didn't know I was feeling needed a new channel. I truly believe the feeling of kindness for others that I felt running through me in the weeks that followed my wife's death helped get me through. But now I recognise that there was rage there, too.

I didn't feel I was angry about Desreen's death. I wasn't blaming people, I didn't curse the heavens and I didn't do the whole *How could you leave me?* thing that I'm told so many people do. Maybe that was largely because the circumstances around her death made it feel unreal. Neither our friends and family nor I really lashed out, because we were denied a focus for any potential fury. We were told that any potential legal proceedings against the driver or the insurance company of the car that killed my wife would take over a year. This made us all respond to the situation in a similar manner: we simply put the question of blame to one side and grieved the loss of the girl we all loved rather than focussing our attentions on a driver whose name none of us even knew.

Although I didn't outwardly display anger towards others, if anyone irritated me I felt a disproportionate amount of rage towards them and I would inwardly rant a soliloquy of disapproving abuse. And the list of offenders was long: people who were in touch too much; people who weren't in touch enough; people who weren't in touch at all; people who hadn't been in touch for a decade but were now all over me; people who hadn't liked me for over a decade but suddenly saw me with newly rose-tinted glasses; and people who I felt wanted to come to my circus, come backstage to meet the ringmaster and then get access all areas. I just couldn't imagine why some people who had shown so little interest in my life, or indeed my wife's, when both were still intact, were suddenly so interested now. I suppose sometimes people only go to a show to say they've been.

I got December over with. I hated every minute. Initially I wanted to enjoy Christmas for my son but then I told myself it was ridiculous to think that he was enjoying it without his mum. The only moment I remember feeling anything close to happiness was on 22 December at Bev and Kelson's house when Jackson handed me a used Manila envelope that had contained a letter from the Inland Revenue, which he'd scribbled all over in black pen.

'What's this, Jackson?' I asked.

'It's Mummy,' he insisted with a smile.

His drawing of Desreen now sits in a frame in our house and I will keep it for as long as I live.

On Christmas Eve I attended a midnight service with Caroline, Lee, Anna and Paul and sobbed as we sang the lyrics 'mother and child' and 'sleep in heavenly peace' from the hymn, 'Silent Night', which we'd all sung in the same church three and a half weeks earlier at Desreen's funeral.

On Christmas Day I sat at her family dining table with her seat next to mine empty. We'd tried hard to make it work: Bev did her best to motivate herself to cook up the usual feast, but with a heavy heart; I ruined a decent piece of beef because I wasn't concentrating and I didn't give a shit; and we exchanged gifts even though we felt no sense of satisfaction from unwrapping what was inside. All we really cared about was making it nice for Jackson.

He was a joy that day. He played nicely with his new toys and wore an outfit that I'd bought him from Liberty, knowing that Desreen would approve.

I remember feeling so much love for him but also so much pain. Christmas had always felt like a magical time for my family – my mum and dad made it so amazing when my brothers and I were kids. But now, as an adult looking at my own child, who had lost his mum before he even knew what Christmas was about, the magic had totally gone. All it felt like now was accentuated pain.

When Jackson went to bed that night I thought about how lucky I was to still be part of the family that had embraced me as one of their own. Bev lives her life doing everything for others and so I already knew I wasn't alone in caring for my son. Kelson and I had supported each other through the awful experiences of arranging Desreen's funeral and handling the legal issues surrounding her death with nothing but respect and affection towards one another. Anthony and I grew closer than ever, even though we'd already considered each other brothers for years. And I thought about all of the friends and family members out there who must have been thinking of Jackson and me while also dealing with their own personal agony over Desreen's death.

Deep down I knew that the people who were trying to help were only doing so because they cared, and yet I almost ended the year angry with pretty much all of them. When Jackson and I came back to London, Bev joined us and watched as I grew more and more irritated. But then New Year's Eve came around and, strangely, it made me come to my senses.

MARRIED FAMILIES

On our wedding day, John, the vicar, spoke about how our marriage would create a union not just between Desreen and me, but also a bond between our families. These words sang in my ears as I looked back at a congregation made up of two families and two sets of friends, which, over the years, had begun to merge into one. That night lots of rum and cognac would further strengthen the bond. Uncles, black and white, would become brothers – at least for one very drunken night.

Six and a half years with Desreen had already made her brother mine, which, in some ways, is a miracle – given that the first time we met I was in bed with his twenty-five-year-old little sister. Her parents, who I met in a slightly more orthodox lunch setting, had also become like a second mum and dad to me. She'd slotted into my family in exactly the same way.

I had taken both Desreen and myself entirely by surprise with my proposal in June 2009. We had always agreed that commitment and children were what mattered to us most, rather than marriage. We had decided that we'd sooner use the money to buy a home and I knew that Dessie could think of nothing worse than all eyes being on her as she walked down the aisle. Beautiful, confident and self-assured, Desreen was also shy and easily embarrassed. Only her skin colour hid her frequent blushes.

I'm still not sure exactly what came over me, but one day I just woke up and decided to go and buy an engagement ring. I suppose I knew that it wouldn't go to waste, even if she were adamant that she didn't want to get married, because she frequently told me that she expected to be bought a diamond, either way.

On that day in June, ostensibly we were just going for a picnic in London's Regent's Park. I was probably behaving a bit erratically, and it probably seemed strange that we were eating lunch by 11.30a.m. 'because the weather looked like it might turn,' but she seemed none the wiser.

We found a beautiful spot by the lake. I'd been to Selfridge's for the hamper. Not for the contents, just the basket. A friend of mine had told me that a handbag designer Desreen loved had made a limited run of wicker baskets for the department store, so it was the only choice. I filled it with her favourite foods, which made for a fairly unlikely engagement lunch: crisps, ham, a baguette, smoked cheese, some olives and prosecco rather than champagne. What can I say? The girl knew what she liked.

I also found these little contraptions to hold glasses, which you push into the ground like tent pegs, so you can't knock your drinks over on uneven terrain. I bought plastic flutes rather than crystal so she didn't get suspicious. I had remembered a night when we went to the theatre, about a year after we met, and instead of getting a taxi, we caught the bus and drank cava out of two plastic cups. I'd taken them from the water cooler at work. She told me how much she preferred this casually romantic gesture to anything more traditional or clichéd.

I would pop the question in a way that only made sense to her. So rarely did we slow life to a pace where we would actually sit and read the papers together, or play a board game, that when we did, the moments stuck out. Just a few weeks earlier we had found ourselves in Shoreditch House, a private members' club in east London, chilling out and playing Scrabble. 'I love this game,' she said, to my great surprise, as she made up another word that she insisted she was counting even if it wasn't in the dictionary.

'My mum says it all the time. You're racist if you don't let me have it,' she exclaimed, closing the conversation down in the lowest way possible.

I loved it, too. I loved to watch her childlike mannerisms at play. I loved the way the game would inevitably result in the kind of quarrels we had on the night we met – petty, flirtatious, aimless, daft and funny. And so a travel Scrabble set went in the hamper, too.

'Oh my God! Crisps, fizz, ham, olives, Scrabble, this is like the best day of my life!' she oh-so-kindly stated to a nervous man who only wanted to make the whole thing perfect for her.

Great set-up, I thought to myself.

Desreen and I were not traditional romantics. Fun and laughter were always too close by for us to drown in each other's gaze as we whispered sweet nothings. And fun and laughter were heading towards us just as I had got comfortable enough to get down on one knee.

Fun and laughter, on this occasion, were a demonic squirrel and a flock of geese. The little bastards were dead set on attacking our picnic and claiming it as their own. The squirrel got closer and more aggressive the harder I tried to shoo it away. In the end we were howling with laughter because the beast – nothing more than a rodent in a fancy fur coat – got off with a slice of tomato, which it took right off one of our plates. Then the geese came over and it all became too much.

Desreen hated most creatures. She had a phobia of birds flying into her hair and not being able to escape. Her view was that if I couldn't prove that something categorically *couldn't* happen then it could. And if it *could* happen, however unlikely, then she needed to be scared of it. It made all sorts of things difficult, including city breaks (because there are always pigeons in open spaces) and going to the cinema (because 'that's where terrorists leave bombs'). We never did see many films together and perhaps in the end she was right to be worried about seemingly unlikely dangers lurking round the corner.

When we eventually got settled in – the flora and fauna finally left us to our lunch – I offered her the bag of Scrabble letters but, for once, she let me go first. I dramatically rummaged around in the pouch, although it was all an act because I was already holding seven letters in my hand. Spelling out *M.A.R.R.Y.M.E.*

Immediately, she accused me of cheating, saying it was impossible to get a seven-letter word on your first go. Then she took another look at the letter tiles, burst into tears and said yes.

Although Desreen seemed confident and outgoing to some, she was naturally quite shy and pensive. I could tell, even early on, because I'm exactly the same. Now she sat on the picnic blanket on the grass and just took it all in, staring at the ring.

It was a very unusual antique piece and I could tell she wouldn't be sure whether it was her style until she'd spent some time studying it. But she soon decided she loved it and in the months and years that followed, she frequently told me that she liked it all the more as time went on.

She was shocked by my proposal and initially very thoughtful, but before long she was ecstatic. She told me that it was time to go out and celebrate in style; I've never drunk more champagne and prosecco in one day.

Having successfully kept the whole thing a secret from Desreen, she turned the tables on me a couple of months later. We took the day off work to celebrate my thirtieth birthday and she booked an amazing restaurant in Kensington that our good friend Hannah, who works in food PR, had recommended. I could tell Des was up to no good because she kept giggling to herself, but I couldn't put my finger on what she might have planned.

All of a sudden the waiter came over to say that he had an announcement to make and a gift to give me. I could only imagine that Hannah was involved and that she had put on a cake to embarrass me in front of the other diners.

A cake did come, but that wasn't the bit that made me break into a shame-fuelled sweat. With all eyes on me, I was invited to open a little box in full view of the restaurant. From it I pulled a white gold and black diamond ring, which a friend of Desreen's had designed and made, and she asked me to marry her, as if we weren't already engaged.

I was touched and mortified in equal measure. Everyone was staring at me as though they had witnessed an unrivalled episode of romance unfold, while Desreen almost wet the plush leather banquette on which she perched. I could hear little snorts of laughter as she tried to contain her amusement at her own joke.

Two weeks before our first engagement, I had visited her parents to ask them both, individually, for their permission. Bev made it easy for me to find a quiet moment. Kelson, on the other hand, did not. He'd picked up the nickname 'Babbling Brooks' early on in life, for the amount he could talk without coming up for air. That weekend was no exception. In the end Bev had to make an excuse to head off with Desreen to the ladies' room of the restaurant where we were having dinner, to allow the two of us a moment. I took advantage of my brief opportunity and pretty much came straight out with it. He agreed, too. And then the following week he had a stroke, though thank God, he turned out to be fine.

Desreen's reaction to my proposal, in the light of her dad's recent illness, reinforced everything I already knew, and loved, about the woman I would wed.

'Did you ask my dad's permission?' she enquired, a few minutes after I proposed.

'Of course I did. I asked him a couple of weeks ago,' I replied.

'Do you think it's your fault he had a stroke, then? He was probably nervous about how much it's going to cost him!'

'I actually can't believe you just said that.'

'I'm serious!' she insisted.

Thankfully, clinical evidence proved I was not to blame. This was not the sort of stroke a person has from living an unhealthy lifestyle and then getting some unexpected news. At the time, I was in my late twenties and Kelson was in his late fifties, but he would easily have won the washboard stomach contest.

Kelson would go on to have an operation and make a full recovery, walk his beloved daughter down the aisle and give a speech at our wedding, which he pointed out was held, fittingly, on Jamaica Day.

Being part of a Jamaican family gave a whole new dimension to my life. Once a mild-mannered, calm and quite shy young man, I learned the benefits (and pleasures) of being direct, telling it as it is and not taking any nonsense from anyone.

Despite having imparted these qualities to me, Desreen would reprimand me for trying to wear the trousers in our relationship. 'We can't both be in charge,' she would insist.

Our vicar would later support her argument. On our wedding day he told a story that somehow involved Jesus walking on water at the Sea of Galilee . . . and Mark Twain. The punchline – his sermons generally conclude with a joke – was about how two people can't stand up in a boat at the same time. The moral of the story was that married couples need to compromise and work together to avoid *rocking the boat* – only one can take control at a time.

The morning after our wedding day I woke to see Desreen already staring into my eyes. 'Benji,' she said, 'please may I stand up in the boat today?'

I secretly loved how she would take the lead. She loved us being together, she loved our relationship but she loved her independence, too.

'Just to let you know, I can't take your surname, Benji,' she said before we got married. 'I've worked hard to build up my name in the industry.'

'I wouldn't ask you to, darling. I just want to marry you. You can call yourself whatever you like,' I replied. 'Anyway, Des Dutton doesn't suit you. It makes you sound more like a snooker player than a fashion agent.'

That was back when my surname was simply Dutton. My wife, Desreen Brooks, didn't take my name when we married but our son and I took hers a month after she died. I wanted us both to carry Desreen's family name as well as my own. In December 2012, we became Benjamin Brooks-Dutton and Jackson Bo Brooks-Dutton. The hyphen was really important to me because it symbolised a joining of two families, one that couldn't be broken by death. I only wish I'd done it while she was alive. Still, I know she would have loved the fact that she had stood her ground as a strong independent woman while I became her 'wife'.

There was another gesture that I wanted to make after her death – I got a tattoo. Thankfully it wasn't a drunken grief-fuelled whim; I'd been thinking about it even before she died. Desreen and I had a family monogram designed for our wedding invitations, consisting of our son's and our own initials – DJB. We were planning to have another child and I made her promise that we would stick to the name we had chosen whether we were blessed with a boy or a girl (her reading *The Secret* meant it was guaranteed we were having a girl anyway, apparently). As the name began with the letter B, I would never need to add another letter or have a difficult conversation with our future child about why I hadn't gone under the needle on *her* behalf.

So I now have the design that was used for our wedding and both Desreen's funeral and headstone, imprinted on my chest for the rest of my days. Every time I look in the mirror I am reminded of our love. And every time Jackson sees it, he points enthusiastically and cheerfully exclaims, 'It's Mummy, Daddy and Jackson.' His broken family forever etched over my broken heart.

NEW YEAR

Friends had invited me to spend a low-key New Year's Eve with them but I was clear on where I would be come midnight – in bed with Valium and a sleeping pill to help keep the pain of grief at bay. Actually, I was in bed by 9.30p.m. but neither the Valium nor the sleep aid did anything to help me nod off. I could hear fireworks outside in the street and explosive thoughts inside my head. My fingers were starting to feel itchy with the desire to write. I knew there was something I wanted to say but I wasn't sure what or why.

I logged on to Facebook and it came to me. There was a pretty consistent 'fuck off 2012' narrative and a 'good riddance to a bad year' tone unfolding online. I suppose I had the right to join in but instead I thought about how sad Desreen would have been if she thought I had written off such a wonderful year just because of the way it ended. I started to think about all the great memories and decided to share my thoughts with my online social circle.

2012: almost half of our son's life; our first (and only) wedding anniversary; tickets to the athletics at the Olympics that very same special day; the year Jackson discovered he loved a little plastic train called Thomas more than most human beings; the pride I felt in witnessing my wife start her own fashion business with an old friend; the humanist wedding of the year; a new job and a big promotion; unforgettable holidays with some of our best friends; countless great times with all of them; beautiful babies born who don't yet know how lucky they are to have inherited such top friends; and then tragedy and loss that has touched so many lives.

But it would be a disservice to my wife to say 2012 was a completely shit year. In October Desreen asked me to buy Jackson a commemorative London 2012 five-pound coin as a memento of an amazing year that he wouldn't remember but that we could explain that he was a part of. It just struck me that we can follow that same gesture of remembrance into 2013 and beyond, for his sake.

So yes, it was the year his mum died, but it was also a year when she had the opportunity to show him how much she loved him every day. And it was the year she always put him first. For those who continue to be part of his life, let's focus on the good times we all shared this year. I know he'll come to cherish the memories as much as we do.

Love to you all for 2013. Here's to remembering the good times and planning new ones xx

I logged off my laptop and I logged out of 2012. It would be 2013 when I woke up, the first New Year's Day in eight years when I wouldn't be able to talk to, touch or hold my wife. It would be the beginning of my first whole year as a widower and of an unexpected journey into raising my son without his mum.

I've never really bought into the idea of *New Year, new you* but when I woke up on 1 January 2013, that's what seemed to emerge. Instead of reaching for the coffee to drag me out of my chemical sleep, I put on my trainers and went for a run. Desreen and I had signed up for the Brighton Half Marathon and I was determined that the one person who still could charge over the finishing line, actually would. That meant I needed to change a few habits.

I stopped drinking and started training. In the weeks and months that followed Desreen's death there was almost always someone staying with Jackson and me. I didn't want to leave him during the day, so instead I would get myself out of bed around 5.00 or 6.00a.m. and go running while he slept, leaving at least one of his grandparents to look after him. Often I would have run ten miles, showered and dressed before he and they even woke up.

I found I had a new energy, one that I'd never felt before. I told myself that it made no scientific sense that the force from a living body went nowhere and that perhaps Desreen's had been imparted to me to help me look after our son. Maybe I'd just been using it on all the wrong things for the last seven and a half weeks.

One day I spoke to Desreen as I ran. I talked about how things were at home, how Jackson was getting along and how much I was missing her. I later thought it odd that I had tried to frame all my news so positively. If she could hear and see me, surely she knew the truth. Until this point I hadn't been able to utter a word to her since the last time I'd seen her, in the chapel of rest the day before her funeral. Now I felt stupid speaking to someone I wasn't sure could hear; I didn't know what to talk to her about. If she still had some heavenly consciousness or was indeed somehow still walking with me, then why would I need to give her updates about our lives? I tell her I love her every night before I go to bed, but I'd say that if she were still alive. If I had spent the whole day with her in person, I would feel foolish recounting everything we had done and she would think me mad.

And that's how I've felt ever since she died. That chat as I ran was pretty much a one-off. I find no comfort at her grave; I just don't think she would be there in spirit. If her soul were anywhere then it would be at home with Jackson and me or perhaps out shopping at Liberty, a place to which she was so devoted that she had told Olive she wanted to be buried there in a text just weeks before she died. Sometimes I worry about how cross she is with me for leaving her in a field, sandwiched between Warblington Castle and Langstone Shore, and not at least trying to honour her request.

When my legs ached and my feet hurt from running I repeated the words *I'm alive! I'm alive!* in my head and I ran faster and further than I ever had before. At first I thought I was running away from my feelings because I started to feel my head emptying of the thoughts that had kept me awake at night for weeks. But before long the tormenting and confusing stream of consciousness that filled my brain – leaping from one worry to another and leaving me confused about where I'd even started – became more orderly reflections and feelings. The questions I was torturing myself with were gradually finding answers: *Should we move house? How was I going to manage to create a happy future for my son? Where was I going to turn for help? What was I going to do about work?*

I dealt with the work question first. I met my boss, Mitch, for lunch at the beginning of the month. Fortunately we had become great friends over the years so his priority was helping me to reach the professional agreement that worked best for Jackson and me. Even before we met up we were both quite clear on what that was most likely to look like: I would have to take a demotion. I could no longer shoulder the burden of being the managing director of such a large company when my priorities were so firmly at home. Nor did I want to. My work hours would need to be flexible because I no longer had a wife with whom to share childcare commitments; and I would need a phased return. I would work four days a week as a creative director: I would arrive late and leave early on Mondays and Tuesdays so I could drop off and pick up my son from nursery. Bev, who worked part time as a nurse, would come to London to stay with us each Wednesday and Thursday, to be with Jackson. And I would no longer work Fridays, giving us as much time as possible together.

Over the next few weeks I kept training, partly to help make sense of all the other concerns running wild around my head. The running gave me the focus I needed to realise that something useful had to transpire out of the tragedy of my wife's death. I just didn't yet know what that useful thing was.

Funnily enough the answer came from a much more dedicated runner than me. I spent the first two weeks of the new year ignoring my phone and wanting people to just leave me alone. My new focus on living healthily and keeping a clear head to tackle the massive challenges I faced meant that I had even less desire to see people than before. My ambivalence about the legions of well-wishers was still in full force. Then, one day, my good friend Dan nipped round to our flat. I stuck my head around the door, hiding my body from view in case his wife had come, too.

'Is Sarah with you?' I asked, before even extending the courtesy of saying hello.

'No, mate, just me,' he replied.

'Phew!' I said, opening the door in relief. 'I've only got my undies on. I'm trying to clean the bathroom.'

In one way, the time following Desreen's death was much like the period after Jackson was born. The house was constantly full of visitors who meant well but who left the place looking like a bloody wreck. When Dan arrived I hadn't cleaned either the bathroom or myself that day, despite it being late afternoon. I had intended to take advantage of a quiet day with no visitors to get some housework done but my son needed my attention.

Dan was one of the first people to actively respond to the email I'd sent to my closest friends and family after speaking to Care for the Family. He walked into the flat and behaved exactly as he had before Desreen died: he was funny, cocky, and sincere. But on this occasion he hadn't come to hang out with me, he'd come to help.

'Don't worry about what you're wearing, mate. I haven't come to see you, anyway. I've come to read to Jackson. Come on Jacko, Uncle Dan's here now.'

I scrubbed the bathroom with a big smile on my face, knowing that as long as I was willing to open up, my friends would be willing to listen. And as long as I wasn't too proud to ask for help, I knew it would always be there. I suddenly understood that it wasn't enough for me to sit at home and sulk about people not behaving the way I wanted. I was going to need to do whatever it took to help them understand how to help me. And I could hear from the giggling in the next room that it was already working.

Half an hour later I emerged washed and dressed from a clean bathroom. 'Thanks, mate. It's hard enough to get everything done when there are two of you but it's impossible to get *anything* done when you're alone with a young child. I didn't know it was possible to feel guilty about cleaning your bathroom until now. I just don't really want to leave him alone for a minute.'

Dan was in full-on January mode. Like me he was running,

but with much more gusto and intent. I was only working towards a half marathon but he was in training for London's big one.

'I've started a blog about my training,' he told me.

'I know. I'm following it.'

I hesitated, then said, 'I've been thinking about starting one myself. I spoke to this guy from Care for the Family the other day and it's clear from what he said that there aren't many blokes out there who feel comfortable enough to open up about loss. That means there are men raising kids alone who aren't able to express how they feel. I find that tragic.'

'Just do it!'

Dan understood the motivation immediately and he, possibly more than any other friend could have done at the time, believed I had it in me.

The two of us had worked together at the beginning of our careers in public relations. Almost every week I was asked by my company's HR manager to take the new starters out for lunch. She knew that no amount of work would stop me from taking time out to bag a free meal. I suppose she also thought I would do my best to make the newbies feel welcome. But the day I met Dan, *I* wasn't in charge. About two years my junior and only really just getting his foot on the ladder, this confident young man was going places. Brash, northern and quick with a jibe, I loved him immediately. We became friends quickly and our respect for one another both personally and professionally has never waned.

Dan told me that he really thought I should go ahead with the blog idea. Having seen me in action both socially and professionally over the years, he suspected that my ability to communicate freely could help other men going through similar ordeals. I suppose he assumed that this, in turn, would also help me.

After he left the flat that night, his encouraging comments ringing in my ears, I put Jackson to bed and thought about my wife. Talking with Dan had reminded me of a conversation I'd had with Desreen the year before when she also suggested that I start a blog. I'd previously mentioned in passing that I was tempted to, and she was right behind me. Her enthusiasm was infectious and so within a couple of days I had designed a homepage and written my first few posts.

'This is amazing!' she told me, gushing at the half-dozen distinctly average posts I had written about something and nothing. 'I think this could be huge for you. Seriously, you might have found your *thing*. I can see advertisers getting on board and everything.'

She knew very little about blogging or digital marketing but she believed in me more than anyone I've ever met – more than I ever have, in fact. In the end my lack of self-confidence got the better of me and I took it no further. The blog never went public and the posts I wrote never saw the light of day. I just didn't think I had anything worth saying or sharing. But then my wife died. The person who had unfaltering faith in me – the one who could make me believe that anything was possible – was gone. It was only then that I realised that maybe I had something worth saying after all. And only after her death stripped me of any of the concerns that I once had about how others might judge me, did I have the confidence to put myself on the line. Desreen inspired me in death just as she always had in life.

That evening I chose a blogging platform, played around with it for a couple of days and then simply wrote from the heart, setting out my stall. My first blog post, titled *Opening Up*, followed on Sunday 6 January, just two days after my conversation with Dan.

In my shock and utter delirium after my wife was killed, I almost started blogging straight away (grief from sudden death does crazy things to your head). I'd always wanted to start a blog but wasn't convinced I had anything that interesting to share.

I quickly realised I had more important things to focus on, in raising a child as a sole parent, than keeping a public diary. That was until I spoke to a man called Steve Smart at a charity called Care for the Family. They offer a telephone support network for widows and widowers, a kind of buddy system for when people connected by the death of a spouse need to talk to someone. He said that, sadly, there were very few male volunteers, perhaps because men find it hard to open up about their feelings. Fortunately for me, I don't. I use the word fortunately because I think that opening up now is going to make living in my own head somewhat less difficult in the future. That's what the books I'm throwing myself into say, anyway.

So, I'm not exactly sure where this blog is going. I'm not sure how I'll tell my story and whether I'll go back to the beginning or start from where I'm at now. But I can't help but think that some poor bastard will wake up tomorrow morning, realise their wife has gone forever and that it wasn't just a nightmare, and search for someone who can relate to the hell they're going through. Perhaps if I keep writing they'll find that someone. Perhaps a few more blokes will be encouraged to open up about how they feel. Perhaps the process might act as catharsis and make things easier on me. Perhaps when the next bloke calls Care for the Family there will be a few more guys to talk to.

Let's see how things go . . .

That night I dreamed of Desreen for the first time since she died. I was desperate for this to happen; I knew it was the only way we would ever be together again. It was amazing to be with her; she looked incredible. She had her hair styled as it was on the day we got married and she was wearing the dress she wore the day after. She was happy, weighed down by the expensive-looking shopping bags she carried. I was elated to see her and as I ran down the stairs over which she elevated towards me, I beamed and told her that I had been scared I was never going to see her again. She said nothing. She just smiled and then suddenly fell backwards until she disappeared out of sight. I woke up with a start and tears ran down my face.

UNIMAGINABLE EXPOSURE

Once I started writing I just couldn't stop. Finally I had an outlet for my grief and a platform from which to share my confused and conflicted feelings and to try to encourage other widowers to open up about theirs. I'd been lying awake at night for weeks, desperate for empathy from people just like me, unable to find what or who I was looking for. This way I hoped that what I was searching for would come to me.

As soon as I started blogging it was as if a floodgate had opened in my head. Writing allowed me to re-evaluate things. 'Be strong!' people had kept telling me. *Oh, fuck off!* I'd wanted to reply so many times. Now I had the means to communicate that sentiment more articulately and to explain why I didn't think that sort of expectation should be made of the newly bereaved.

On Monday 7 January I wrote and shared my second blog post.

BEING STRONG

I've decided I'm not going to write about the incident. It's really easy for people to say you need to see a counsellor and go over what happened on the night but I'm not convinced. I know what happened better than anyone else at the scene, I know the outcome and I know that I can't do anything to change it. So why revisit it publicly? Fortunately the professionals seem to agree. I imagine I'll replay it in my head every day for the rest of my life, but I don't think it helps me or other people to discuss it at length. That said, I am seeing a counsellor. In fact I'm seeing about twenty, because if you can open up, then suddenly your closest friends and family have invisible letters after their names.

I want to voice some points here about grief.

Point 1: *Grief is fucked up.* I'm planning on using swear words sparingly on this blog and only when I really mean them, but in this case I do.

Grief (the shock and numbness phase) made me crack jokes minutes after I saw my wife die. It made me check that everyone was okay for drinks when her best friends came to my house in the middle of the night. It allowed me to plan a funeral for my wife with as much gusto as our wedding. It enabled me to stand up in front of countless people in a packed church and speak about her without really shedding a tear. It's tempting to say that Valium and rum played their parts too, but in my heart I know I could have done it without, because shock is more powerful a drug than either.

Point 2: *Grief is totally unpredictable.* I wanted to be strong on the day of the funeral because I felt it was my duty. People have told me how strong I've been or encouraged me to be strong along the way. But it's really not a badge of honour when your wife has just died; it's simply a matter of wanting to do her justice. Now I wonder whether it would be better if people said be weak. Because if I'm strong the whole time then I'm not letting grief have its way with me and, trust me, we're all grief's bitch in the end. It just depends how long we're prepared to flirt before letting it take control.

Point 3: *Grief shouldn't be hidden from children.* If we are only ever strong and hide our true feelings (and tears) from our kids then perhaps they will think they shouldn't cry or show their feelings in later life. I can only use my son as a reference, and I'm no psychologist, but if he hides his tears from me because I was strong and hid them from him, then I'll have failed him.

Sadly for me right now, when he does see me cry he snatches my hanky, wipes fake tears and says, 'Oh, boo hoo hoo, Daddy,' while throwing himself around the room dramatically. One day he'll know that this is the worst time to mock his father's feelings, but for now I just have to believe it's his way of making me laugh. So it's just two guys trying to make each other feel better — one of us two years old and the other thirty-three.

That day I was unstoppable. I imagine anyone reading might have thought I had reams of notes already written and that I was just posting existing content frantically, but that was not the case. I scribbled down my thoughts as they came into my head and shared them while they were still raw, painful and as difficult to write as they probably were to read. I realised that if people were going to sit up and pay attention to the message I was trying to convey – and indeed to the people I was trying to help – there needed to be more than a couple of posts rattling round an otherwise empty web page.

I took a breath after writing the first two posts and thought about what people might actually want to read. Almost everyone who spoke to me after my wife's death told me that they couldn't imagine what I was going through, as if that might be a surprise to me. Not wanting to appear rude by asking them to be more original and less prosaic, my stock response became, 'Don't try; you wouldn't like it.'

People generally seem to feel the need to fill the silences in the company of the bereaved, even if they don't know what to say. I quickly came to the conclusion that we don't have the words in English because, as a nation, we're not well trained in dealing with death. Yet I found that nearly everyone attempts to offer some sort of consolation for loss through pedestrian comments and clichés. Even now I still find myself lost for words when a friend's goldfish dies, so God only knows what happens to a person's larynx as they stand before a newly widowed young man with a two-year-old son. And perhaps this is part of why I started to write. How would a person ever know what it *could* feel like if no one ever took the time to explain? And so I did.

IMAGINING IT

It feels like guilt. Guilt because I'm still alive and she isn't. Guilt because the papers called me a 'hero' for saving my son, when my wife still died. Guilt because my parents still have a living son, but her parents don't have a living daughter. Guilt because Jackson will be brought up by the less natural parent. Guilt because Desreen carried our unborn son for nine months, took ten months out of her career to care for him after he was born and took him to bloody Rhyme Time every week when he may now struggle to remember her for real.

It feels physical. Physical because it's not all just in my head: I need the toilet more; I'm hungry but can't always eat; I'm thirsty but I often can't drink; my stomach aches from the pain; my head hurts through lack of sleep; my tears have become more saline and they sting my eyes.

It feels like anger. Anger because my temper is out of control. God help any glass or crockery you own if you break the ring pull on the tin of spaghetti you're trying to feed your child after your wife dies. Anger because what used to be a tantrum that we would both have rolled our eyes at just ignited a volcano inside of me. In fact each time my son has a tantrum he transfers it to me and I'm stood letting it loose in the park in front of all the parents from nursery.

It feels like confusion. Confusion because I think she's still coming home from her Saturday morning run when I look out the kitchen window. Confusion because I find myself sitting in my favourite seat on the bus on a route I travel every day, reading something in a newspaper that I know will make her laugh and I reach for my phone to call her. This despite having spoken at her funeral and thinking about little other than her death for weeks.

But most of all it feels selfish. Selfish because I don't think I should allow myself to indulge in grief when I have a two-year-old son to take care of. Selfish because I feel like I'm getting the lion's share of sympathy when her parents have lost their daughter, her brother has lost his sister and her mates have lost an irreplaceable, loyal, witty, funny, kind and outrageous friend.

How can anything be so cruel? You lose your wife, the head of your family, your child's mum, your best friend and the person with whom you'd planned the rest of your life and grief comes along and makes you feel worse than you already do. It makes you feel bad about feeling bad. It tells you you're selfish to think of yourself.

Grief is Gollum.

This post touched a nerve. The blog received around five thousand views in the first couple of days, something that I never anticipated. But my surprise about the number of hits was soon left in the shadows by an email from *BBC Breakfast* inviting me to join the show's presenters on the sofa for a chat. It was only then that I really began to appreciate quite what a chord it had struck. Just three days after I set up the blog, the BBC was asking me to be in the studio the following morning.

I had to laugh at the gulf between my circumstances and the demands of the TV producers. I imagine most sole parents, widowed or otherwise, would have found it impossible to drop everything to jump on a train from London to Salford that very same day. For the first time, I felt like a man raising his child alone. Spontaneity and flexibility were instantly made a thing of the past.

Having spent my entire career leaping at opportunities to get clients television exposure, all of a sudden this was my life and not my job. I cared about getting the message out there, otherwise I wouldn't have started the blog, but I cared more about my son. Any activity built around the blog had to be on terms that suited the two of us. I suggested to the researcher that we speak again the following week if the production team could find another appropriate slot.

In the meantime the *Guardian* also made contact by email. My friend Julie had shared the blog with a friend of hers on the newspaper's beauty desk, who was sufficiently moved by its content to share it with a colleague on the fashion desk, who was, in turn, touched enough to send it to a colleague on the family desk. That colleague, Steve Chamberlain, then wrote to me and asked if I would consider writing a feature for the *Guardian* Family supplement about my experience of losing my wife and becoming a sole parent. I told him I'd call back once I'd had time to think about it.

I sought my mother-in-law's approval straight away. 'What do you think, because I won't do it if it makes any of the family feel uncomfortable.'

Never a woman to mince her words or to labour a point she simply said, 'I've said it before and I'll say it again, I just want something good to come out of all this mess. And good is good. So just go for it.'

I couldn't have agreed more. When I thought of Desreen's completely unnecessary death being entirely in vain, it left me cold. Her ambitions for her future, after building a successful business, were to help other young black women into the fashion industry and address its huge imbalance of colour. I knew it was time for me to try to do something that might help others, too. That would be my way of honouring the memory of my wife and attempting to be more like her, as I'd asked of others when I gave her eulogy.

The idea of writing for publication in a national newspaper was daunting and the thought of being interviewed on TV terrified me but three things spurred me on to tackle both: believing that the worst thing that could ever happen to my life had already happened; a total lack of interest in any judgment or criticism that might come my way; and the desire to help those 'poor bastards' I referred to in my first blog post.

So while I thought about the content of the *Guardian* Family feature – glad that I hadn't been given a deadline for the first time in all my years of working with the media – the BBC called back to confirm that they would like to see me the following week.

I knew that no newspaper was about to let a story break on national television and then casually follow up with a feature a few weeks later. I called Steve at the *Guardian* straight away to let him know and sure enough the deadline was brought forward.

At that point it was the end of the day on Friday 11 January and I had until the evening of Tuesday the 15th to file my copy. Four days on paper but not in real terms because I had a child to look after, alone. No one else was with us that weekend. I had promised myself that I would be the very best father possible to Jackson and that meant taking him out, playing with him and reading to him. What it didn't mean was him trying to drag me away from a laptop. So the weekend was off the cards and I had commitments all day Monday. That left me with about twenty-four hours to turn around a 2,500-word piece, which I'd suggested should be about how I told Jackson that his mummy had died.

I had a day, but as it transpired I only needed a couple of hours. My friend Lydia brought round dinner on the Monday night, and we played with Jackson. It was then that we witnessed something that took my breath away and which, I suppose, became one of the most significant parts of the story that I would file the very next day.

A week before Lydia came round, Jackson had been struggling. We'd spent the weekend with Lee, Olive and their delightful then three-year-old son, Albie. The moment Olive walked through the door I knew we had a problem – to Albie she was of course 'Mummy'. They would be with us all weekend and Jackson would have to hear that name the whole time. It wasn't as if we could ask another child to start calling his mum by her first name, just because of what had happened to Jackson's. But I saw the confusion in Jackson's little face every time he heard the word spoken. And the confusion turned increasingly into frustration and anger as the hours and days went by.

This was never more evident than the morning after our friends arrived. As we all walked down our local high street Jackson paused at a bus shelter to stare at a young black woman waiting for the number 185 through East Dulwich. She looked nothing like Desreen, apart from the colour of her skin, but sometimes hope can do funny things to our heads, big or small. Not immediately realising what was happening, I gently pulled him away and told him not to be nosey. Not because I cared about him gawping, but because I know he likes the sound of the word. 'I'm nosey, Daddy,' he would repeat, with a large smile.

Not today. He was silent and I could tell he was cross and confused. He refused to walk any further and he told us all to go away. You can't ever really *go away* when a toddler tells you to, but certainly not when you're in a street full of cars. So I asked the others to carry on so Jackson and I could have a chat.

I had learned from the child bereavement charity, Winston's Wish, that it can be helpful to encourage children to vent their anger caused by grief in a controlled environment and before it actually manifests itself. So I explained to him that I get angry about losing Mummy, too, and that when I do I like to run really fast in the park. But by now it was too late; he was already lashing out and getting really cross with me, so I took him down a side street, kneeled down to his level and tried to calm him down. He started kicking the shutters on a shop window. I nearly told him not to and I almost told him off but I thought about how I would feel if someone tried to tell me I couldn't express my grief at that moment. So I let his infant size fives give the shutters a good whack to help release his frustration, knowing that he was too small to do any damage to himself or to the shop. Then I gave him a hug and together we went and bought him his first ever croissant. He wasn't his usual self for the rest of the day – he was quiet and short-tempered – but at least he had been able to show me how he felt, even if he couldn't put it into words.

After Shuttergate, a very different boy emerged. As Lydia and I tidied the kitchen after dinner, Jackson pointed at the many photographs of the family we had on the kitchen wall. He often did this, but this time he seemed to want to hold one. So I lifted him up and let him take his pick. To my surprise he didn't choose the one of Desreen and himself, he chose one of Mummy and Daddy. He pulled it off the wall and exclaimed, 'Poor Daddy! Poor Daddy!' Then he brought the picture to his face and kissed it, saying, 'Kiss Mummy!' He wasn't letting go so I let him keep it and we stuck it to his little play kitchen station in the living room.

Then two things happened that made my heart truly swell with love for my son. As we turned out the lights and left the living room for bed, he said, 'Night night, Mummy.' He knew that she wasn't in the room but that her memory was. The two of us went up to bed and he began to sing the few words he knew from Alicia Keys' hit 'No One' – the song played at my wife's funeral as her body was carried into the church.

I could barely drift off as my mind raced with thoughts about what had happened that night and the copy that I needed to provide the next day. So I hauled myself out of bed at about 4.00a.m. and just spilled everything out onto a page. I wrote 3,000 words in about an hour and a half, while quietly reminding myself that if the paper hated what I had written then it didn't really matter to me. All it meant was that they wouldn't run it.

I wasn't looking for recognition, I wasn't hoping for a career in journalism and the only thing I wanted was to reach the right people with a message that really mattered to me. The worst thing has already happened, I told myself again. And if they don't like it, I can publish it myself on the blog.

I'd already hit send by 8.00a.m., eleven hours before the deadline. I promised myself from the start that any writing, whether for my blog, a newspaper or a magazine, would never come ahead of my son. So I sent it before he woke up and asked that any feedback come in time for his afternoon nap.

Fortunately Steve was moved.

'Blimey,' he replied over email. 'I've been on this section for seven years and read quite a few stories that have left me stunned but this one tops them all.'

I suppose that could be seen as a huge compliment to a young guy who had never written a word for a newspaper before. The paper barely edited the copy at all. But I felt nothing. And this feeling of nothingness, I would come to learn, would not go away.

The feature was scheduled to run in that Saturday's issue. For now, though, it was time to turn my attention to the BBC. I planned to take a train up to Salford late that afternoon; I had a few hours to catch my breath. Or at least that's what I thought.

A steady stream of calls and emails started to come through. *The Camden New Journal*, *Mail on Sunday*, *Daily Mail*, *ITV London Tonight* and a handful of freelance journalists and women's magazines all made contact. They either wanted interviews or for me to write for them.

I was completely taken aback; the blog was only in its ninth day and I'd only published seventeen posts. But I felt no sense of pride or achievement; how could I, the whole thing was borne out of my wife's death. So I simply said yes to the stuff that felt right and that I could fit around my commitment to Jackson.

I tried to get some rest on the way up to Media City, the BBC's northern headquarters, but my mind was too active. The trip involved an overnight stay and I left on the latest train possible from Euston to Manchester so that I wasn't away from Jackson – who was being looked after by Bev – for too long.

As soon as I boarded the train, two actors from *Coronation Street*, a programme Desreen loved, apologised for bumping into me as they sped to their seats. This was just one of the many times I would feel a surge of excitement as I reached for my phone to ring my wife, before my heart sank and the remembrance that it would be a wasted call hit me.

I had to keep my phone on charge the whole way there – the blog was rapidly amassing followers from all around the world; comments, emails and messages were flying at me. I had set up supporting Facebook and Twitter pages so that I could share news, such as writing for the paper and appearing on TV. I wanted to ensure that the blog's content remained entirely about grief and for it not to become some kind of promotional tool for itself. But the interactions created by the blog posts were becoming almost overwhelming. They fuelled my adrenaline and left me exhausted all in one go. I was no longer just living through my own grief and that of those close to me, but also that of strangers who sent heartbreaking messages about their own devastating losses.

I got very little sleep that night. I was staying in a hotel opposite the television studio and all night long my phone beeped and flashed with messages of support from friends, family and strangers. I missed Jackson, too. As a family we had shared a bed for the last two years. I was already having to adjust to Desreen's warmth no longer being there at night and now, for the first time in as long as I could remember, I was completely alone in bed.

I lay awake thinking about the TV appearance the next day. Pretty much everyone I knew would be watching, but I felt nothing. Right before going on air I still didn't feel any nerves, but I took some Valium just in case. Looking back now I know I didn't need it – I didn't even care if I cried live on air – but I did want to articulate my point well and I wanted to reach out to other men who had been left widowed and caring for young children.

It's difficult to decide whether a television appearance has gone well when you have nothing to gain and nothing to sell from it. But I was composed; the interviewers were sensitive; judging by the social media interaction, the show's viewers were moved; hits to the blog went through the roof (by the time I left the studio it had received 60,000 views and that was about to grow massively); and I got a thousand compliments that day.

None of that mattered. What did matter to me was that I might be able to help and encourage people to support widowers and their children through the pain of grief and, hopefully, to offer some consolation myself. By that measure, I started to feel that the BBC appearance had definitely been worthwhile.

In between leaving the Salford studio and arriving at Manchester Piccadilly station I received an email.

My wife died eight years ago this week. My grief is buried really deep inside me but it's still there big time. I broke down in tears uncontrollably as I looked at your blog. You know the type of tears? Massive deep sobs, deep breaths — my goodness it's still there after all these years. I haven't cried like this since around the time she died. I've never really addressed it.

I've just found a way to live with it and I never realised it was still there. My God! I had such a powerful emotional experience this morning; I just had to tell you. Think I'd better go and see someone now to talk because I never really talked to anyone before.

I'm with you all the way, brother. Hope that you are okay. Be well.

I realised then that this wasn't just about me being helpful to others, it was also about seeking support for myself. I had found what I had been looking for – empathy. Perhaps someone to talk to, someone who might really be able to say, *I know how you feel*.

What I didn't appreciate that day was that the thing I'd started was not just about men who had lost their wives. They were the group I particularly wanted to help but I soon realised that by opening up about my own grief, other people – male, female, young and old – felt more able to open up about theirs.

Over the following days and weeks people from all walks of life started to get in touch. Friends and family told me that the posts were helping them articulate how they felt; that the blog was helping them to understand how they could best support my son and me. Strangers said the same about their own loved ones suffering loss.

On the one hand, this was great. But ironically, it wasn't long before I began to wonder whether it was that good for me. I wondered whether wearing my grief so openly was becoming a way of hiding it away; whether it was in fact a diversion from the real emotional issues. I felt concerned for the many widowers I eventually came into contact with who explained that they had thrown themselves back into work to distract themselves from their loss. Then I would have to question whether I was in fact doing exactly the same thing. I may not have been at my desk in the West End PR agency that I helped to run, but I was effectively doing the same job from my bed in southeast London – perhaps at an even faster and more obsessive pace. At work I could call on the assistance of dozens of colleagues to help out, but at home I was working alone and the subject matter was my own life.

The campaign I had started became a release but doubtless also an escape, though it didn't feel like that for long. The more I wrote, the more people got in touch. And the more people got in touch, the more I realised that I was becoming engulfed in grief.

'It must help to know you're not the only one out there going through this,' my mum once speculated.

'Not always,' I replied, beginning to question the value of the empathy I'd been so desperate to find. 'A big part of me wishes I were the only one. After all, why would I want anyone else to be in this much pain?'

UNCOMFORTABLE COMPLIMENTS

Conflicting emotions have played a huge part in the complex condition of my grief. One minute I could be talking to a friend about how I believed that kindness towards others would get me through the pain and the next I would want to tell that same person to fuck off.

The weekend before my appearance on the BBC I wrote a blog post about how grief had robbed me of certain feelings. Most of the time I felt nothing but numbness. Now there was an additional dimension to this problem: people had suddenly shifted from offering their condolences to paying me compliments for what I wrote and what I'd set out to achieve. The praise made me feel hugely uncomfortable, even dirty: like I was receiving acclaim while my wife lay dead – *because* my wife lay dead. I didn't like the way people's kind comments left me feeling emotionally, at all.

I wanted the compliments to stop, but I couldn't simply tell everyone reading the blog to piss off only a week after inviting them in. Still, I knew I couldn't bear it for long so I wrote a post in the hope that it might help temper the readers' compulsion to praise.

FEELING NOTHING

I used to crave constant praise from Desreen, which is perhaps why she offered it sparingly and only when she really meant it. She was big on self-improvement and probably worried that I would turn into a comfy thirty-something male if she didn't keep me on my toes.

I sought approval from others, too. I was the kind of guy who liked to please people, which is, when I think about it, probably why I so often cooked for friends. It tends to have the effect of instant glorification, which I think most women would say is typical of a man's motivation. It's why we expect thanks when we half-heartedly push a Hoover round the living room, although it probably wouldn't occur to us to acknowledge the women in our lives for carrying out the same chore.

I refer to the kind of man I *was*, because he seems to have disappeared at Desreen's funeral. Ever since the moment I returned to my seat from giving her eulogy, every compliment I've been paid has fallen on deaf ears.

I've been called strong; brave; a good father; a hero for saving my child; an honest, powerful writer; witty; an inspiration. People have said they are proud of me. Yet I feel nothing. I feel the kind of nothingness I first felt when I took Valium three days after Desreen died, naïvely thinking it was a kind of sleeping pill.

For those unfamiliar with it, Valium (in a strong enough dose) almost stops you from grieving. So when I woke up at 2.00a.m., confused about why I'd woken so soon after taking such a strong sedative, sleepless and with a head full of dark thoughts that I wasn't able to *feel*, I was deeply confused. I wondered what was wrong with me. How come I didn't feel emotional even though my wife had died. I felt nothing.

That's what a compliment feels like to me now I'm grieving. The endorsement I have sought my whole life becomes redundant. Perhaps the acclaim I was seeking before was arrogance; perhaps it was insecurity. But either way it was a feeling. Yet another feeling her death and my grief have stolen from me.

Three days later I would step out of the BBC studio feeling entirely different. I went back to my hotel room to collect my things feeling like a different man. I was crying but I had a feeling that I had done some good, that I might have had an impact on the audience. I dared to hope that something positive might emerge from all the negativity, just as Bev wanted. I jumped in a taxi, got on the train and immediately published another post.

FEELING AGAIN

Three days ago I wrote a post called *Feeling Nothing*. It seemed to sadden people close to me, resonate with the unfortunate people who could empathise with my loss and make the compliments many people had so far offered dry up.

This morning I was given the incredible honour of being asked to talk about my blog to millions of British TV viewers on *BBC Breakfast*. As I sat in my hotel room last night preparing — or rather, completely crashing out, in the knowledge that I wouldn't have a toddler whacking me in the head all night with his twitchy little limbs – it was my turn to be saddened by someone close to me: my mum. She sent me a text saying that she knew I didn't want any praise but that she was proud of me. It upset me that I'd made her anxious about saying how she felt, especially when my blog is all about opening up. I noticed a little of my old insecure/cocky self in my reply. 'I never said I didn't want compliments,' I challenged her, 'I said I just felt nothing when they were offered.'

I've tried all sorts of things to bring pleasure back to my life over the last two months: the Mr Porter sale; Kalms; my favourite cognac; wine (lots of it); exercise; expensive new Nike running gear for my half marathon; plans to have my teeth straightened; new shoes; booking a holiday; getting a tattoo; changing my name. But none of it did what I hoped it would. I probably never even expected it to. I guess I was just clutching at anything to distract myself from my pain.

This morning I realised it's possible to feel again. I was a little surprised to learn that, for me, it doesn't come from material things and it doesn't come from running away. It comes from facing your demons, offering and receiving kindness, doing good, accepting and offering support from the people who care about you and to those less able to express themselves. And it comes from love.

When I left the BBC studio, where I was able to compose and articulate myself well, I broke down. I broke down because, of all the things I've done in the eight years since I met my beautiful wife, I knew she would have been most proud of this. I knew from the conversations we had towards the end of her life that her career was just a bridge to the good she wanted to do when she retired (at forty – you can't knock the girl's self-confidence and ambition). It was her intention to help more young black women break into the fashion industry because she felt there was too great an imbalance.

Typically, I was several steps behind her on the to-do list and hadn't even thought about what positive impact I could make in my future life. But last week her memory told me, and it has guided me all the way. I like to imagine she has bequeathed me her strength of character and desire to help others so that they weren't lost upon her death.

I can't end this post here because if she has indeed passed any of her qualities on to me then it would be only fitting to end with a gag. Desreen would have pissed herself laughing at seeing my gaunt mug on the telly today. She'd have told me that I'm always too pale in January to go on TV without fake tan or a sunbed session. And she would have been cross that she didn't get to select the pictures that were broadcast across the nation. 'Benji, what have I told you about sharing photos of me without my approval? You idiot!' she would have shouted. But she would have forgiven me an hour later on the condition that I buy her a present.

I love you Dessie, and everything I'm doing is for you. X

I felt reborn. I had adrenaline rushing through my system and all the empathy a widowed man could ever have wanted was flying at me from every direction. Emails, calls, Facebook messages, tweets, you name it. All of a sudden I had *virtually* met a group of young widowers numerous enough to start a private Facebook network. We were chatting, sharing stories, even cheering one another up. I was far from cloud nine, but I wasn't alone in grief's gutter any more. Despite having had all my friends and family at hand, I had spent too long feeling like I was alone. All I ever heard was 'I just can't imagine what you're going through' and it was a relief to finally talk with people who could.

The thing that struck me most was the other widowers' humour. Bereavement can steal a lot of things away, but one thing I was determined to retain was the ability to laugh and make others laugh, too. Of course we weren't going to be picking up any comedy awards any time soon, but I was relieved to find a place where it was okay to crack jokes and not be seen as insensitive or sick in the head. Our in-jokes made it easier to be part of the tragic club that none us had ever wanted to join.

All of this was above and beyond what I had hoped for or set out to achieve. But as well as the cringe-making compliments, there were other responses that I didn't relish. And this part wasn't going to make me feel good, about others or myself.

A message from a happy couple read, 'I wanted you to know how much what has happened has affected us (*our relationship*) in a positive way, if that doesn't sound selfish.' It did. Messages from dozens more people said similar things. 'Your story has really made me think about just how much I love my wife/husband/partner. Thanks!'

No, thank you. *I'm glad you still have one to mostly take for granted,* I thought bitterly.

People just couldn't wait to tell me that they were learning to appreciate what they had in life. At first I found this so difficult to hear because while they could take a fresh look at their own lives, I was still sitting at home, a widower grieving the loss of the wife I love (not loved) so much. I tried to focus on what Bev said, soon after Desreen's death. 'I just hope some good comes out of all this mess.' We discussed that point again and once again agreed that 'good is good'. I pushed myself to shed the frustration that had been building up inside of me. Long may people learn to love life by learning more about loss, I told myself.

There was another type of comment that I found pretty difficult to hear. Some people got in touch to encourage me to slow down. I'm positive it was advice offered with compassion, concern and from the harrowing hindsight of living through loss while still running at a hundred miles per hour, but it infuriated me nonetheless.

The great strength of blogs, but also a potential problem, is that they allow intimate conversations between strangers. I was being so open about my life, so lots of people felt they were getting to know me, but these readers didn't know anything about what I was like in normal pre-grief life. This meant that inevitably, some of their comments and advice felt wide of the mark (and some of it felt downright out of place).

I've always been a pretty restless kind of guy. I work hard. I would rather go for a run than a walk. I've never enjoyed lying on a sun lounger for more than fifteen minutes at a time. And grief didn't change any of this. Looking back at the 'down time' after my wife's funeral, I can see that sitting around doing nothing made me spiral into a dark, gloomy and lonely place, one I never want to revisit. I hated it, and I also hated myself when I was there. Once I had escaped it, I got busy. Other people saw a guy creating a blog, writing for newspapers and taking part in broadcast interviews. Some saw a man potentially pushing himself too hard. I saw myself running at half capacity. And so I decided not to listen to opinions I found unhelpful (and to try not to get wound up by them, either) and to keep going at my own pace.

So gradually I found ways to deal with most of the more challenging comments, and my own negative feelings about them. The compliments, though? They weren't getting any easier to deal with. After the feature ran in the *Guardian* I started to feel deeply uncomfortable again. Unwanted and unsought praise was pouring in. I felt guilty for having become a focus of attention when all I could focus on was the life and death of my beautiful wife.

That Saturday morning I published a message across my Facebook page and Twitter feed. *Paying me a compliment for my campaign? Thanks, but I don't need it. Instead think about how much more a bereavement charity might benefit from the payment of a pound or two than my ego will benefit from praise.* A link then took readers to a Virgin Money Giving page where people could make donations that would be split between four charities: The WAY Foundation, Grief Encounter, Winston's Wish and Child Bereavement UK.

The message began to sink in, the uncomfortable compliments began to die down and those that still came generally started with the words, 'I know you don't want praise but . . .'

Suddenly two weeks had passed; the blog had received 165,000 views; the supporting Facebook page that I set up a week after the blog had hit 3,000 'likes'; and the number of people following the cause on Twitter had rocketed. But more importantly, people were sharing their stories of grief and supporting one another through all three channels. The empathy that I was looking for when my wife was killed was being found and shared by others, too. And loads of money was raised for charity, to boot.

I had started a blog that aimed to reach out to other young widowers, but something bigger had emerged. That brought challenges. I felt it was time to think about the direction and limits of what I was doing. I needed to put a stake in the ground.

Where do we go next? Well, one thing that I have had to clarify in interviews this week is that I am not a counsellor. Even if I were, I'm sure I wouldn't be working right now because my own grief is still too raw. I urge people to share their stories on the blog, Facebook and Twitter but I can't offer any answers. I will simply share my own experiences of grief, as a widower with a child, and what I learn along the way. Hopefully they will offer consolation and insight to as many people as possible. I'm also hoping to be able to use the blog's profile to get in front of experts on grief and child bereavement. When I do I will share their advice rather than mine. I'll find it a great comfort if this can help others in a similar situation to my beautiful boy and me.

BABY BOY

Jackson came along ten months before our wedding. A couple of weeks after I had surprised Desreen by proposing, she became a little irritated about something.

'What's wrong, darling?' I asked her – she had been quiet all evening.

Desreen knew her mind, she was a very strong character and she never minced her words. Sometimes, however, they needed a little coaxing out.

'You're an idiot!' she eventually snapped.

'Huh?'

'Well, you promised we could have a baby first and now you've asked me to marry you.'

'I love you too and I can't wait to marry you, either. Thank you for your kind words,' I replied sarcastically, sparring with her.

'I'm being serious, Ben.'

'Listen to me. I never said we couldn't have a baby first. I still want to. We can get married any time.'

We both wanted to be young parents. And on Valentine's Day 2010 we got the good news. I begged Desreen to do a pregnancy test, but she said she wanted to wait until the next day. We'd had such a good time together, relaxing with a glass of prosecco, a table picnic and a battered Scrabble set at

Shoreditch House. Dessie was determined not to spoil a great day with disappointing news. By then we had been trying and failing to get pregnant for six consecutive months.

'But imagine how cool it'd be if we found out that you were pregnant on Valentine's Day,' I pleaded. 'Go on, just do it and then I'll run off with the stick and tell you the result tomorrow.'

She relented, did the test and watched the stick turn blue. We were overjoyed and then suddenly very nervous. We promised each other not to tell anyone until the time was right.

The next few months passed slowly as we waited impatiently for our first, and ultimately only, child to be born. We opted not to find out the sex but the baby had a strong kick and Dessie would get so cross when it attacked her just as she was getting into bed.

Everyone commented on how beautiful she looked when she was pregnant. She looked so stylish the whole time; not one of these women you couldn't tell was carrying a child but just really at ease and cool with it.

She was hilarious to live with, too. Peculiar in her habits at the best of times, when she was pregnant she developed a taste for soap and washing-up suds. If anyone had seen me trying with all my strength to stop her dipping her tongue into the bath's bubbles or filling her mouth with Fairy Liquid lather, they might have thought they had walked into a wrestling match. I thought it couldn't be good for the baby but she had become a foam junky and nothing could stop her from getting her hit when she needed it most.

'Oh, she's very Jamaican,' her mother, a nurse by profession, explained. 'Pregnant women eat soap all the time back home.'

With this comment I came to understand how Desreen had developed her habit of making sweeping generalisations.

'And if they haven't got any soap, they'll eat dirt,' Bev

continued. 'Clean dirt, though. The sort you get on the back of a stone. You see them grabbing one on the side of the road and giving it a lick.'

Studies have shown that a baby's taste develops in the womb. That's why French children generally take easily to garlic and Mexican children like chilli pepper. When Jackson was old enough to sit up in the bath he was suddenly old enough to start weaning himself on soap – great fistful of soapy suds. He's always been able to out-spice even the fieriest Jamaican palate, too.

His mum's tastes while she was pregnant were not exclusively Caribbean, though. For many weeks she couldn't face anything other than fish fingers and beans at dinnertime. As the cook in the relationship, it was my duty, perhaps more so than ever, to make sure she was fed. I've tackled more challenging dinners but never, I think, a more challenging diner.

'Benji,' she whispered to me as I updated my dad about Desreen's progress over the phone, while serving up her distinctly orange plate of processed pollock and pulses, 'I don't like orange food anymore.'

Our baby was interrupted in the development of his tastes when contractions started at lunchtime on Thursday 14 October 2010. But he didn't arrive until 9.17p.m. on Sunday the 17th. It proved to be hard work but Desreen was nothing short of amazing. When her waters finally broke early on the Sunday morning we dashed to hospital. It was frightening at first because a midwife quickly checked her over, then warned us the room would be filled with doctors any second. The baby's heart rate was all over the place, fast one second and then worryingly slow the next. They were concerned it was a problem with the umbilical chord effectively chocking our unborn child. Soon the panic calmed and we faced something like a normal labour.

Two epidurals, ten episodes of *Desperate Housewives*,

countless probing doctors and lots of gas and air later, there was still no sign of progress. After around fourteen hours in the ward, a consultant finally made his way into the room and scolded the doctors for not having performed a Caesarean hours earlier. He said Desreen was now too tired and weak to give birth naturally.

Dessie shivered in the cold theatre. Teeth chattering, she looked at me and simply said, 'I'm scared.'

'Don't worry,' I replied, 'we'll be home to watch the next episode of *Desperate Housewives* by nine o'clock.' It was already gone eight, so I knew we wouldn't, but I wanted to help her to relax.

'Can I have a lemonade, please?' Desreen asked the highly qualified surgeon, perhaps confusing her for a waitress in her delirium.

'You're not allowed to eat or drink anything until after the procedure,' she replied gently.

Minutes later she held up the most perfect little baby.

'It's a boy,' she confirmed, as he squealed and showed off his willy to everyone in the room.

'How do you know?' Dessie asked, much to my amusement. She was completely spaced out from four days without sleep and a day taking enough drugs to floor a stallion. It's a memory I'll never forget. Desreen was the only woman in the world with the capacity to make me laugh so hard in such a cold, sterile operating theatre.

'Can I have that lemonade now?' she repeated. The girl never stopped.

Our children, we had agreed, would take our maternal grandmothers' maiden names as their Christian names. We called our son Jackson after my grandma and our next, boy or girl, would be called Bailey. When she died I discovered that Desreen had written the name in the back of her diary because she truly believed that positive thinking, especially when committed to paper, would bring her the things she most wanted in life. She had also planned the holiday destination for the conception, and the month to determine the next baby's star sign – some signs were completely out of the question. Sadly this dream was not to be.

Jackson came home and was an instant hit with everyone he met. With big brown eyes and a head of thick black hair, just like his mummy, he was the most beautiful baby I had ever seen.

'Is it bad for his own father to say that?' I asked my mum.

'No, darling, it's a fact,' she replied. 'He's beautiful.'

'You see, the thing with Jackson,' Desreen's dad went on to say when Jackson was only nine weeks old, 'is he's just a great bloke – everyone likes him.'

As with his daughter's comments about lemonade and willies while she was undergoing surgery, Kelson's statement made me laugh and will stay with me for the rest of my life. With just a few short words, he'd shown how much faith and pride he had in his brand-new grandson; the same faith and pride he always had for his beloved daughter.

After Desreen and I got married, Jackson started nursery and Desreen set up her own fashion business with her friend Cathy. Dubious as she was about leaving Jackson in someone else's care, all the nursery staff took a shine to our son. So my wife embarked on the challenging task of being a new mum and setting up a business from scratch.

She and Cathy built this incredible company, Saint Luke, from nothing. They launched during February 2012's London Fashion Week and quickly there was a buzz. They worked as fashion agents representing artists in the industry, including photographers, stylists, designers and hair and makeup artists. Every day

Desreen would call me with more exciting news: a huge name would have approached them about representation or booked one of their artists for a job. They were finding exciting emerging talent, too, and Desreen was so keen to nurture these artists and to be a part of the success they would inevitably experience in her charge.

Desreen was evolving again. Since becoming a mother she had more drive than ever before. She wanted the very best for her family and she had listed all of the things that she wanted us to achieve in her diary. She was going to work hard to provide the material things but also put her heart into safeguarding us all emotionally. She strived never to rest on her laurels, so her aim was to look and feel better than ever before. She wasn't going to allow her standards to slip as she approached her mid-thirties.

And it paid off. Before long the business was starting to thrive and she looked better than ever before thanks to regular exercise and a beauty regime that would leave Naomi Campbell with time on her hands. She was slim but not skinny and her hair and skin looked amazing.

She persuaded me to go on a detox that she'd learned about through a website set up by Gwyneth Paltrow called goop.com. We had to give up alcohol, wheat, gluten, dairy and red meat, and eat and drink only at allocated times of the day for three weeks. I would get up early to make the two of us breakfast, mid-morning smoothies, lunch and snacks to ensure we stuck to the programme's every word. Before bed we ate raw garlic and drank olive oil, and then Desreen would make me scrub my skin with a hard bristly brush before bathing in scalding-hot water filled with pink salt from the Himalayas. We would then brush our teeth with aloe vera toothpaste, which contained no fluoride and only natural ingredients and probably did nothing to cut through the odour of uncooked garlic.

I imagine most people might regard this regime as torture but we had so much fun. We would sit up in bed and compare notes from the day: first how sick we felt from the detox, then how disgusted we were by the cold raw vegetable soups we had to drink for dinner and then, ultimately, how energised and completely revitalised the whole experience left us feeling.

I can't remember ever being happier than we were right then; we had everything. She was successful, fulfilled and happy, all of which made her more attractive than any beauty treatment ever could. I caught her eye across the room at Jackson's second birthday party in October 2012 and I remember thinking how lucky I was that the woman I had married just kept getting more and more beautiful and focussed with every year that went by. That she had more drive to be the best she could be since she'd had a child, rather than less.

I was doing well, too. I'd got the job I had been working towards for twelve years and we could see a future for ourselves. One that would afford us the house we wanted, the second child we were planning and a month off in Ibiza, which Desreen insisted we were taking the following summer – she would be the one to tell, not ask, my boss. But disaster was looming; our lives would change forever just five weeks after Jackson's party. And tragically there would be no more summers in the sun for my wife.

DADDY'S PROMISES

As the profile of *Life as a Widower* grew and the world around me came to view me as a blogger, I continued with the hardest role of my life – raising a toddler bereaved of his mother, as a grieving father and husband. A great deal had happened since my wife's death and some people probably saw me as stronger than ever but the fact was, Desreen had only been dead for eight weeks. Shock had given me the internal resources I needed to get through those two months but it was fading; now I had to manage without its chemicals running through my veins. I needed to face up to my future as a sole parent and do everything I could to help my son through the trauma of losing his mum.

I was discovering that there was a lot of expert help out there. In addressing the sensitive (and often hidden) issues of child bereavement, I had created a channel for people who knew much more about it than I did to come to *me* to offer advice.

I realised I had found a way to allow the best possible intelligence, insight and guidance to filter through to me on behalf of my son. I could then share my experiences with other widowed parents through the blog. I would never try to be the expert; I would simply share my stories in the hope that they might help others.

In the days and weeks after Desreen was killed, I lay awake each night as Jackson snoozed next to me in my marital bed.

We needed each other's company and closeness. Somehow, at night, all of my thoughts turned to *his* future rather than my own. I wanted to be able to put things right and to somehow make amends for how short-changed he had already been so early on in life.

I suppose, like most people these days, I wanted quick fixes, answers and immediate resolutions. In hindsight these were ludicrous expectations to have had when I already knew that the only thing that could resolve the situation – waving a magic wand to bring Desreen back – was impossible. Slowly realising that our once perfect little life had become incredibly hard was the first step I took away from wishing life better and towards making it that way.

I read books, I scoured the internet, I spoke to child bereavement charities and I soaked up any advice I could get. I would try anything to make my son's life as positive as possible, but I promised myself not to try to make it perfect. That ship had sailed. I knew that I needed to be realistic.

I soon realised that the biggest problem with trying to understand more about how a baby or a toddler grieves is that by the time they are articulate enough to be able to tell you how they once felt, they almost certainly can't remember. This means that a widowed parent can be offered advice that ranges from one extreme to another. Try to imagine – or perhaps you *know* – being more tired, confused, conflicted and heartbroken than you have ever been in your life. Then add in a feeling of being desperate for good advice to help you through, only to find that as soon as someone tells you that you must turn right, another says left.

I remember feeling incredulous that a health visitor had been to our home when our baby was born but no one had checked in when his mum was killed. Did they think he could stand on his own two feet now that he was two? Was there no mechanism for assessment of whether the bereaved parent was fit to care for the child? Only via a chance episode in A&E when Jackson's temperature soared to above forty degrees Celsius did the authorities realise that his mother was no longer his next of kin. And only once that had happened did I receive a letter inviting my two-and-a-half-year-old son, 'Benjamin', to visit a clinic for his two-year check-up. The health visitor we met that day turned out to be very kind (far more sympathetic than the doctor who was only prepared to prescribe me Gaviscon for my grief), but she didn't have a great deal of advice to offer. In fairness, of course, she was no expert, but I felt entirely condescended to as she overused the words 'well done'. They felt like the sort of reward you would offer a pet for good behaviour, as if she were surprised that a man was actually able to care for a child.

I've grown to hate the words *be strong*, but I knew I would need to find the strength of character to be the only judge of what was right or wrong for my child. The only other person who, ultimately, would really get a say in the matter would be him. I resolved to open my heart, open my ears and keep an open mind about the idea that perhaps a child, who was still barely two, might already know what was best for him. Maybe my little apprentice could one day prove himself to be the master.

Toddlers aren't always the most sympathetic of creatures, however. As much as I tried to do what I believed was right by my son, he didn't always appear to be on my side. Something that he responded to positively one day might leave him reeling the next. I suppose it's a bit like the first time a child shows a liking for a new food – one taste of broccoli and they are labelled as a wonder-child, their palate so advanced they will probably be the next Michel Roux. The following day, however, it's as if it never happened – now only chips and ice cream will do.

When I first noticed that Jackson was more honest with his grief the more honest I was with mine, I thought it would always be okay to let him see my pain. One day we just lay in bed and cried together and then silently cuddled away the tears. The very next day, however, was the day he looked at the tears in my eyes and asked, 'What are you doing, Daddy? Are you crying?' before throwing himself dramatically onto the floor and *pretending* to sob. 'Oh boo hoo, Daddy! Boo hoo hoo!' he mocked, flipping between faux-tears and hysterical laughter. Once he came round from his fit of giggles and the lingering 'Oooooh' he always adds when he's found something exceptionally funny, he looked at me and told me I was a 'silly daddy'.

He had a habit of making already tough times even tougher. I had received an invitation for a joint birthday party held in honour of two of his friends from nursery, in mid-January. I really didn't want to go, but I wanted to make sure that I still included Jackson in 'normal' toddler activities. He completely stitched me up and fell asleep on the way there so I couldn't even hide behind him when we arrived. When I was offered either tea or cava I said, 'Oh, definitely cava please,' much quicker than a parent at a children's party probably should.

After her death, Desreen became my benchmark as a parent. If I could heed my own words from her eulogy and try to be more like her, then I knew that I could still give Jackson the best possible start under the circumstances. And I knew I could also continue to raise him the way she had and would were she still here. While her sense of fun and her ability to make our son laugh was going to be a tough beacon to relight in such dark days, her devotion, dedication and unconditional love for him would be the baton that I would carry for the rest of my life.

My father-in-law's words (words that Desreen would repeat,

mostly to get a laugh from her friends who had heard his mantra over and over when they were teenagers) rang in my ears: *proper preparation prevents poor performance*. So I got myself prepared properly to prevent myself performing poorly, and made some parenting promises.

I would be honest with my son

'Jackson, Mummy's gone away and she can't ever come back. She didn't want to go. She would never have left you out of choice because she loved you more than anyone or anything in the world. But Daddy's still here and he's going to look after you now. And I know how to look after you because Mummy taught me.'

I'd seen my wife die. I was the one who told my son. I'd already done the two hardest things I could ever have imagined, and I had survived. I would comfort him, love him and care for him, but I would also respect him enough to always tell him the truth. Father Christmas, the Easter Bunny and the bloody Tooth Fairy would soon become real moral dilemmas.

I would listen to him and I would never marginalise his grief

'It's probably a good thing that he was the age he was when she died,' people would say. Bullshit. Who wouldn't want another day, week, month or year with their mum, however much it may still hurt to eventually lose them? I would never brush his loss under the carpet nor tell myself that his sea of grief was any shallower than mine just because of his age. Instead I would teach myself to better interpret his and I would become the person he could trust to share it without judgment, reservation or limits. I would treat his grief no differently to my own.

I would always put his feelings before mine

'My mum died when I was young but we were never allowed to talk about her with my dad. We didn't want to hurt his feelings.' These were words I heard from so many people. But I never really *chose* to allow Jackson to maintain a conversation about his mum. I knew it was the *only* way. I knew right away that my pain couldn't be any worse than it already was. Why would I stop my child from talking about the woman we both love more than anyone else? How could that possibly make the hurt any worse for me?

I would be firm but always try to give him the benefit of the doubt

As long as Jackson lacked the vocabulary to express his feelings in words, I could never truly know what was a tantrum and what was an expression of grief. I would endeavour to put myself in his little shoes and consider how I would feel about being yelled at when I was already upset, simply because someone who misunderstood me thought I was being naughty. I would remove him from any situation that made him uncomfortable, come down to his level and talk as man and boy. But I would not be taken for a ride. Daddy would remain in charge, or life would become unbearable.

I would guide him as a child but also let him guide me as a father

The boss I might be, but not the dictator. I learned quickly that I could learn from him as much as he could learn from me. The two of us would just need to find our own way of communicating our own lessons. Which was tricky when one of us possessed a reasonable grasp of the English language and the other mostly expressed himself through the names of toy trains from the fictitious Island of Sodor. It would be tricky, but not impossible.

I would play with him every day

A play therapist called Emma Latchem contacted me through the blog to offer some advice on how I might learn to *hear* Jackson's lessons. This was a huge breakthrough in understanding and recognising his grief. Play therapy would make him the teacher and me the pupil, simply by letting him lead our games. Through the simple act of taking time out to play with my son on his own terms, I would enable him to express his feelings to me in a way that would feel natural and safe to him. And no, the games weren't all easy. There were tears, rage, anger and upset. But then why would any *adult* visit a therapist if they were only looking for a friendly chat?

I would allow him to make me happy again

It was a crime that his mummy was taken from him so soon. I decided that, however hard it might be to get there, it would be another crime if I could not allow my son to make me happy again. In fact, I found it impossible to resist the joy he brought me. Perhaps my smiles would fade as quickly as they appeared but I would be grateful that my beautiful wife had left a legacy of love and laughter.

I would love him unconditionally

It was inevitable that there would be difficult days ahead. Children would say mean things at school, teachers might even be insensitive too, and one day his grief would probably manifest itself as something challenging. But I would weather the storm and always try to ensure that my heart was filled with enough love for two parents.

I would keep the memory of his mummy alive

We would talk about her every day. Pictures would go up on the wall and not come down. I would teach Jackson about his mum through stories, photos, drawings and songs. I would tell him how much she loved him and how proud she would have been to see him making progress in his life. And I would be able to do both with such credibility, authority and sincerity because I knew that she had never felt a stronger sense of love and pride for anyone than she had for her son. I knew because she told me. And not just through words but through her actions, expressions and plans for the future.

None of these promises would be easy to keep. I quickly realised that, while toddlers have a wonderful way of lifting you up in times of grief, they also have a knack of kicking you while you are down. *Remember, they all behave like this. Yes, they all behave like this,* I repeated in my head over and over when Jackson made the already difficult journey up north for our first Christmas without Desreen even harder. I was quietly breaking down while he screamed hysterically for me to remove a dark chocolate button from his mouth, which he couldn't quite grasp had already made it halfway to his colon.

THE HOLIDAY

My loved ones wanted to fill our futures with plans. They needed to show they were there and I imagine they intuitively knew that they might need to fill the void to help prevent me from plummeting too deep into it. I said yes to most things. Shock left me feeling like I was simply filling out dates in my social calendar, no different to before. I couldn't just stay at home grieving all day after all, could I? What did I know? With no guidebook, I would have to feel my way myself.

But there were two things that I was sure of at that point: that I needed to try to make sure that my son still had fun and that my life couldn't stop just because my wife's had. Somehow our lives needed to continue, however impossible that might feel. Only time would reveal the extent to which these self-imposed expectations were premature.

Perhaps I should have paused. Perhaps I should have treated my two-year-old son's emotional intelligence with a little more respect. Perhaps I should have thought that all he needed was love, understanding and care. But instead I took my friends – Woody and Katy, Lee, Olive and their son Albie – up on their generous offer and booked a holiday in the sun just three months after Desreen died. Surely we'd be ready by then, right? Wrong – it was a disaster.

I couldn't have known it would be so bad, but I could have

pressed pause on our lives and slowed them down to a manageable pace for a grieving child, husband and father. I've come to believe that toddlers are adept at telling you how they feel and how to care for them, even if they don't have the words. In my son's case he told me through his body heat. Two days before we were due to travel he was radiating temperatures between 38 and 40°C. He was attached to me constantly, gripping on like a baby koala but also sloth-like when he awoke drowsily, only to check that he was still in my arms.

I did what I could to bring his body temperature down through medication, but to little avail. His bug was just too hot and bothered and it wasn't going to chill out until it was reunited with its nasty little friends at A&E.

There were undoubtedly better places to pass the time, given my state of mind. The words 'trauma in six minutes' announced repeatedly over the speakers weren't helping me to relax. The doctors and nurses weren't of much assistance, either. One nurse rolled her eyes at my distressed two-year-old's lack of cooperation, a doctor called him 'naughty' and the registrar was openly judgmental about the fact that he was eating plantain chips.

I bit my tongue, although I wanted to ask her to step behind the curtain so that I could explain my son's heritage to her, that the plantain is a type of fruit common to the West Indies, and that in any case, we couldn't get him to eat anything else that day. I also wanted to tell her to get back to her ivory tower and be grateful that she was well enough to stomach her quinoa and three-bean salad. But I refrained. I was too afraid that if I started, I might take every member of staff down with her, and then make for the exit saying, 'Well, thanks very much, docs. My son still feels like shit but I feel so much better.'

I'm sure there are few parents out there who would class themselves as perfect, but it's hard to feel even slightly good when your child is suffering the pain of grief every bit as much as you and there's nothing you can do to make it better. When I couldn't get his medicine down his little throat my devastated mind would tell me that his mum would have managed it. When I spotted that his T-shirt was on back-to-front I felt like handing him the phone to dial ChildLine and scripting him to ensure he didn't leave out any of the details of my shocking parenting skills. When the only thing he would eat, for days, was Cheerios, I felt as though I was knowingly feeding him poison. And all this was before we even got on the plane.

In fairness to Jackson, he could hardly have behaved better. So sedated was he by the medicine slowly making its way around his little system that he slept for most of the four-and-a-half-hour journey to Gran Canaria. When he awoke for the landing he knew that two things were wrong: he had never taken a flight without his mum before and he had never had to sit in his own seat. Since he had just turned two, I'd paid for two full fares, although he remained on my knee the whole way there.

'You're going to have to put him in his own seat,' the cabin crew told me as he screamed at the top of his voice in sickness and in fear.

'Sorry, but it's not going to happen,' I replied, knowing that if pressed I had the potential to be much less polite.

'You've got no choice, sir. You really have to put him in his own seat right now.'

'Have you seen the state of him? It's not going to happen – unless *you'd* like to try, of course. Perhaps you should just get me a child safety belt,' I suggested as a compromise.

Jackson was confused and petrified. I was dying inside but also full of rage and yet suddenly I was faced with a small army of flight attendants.

'Listen to me!' I exploded. 'His mum has just died. He's scared and he's ill. So why don't you just get me the fucking belt and let him stay on my knee.'

'What do you say to that?' I heard them whispering at the back of the plane.

You say, 'Yes sir, no problem at all,' I thought to myself as I stepped off the plane with a slightly calmer and completely unharmed child.

Of course, they were just doing their jobs, but at the time it felt like everyone was being paid a bonus for making me feel like a father who couldn't cope.

Things didn't get much better after we landed. In fact, it was no holiday at all. The sun shone every day but Jackson didn't want to be outside. It was hot but I was hotter because I was stuck indoors with a little boy who had a high temperature and who just wanted to use his daddy's chest as his pillow. I learned every word to every episode of *Thomas the Tank Engine* ever made and came back paler than when I left.

The return leg of the journey was even worse than the outbound. I came back so dejected, so disappointed and so distressed by what happened while we were away that I couldn't even find my own words to share on my blog. So I started to write as someone else. To understand the grief and pain that my child was suffering I would need to see the world through his eyes.

Dear Daddy,
I feel like I need you to see things from my point of view because you're giving yourself a very hard time (good at spelling, aren't I?)

I'm going to keep this brief because I get bored really easily and although I said I don't like Thomas the Tank Engine anymore when we left the house this morning, I've changed my mind and he's all I can think about right now. Frankly, I also find writing letters a real bore and I don't understand why this archaic laptop has keys when I prefer to touch-type directly onto the screen with sugary yoghurt on my fingers. But I love you, Daddy, so I'll persevere. Big word for such a little guy, *n'est pas*? Oh yeah, they make kids' TV shows that teach you French and Spanish now. Oh, and Patois too if you include Rastamouse, man.

Where was I? Oh aye, three things happened last week that I think I ought to explain from my perspective because they seem to be crushing you up and I need you to be in a better state of mind to build my train tracks. I might be able to write well, but those bloody bridges get me every time.

Incident one: Daddy, last week you took me 'on holiday' to the Canaries when I was really ill. I had a huge fever, you pumped me full of drugs and I think you probably wanted me to be on form. Well, let me tell you something, man flu starts young and I had it. You grown-ups think kids' medicine is the answer to everything but if it's that great then why don't you take it when you get ill? Are you with me?

So there we were, sharing a sun lounger, recently bereaved of the one person who meant most to us in the whole wide world and you reckon a swimming pool and a scoop of ice cream is going to sort it. Did it make you feel any better? That's what I thought.

I'm not trying to make you feel bad for taking me, I thought you really made an effort and you barely left my side. But that's my point. I needed you last week, not a holiday. And on reflection I think you did a pretty good job at putting me first, so please don't beat yourself up. Let's just move on. We're both home now and we're closer than ever, so take a chill pill.

Incident two: While we were away I heard you sniff. It's a filthy habit and had I known you didn't have a hanky I would have reprimanded you but, more fool me, I thought you were crying. So I ran across the room and asked, 'Ooo okay, Daddy?' (God knows how come I write so well but can't even pronounce the word you, but you're one to talk, you had a lisp until you were five.)

I also offered you a plantain chip to comfort you because I know from previous experience that dummies aren't really your thing (while we're on the subject, that doctor from A&E can kiss my tiny ass if she thinks I'm giving her one of my plantain chips – bloody nerve of the woman.) I did this because I want to look after you too, Daddy. We're both crushed by what's happened but we really need to support one another. You looked genuinely shocked that a child could be so sensitive, but I love you, man, and I've got your back. That's how toddlers roll these days. We're not as dumb as we are small.

Incident three So I had you covered when I thought you were blubbing in the villa but then you got all like 'Oh God, I mustn't cry in front of Jackson anymore' at the airport when I got overtired and cross and spat on the floor and took my shoes off and threw them out of my pushchair across the arrivals lounge when you seemed to be welling up. I guess you thought it was a good idea for us to get a night flight because I'd probably nod off. Well, for once you predicted my sleep patterns correctly and for that you must be rewarded. I have a plantain chip with your name on it.

But what you failed to realise is that toddlers don't react too well to being woken up to get off a plane at 1.00a.m. What they like even less is when the taxi that is meant to pick them up at 2.00a.m. fails to arrive (don't get me started on that taxi firm, but rest assured we will take them down, Daddy.) The only thing a toddler appreciates even less than that, is when the next taxi firm turns up with a baby seat and not a child seat. I can't fit into one of those anymore. So when the taxi driver suggested he just 'drive slowly', leaving my life at risk just three months after my mummy was killed by a car, I think you were right to tell the punk to go fuck himself.

However, what a toddler enjoys even less than all those things put together is to see his father so upset at nearly 4.00a.m. That broke me, and while you called a friend and asked for help, my verbal vocabulary doesn't stretch that far yet (which is weird because I type like a demon), so I had to show my feelings. And yes, I threw my dummies on the floor (I like to have at least three to hand, especially when upset, because one alone doesn't have the same effect). Yes, I removed my shoes and threw them out, too. Yes, I screamed the place down. But it wasn't because you cried, I'm totally down with the tears, dude, it was because I was knackered, you pushed me too hard and every single fucker seemed to have it in for us that night.

But have you noticed how well I've behaved since we've been home? And have you realised that we've actually both laughed a few times? Also, have you noticed how I keep asking you for a cuddle because you're my main man and I need you so much right now?

Anyway, I just wanted to let you know how I see it all and say I love you, Daddy. We both know Mummy was the best, but you're doing alright so don't be so hard on yourself. We'll get there.

Love, J-Bo xx

But I couldn't just write the holiday off as a mistake. I saw it as an innocent but naïve symptom of my own middle-class materialism and machismo. It reminded me of the way I used to behave when I had barely seen my son all week because of work and then made plans that involved me spending more time trying to buy *his* affections than giving him *mine* freely: refusing to relax and read him his favourite story so we could make a mad dash to the park, when he had already told me he didn't want to go; rushing him to a toy shop when all he wanted was to play with me and the toys he already had.

After that holiday I made myself another promise. I would take things easier on the two of us. I would slow down the pace. I would give us both the time we needed to *just be*. And we would *just be* for better or for worse. No judgment, no expectations and no timescales. I suppose I retaught myself what it meant to be a dad. And to me that didn't mean trips to Disneyland, a pony for Christmas or working so hard to buy material things that my son, who had already lost his mummy, ended up with a daddy he rarely saw. From that point on, the only things I would strive to give him were my love and my time.

LE COURAGE

My friends were all so supportive after Desreen died: Zac and Laura would come round and play with Jackson all the time; Lee and Olive would both find excuses to get to London through work even if they only ended up with an hour to spare; Woody had recently moved from east London to St Albans in Hertfordshire but spent more time with me than ever before, and all of Desreen's friends came round to visit and help often. I was so conscious of my own unhappiness and all the affection people were lavishing on me, however, that I encouraged a few of my friends to start putting themselves first and not to feel that they always needed to be there.

Two of my closest friends, Michael, who I lived with when I first met Desreen, and his wife, Victoria, had their first child just weeks after Des died. They asked me to be godfather to their beautiful daughter, Jemima. I remember thinking that the best thing I could do for her was to encourage her parents to enjoy their first few months with her, in spite of the tragedy that had hit us all so hard.

At the time I just couldn't find the words to say this to the two of them, but I did echo the sentiment when I suggested to Woody that he should try to make sure that Katy came first. Since they met, both his mum and his best friend's wife had died. She had been a tower of strength and support through each tragic event.

After a while I told my friends that I would rather think of them being happy than all of us being miserable; that I was going to be unhappy no matter what they did or how much time they spent with me.

I suppose I had also realised that sometimes I needed some space. Lots of people were inviting me for dinner or even offering to come round to my flat and cook, so I really needn't ever have been on my own. And yet I didn't always want company. I would take Jackson out to the park or to a museum to keep us both entertained but when he took his midday nap, I would wheel him into a restaurant in his pushchair and eat my lunch alone.

During these times it was never just any old company that I missed, it was Desreen's companionship. I already knew that I would have to help Jackson to understand that other people hadn't suddenly replaced his mother's presence, but it took me longer to appreciate that I had to learn the same lesson for myself. When I went dining alone, I didn't feel lonely, desperate, inadequate or as if I was cutting a sad figure at a table for one. I just felt that I wasn't with my wife and I would take that time to get used to the empty space across from me. On the rare occasions when I got to be completely on my own I would allow myself to think about her, remember her and really really miss her – something that I knew I had been denying myself because it just hurt too much.

Soon after we returned from holiday, however, I met up with Zac for lunch, near my home in East Dulwich. He, Laura, Jackson and I had spent a lot of time together since Desreen died. We'd all witnessed her death and that had created a tragic, if inevitable, bond. One night in December I had even (foolishly, in retrospect) gone back to their flat to try to face the demons; it was too soon. I stayed the night because I couldn't let myself step out of their house around the same time as my wife was killed, but I had to leave at dawn because I couldn't bear to be surrounded any longer by the same four walls where we had taken shelter immediately after Desreen's death. I couldn't be on the street where she'd been killed for a moment longer and I ran past the spot where she died, in tears, because I thought if I didn't, I might be next.

As with most of the discussions I had around this time, our lunchtime conversation flipped from Desreen's death to a result of her death – namely my blog. Zac and I talked at length about the issues raised in the posts, the debate they had begun to drive and our own personal experiences of grief, and we discussed the topic that really inspired me to start writing in the first place: the fact that when someone close to us dies we are so often told to 'be strong'.

Zac's bilingual, having spent his childhood in both the UK and France, and he speculated that perhaps it's the English language that makes us say things that we sometimes don't actually mean. He wondered if the word *courage* used in the French way might be more apt. It's the same word but with slightly different connotations; as well as the courage (the English word) it can also mean bravery, energy and motivation.

This really struck a chord for me because, unlike telling a person to be strong, which directs their behaviour, wishing a person *courage* is more generous and less controlling. To me *being strong* meant hiding my feelings; it was shorthand for *be a man*. It meant *keep a stiff upper lip* and *be stoic*. At its most extreme it meant *don't grieve*.

At that moment I decided I was going to approach my grief with courage and not strength. Courage would allow me to cry when I wanted to, scream when I wanted to, laugh when I wanted to and be brave enough to *just be*.

That evening I published a post on my blog that touched on our conversation. A widower who had lost his wife in a motorcycle accident sent a moving reply based on his own experience of grief.

Some of the best advice I received was from a fellow widower, a month after my wife's death. It was two words: courage and patience. Courage to cry when you need to. Courage to make it through the next day, hour or even minute. Patience with yourself and with others. With yourself because, even though it feels like the end of your life, things will eventually get less bad. Patience with others because they can't understand what you are going through and, while they are trying to help, they may say or do something that you just can't understand or that you find hurtful.

A French woman living in London who had also recently lost her husband in a tragic road accident replied, too.

Courage et patience, que de beaux sentiments pour nous aider à depasser notre peine!

Looking back, I think that speaking just a little French over a glass of white wine from the Rhône Valley that day completely changed my life. I realised that, for me, strength was not going to be about hiding my tears and feelings, it was going to be about being man enough to show them.

MASTER JACKSON

I made a big mistake when Desreen died. I tried to hide my grief from my son, thinking that he wouldn't suffer so much if I seemed happy and kept playing with him and his train set as if nothing in our lives had changed. I had no idea what I was doing. I had never lost a wife before, or a parent, and neither experience was covered at any point in my education. I suppose I just enrolled myself in the school of 'he's probably too young to understand'.

It's a popular school, that one. The classes are easy and there are plenty of teachers to go around. Anyone can qualify because it takes so little effort to pass the test. Sweeping statements, wild stabs in the dark and reciting archaic sentiments verbatim are quite enough to get the grade. Perhaps that's why there are so many people out there who deem themselves qualified to comment.

Fortunately, I found myself a different tutor. While his formal education and verbal skills were limited he had an indisputable advantage over anyone else who considered themselves an expert on the subject of *my* child's grief. He *was* the subject matter; he was the very definition of it. And while he didn't teach through lectures, seminars or sermons, his lessons went straight to my heart. I would just need to learn how to speak his language, hear his instructions and be patient enough to wait at my metaphorical desk until he was ready to begin the class.

Once my little student, Jackson now became my teacher. I opened my heart and my mind to his subtle lessons and he showed me how to better understand a child's grief. He taught me how to better deal with my own. He taught me to try to see the world through the eyes of a child. He taught me to make happiness feel welcome in my life again. He taught me about unconditional love. He taught me to balance intuition and education. He taught me to take children seriously. He taught me how to be a better father. In short, my little man in shorts taught me more about life than any big person apparently wearing the trousers ever could.

Very quickly, Jackson also taught me that you can't hide the truth from a toddler. They are much too sensitive and perceptive not to notice when your world has shattered around you. One night in December 2012, only weeks after my wife's death, I let down my then stoic guard and quietly sobbed my heart out on the sofa during *The X Factor* final, while Jackson entertained himself with his tracks. My son knew me well enough to appreciate that his daddy much preferred that year's series of *Strictly Come Dancing*, so understandably he was taken aback to see the tears streaming down my face.

But it was his reaction that turned my tears' steady stream into a river. He weighed up all the people in the room including my parents, my in-laws and my cousin, Graham, to try to establish whether any of them had upset me, gave them all a dirty look just in case, and then tenderly wiped my eyes with his soft little hands. His actions upset me even more because I felt that I should be his rock, rather than he mine. So in the daytime I started acting as if I were happy and then retreated to my room at night to unleash the pent-up grief. I was trying to protect him from my feelings, as if seeing me upset about the death of his mum were in someway unnatural or unhealthy.

After a few days I thought better of this. I tried to see things through his eyes. I thought to myself: what kind of husband and father would I look like to him if I showed no signs of hurt about his mother's sudden disappearance from our little world? I wondered: why would a small child, who used tears as a regular and vital means of communication with the adult world, have a problem with seeing things the other way round? I asked myself: was I protecting my child by not showing emotion around him, or teaching him that feelings are best hidden? I was never taught to keep things inside by my parents, so what was making me do just that?

I suddenly found myself thinking a lot about my upbringing, and feeling very grateful. I could talk to my parents about anything. My maternal grandparents were way ahead of their time: affectionate, open, warm, liberal, and friends as well as parents and grandparents to their children and grandchildren. They passed all these qualities down to both my parents, who in turn passed them down to my two older brothers, Mat and Nick, and me. I think that my paternal grandparents were much more typical of their stiff upper lip generation, so I was always so proud of my dad for turning out to be such a thoroughly modern and sensitive man and parent. And yet here I was, just about to let myself become Daddy Dark Ages.

Something wasn't right; *I* wasn't right and Jackson wasn't either. He mirrored my behaviour and hid his feelings from me, too. He would smile for me all day, only mention his mum when I was not around and then, very suddenly, would shift from giggling through his dreams to crying out and screaming agonisingly in his sleep. 'Help me! Help me!' he cried out one night without waking, words I had never even heard him say while conscious.

I didn't know the answer to my emotional dilemma so I looked to my son for his guidance. One night I took him to bed and we lay down together without saying a word. We just stared at each other and remained silent. My head was rushing with thoughts about Desreen and I imagine his was too, because she was so obviously absent from our bedroom, which was still filled with all of her things. A tear fell down his cheek and then one fell down mine. Suddenly his tear became a sob and that sob became a howl. This time I mirrored *his* behaviour and there we both were, crying loudly and uncontrollably and we didn't stop until the tears ran out.

Some days later I thought a lot about what had happened that night. For the first time since he was born I hadn't said the words 'don't cry' to him when he was in tears. I didn't say 'shh'. I just let him cry and allowed him to show me the depth of his upset. It was our first real moment of shared, honest and raw emotion as father and son and despite the devastating circumstances, it somehow felt positive. From that moment on 'don't cry' became 'good boy, let it out'; 'shh' became 'I know, darling.' Jackson's life was going to be challenging enough without his mum there to guide him, but to have a father telling him not to *feel* would surely only serve to make it harder still. I promised myself then that I would meet his emotions with understanding and without judgment.

Soon we were talking openly about his mummy every day; I wasn't afraid to bring her into the conversation anymore and I didn't freeze when he did, either. She was always a sucker for exposed floorboards in life, so there was no way we were going to start brushing her memory under the carpet upon her death.

Allowing one another to express these little eruptions of emotion and distress in our home ironically made it a happier place to live.

I briefly went to see a counsellor right after Desreen died in the weeks that preceded and immediately followed Christmas. At the time I was going through a phase, which, with hindsight, I can only describe as grief-crazed. For some reason part of me felt a desperate urge to be seen as someone who could cope with the pain. It was almost as though I wanted to be good at grief. I found myself trying to learn all about it through books, case studies, medical documents and online articles; as if by doing so I might arm myself against it or fight my way through it at a pace. I suppose I naïvely thought that it was something I could get over, and that by knowing more about it I could get over it more quickly. The counselling, therefore, became little more than a box-ticking exercise for me – just something that my doctor suggested and that I agreed to out of academic interest as much as anything else.

After the first session I left thinking that I must have been a terribly disappointing patient. My psychotherapist had my life story in about fifteen minutes, and all she'd said was 'Hello'. At one point I asked, 'So what happens now?' If it weren't for the manners my parents taught me as a child I probably would have rolled my eyes when she asked, 'What would you like to happen now?' Looking back I think I was in a state of mania, which made me feel like I was cleverer and better versed in the condition of grief than the therapist. I went in there armed with my own conclusions and left little room for her to work with me.

After three sessions she suggested that perhaps I had enough 'internal resource' to see myself through for the time being. Maybe she sensed that I was putting on a show and that I wasn't really open to the process quite yet. Her parting advice, however, was not to dismiss the idea of counselling should I ever feel the need to talk to someone again in future.

Having since crashed back down from this frenetic state of shock, I am now going back into counselling and I suspect that

I will need to revisit psychotherapy at many different stages throughout my entire life. Time moves on and people move on too, so I imagine it will become increasingly difficult to open up about the same feelings of loss that I have covered with friends and family so many times before. And as Desreen died at such a young age, there are many people who also feel her loss acutely. At times this can make it hard – selfish even – to indulge in a one-sided conversation with friends or family members about how I feel without it straying into an exchange about how *we* feel. Sometimes I just want to talk about how much I love and miss my wife without risking having to comfort the other person in the conversation, and I suppose that may mean getting support from a professional stranger from time to time.

Although I initially only went to three sessions the first time I tried psychotherapy, I quickly learned a very valuable lesson. I learned that doctors and psychologists believe that the act of opening up is in itself positive therapy. So how could encouraging my son – a child of two who hadn't the capacity or emotional intelligence to work through this alone – to open up and show his feelings be a bad thing?

Evidently not everybody agreed. People often have very strong opinions about how to behave around bereaved children.

'You mustn't let him see you're upset,' some said. 'You must be strong for them,' I read. 'You must keep your feelings from them,' people who didn't have any experience advised.

One person even went so far as to set up a Twitter account, make me the first and only person they followed, and sent me their inaugural tweet begging me not to show any emotion in front of my son. I have no idea who they were or why the hell they felt the need to intervene in how I chose to raise my child, but I felt sick with anger. Why would a stranger tell me to play happy families when our family's happiness was dead and buried? I asked myself. I had tried that and when I did I felt like a liar and a fraud. I had cheated him and I vowed never to subject him to emotional lies again.

But as with most aspects of grief, it wasn't as simple as that. Sometimes Jackson would cry spontaneously, completely out of the blue and for no immediately apparent reason. He would tell me that he missed his mummy through his tears, and in doing so he subtly gave me permission to cry, too. But then there were other times when he would show signs of insecurity, confusion and fragility; implicitly, he was asking me to be his strength. If I cried at this point his insecurity sometimes turned into anger and he would lash out at me for not being the beacon he needed to get him through his red haze. So I suppose it would be fair to say the secret Twitterer had a point.

The compassion I've learned as a result of my wife's death means I tend not to stay angry with anyone for long. And yet I have found grief to be laden with contradictions. That same message could make me spit venom one moment or feel humbled that a stranger might care from afar, the next. But in times of intermittent rage I would look at that tweet and want to type a reply along the lines of *If you're comfortable enough to tell me how to bring up my son at least have the fucking spine to introduce yourself and tell me why you know better than me, or indeed him for that matter.* I may have also added the words *you prick* at the end but I was unsure whether I was addressing a man or a woman – and that's no word for a lady. Also, Twitter only allows 140 characters per message, which I find makes ranting quite the challenge. Clipped fury is tricky to perfect.

This message would be the first of a handful criticising my approach to managing both my son's grief and mine. I found that for every hundred positive messages of encouragement that left me feeling as numb as ever, a single critical one would floor or enrage me. I suppose that's human nature: many of us have an unfortunate tendency to focus on the negative. And it's amazing what a delicate emotional state can do to the brain. Yet I somehow managed to stay on course, working through what *I* believed was either right or wrong for the two of us, rather than relying solely on the guidance of others. Grief can kill a person's confidence and sap their strength, but maybe it's intuition that we really need to get us through the toughest times and to keep us on track. And my intuition told me to continue to let my son lead, which brought me both occasional mild pleasure and frequent intense pain.

When I opened my eyes to the power a child has to make a dark world a brighter place, my heart followed. I began to anthropomorphise Grief and imagine 'him' being at battle with my son and me, which helped me to start to have more positive minutes, hours and even days.

I played Luke Skywalker, dressed in white and ready to rumble, while Grief was Darth Vader, dark, dangerous and trying to lure me to the shadowy side. Grief would put up a good fight – a physical and emotional exchange mixing hard-hitting blows and mind games. He told me it was my fault that my wife was dead and that I had nothing left to live for. He told me I would never again be able to feel as if I were really living. He made me think the darkest thoughts I had ever thought and feel the most negative feelings I had ever felt. And when I tried to laugh in his face and beat him with positive retorts, his harsh hand would slap me back down and put me firmly back in my wretched place.

But my trump card was that I was not trying to win. I knew Grief would be back for more if I put up too strong a fight so I decided to settle for a draw. When Grief threw blame at me,

I went for a run. I'm a pretty fast runner and I could go for miles without him catching me, so I got some time off to empty my head or think about other things.

When he suggested I had nothing to live for, I would spend time with my son. At just two years old, he confused the hell out of Grief. He would throw little soft punches made of joy, laughter and mischief that Grief couldn't defend. Just as Grief thought he had got me, my son would say something random like 'I love music, Daddy. I love Mickey Mouse!' Or he would try to do the bum wiggle, which Olive had taught him. His bottom didn't actually move but he thought it did because it was up in the air and his excitedly clenched fists were shaking from side to side. If I was really lucky he might even be my second in the duel and follow me around the house while biting on the tail of my shirt, pretending I was the train to his carriage.

When Grief made me think dark thoughts, I would summon up memories of the good times with my wife. It hurt like hell because they made my eyes go misty and I couldn't see that Grief was about to throw a sharp jab, but I would keep doing it anyway because it was worth the pain. And if he did slap me back down, I crawled off beaten, waited for the wounds to heal and came back for the next round.

Bereavement can be a dark place where light seldom shines, but when a spark occasionally flickers it's unfair of Grief to torture us for our moments of positivity. Sometimes, when I felt frustration at my somewhat cactus-like eyes, which could go days with no sign of water, I would hear my wife saying, *Benji, you're not sad enough for my liking. I deserve a lot more tears!* She did, too. But she also deserved a happy little boy, so I soon decided that I wasn't going to beat myself up if I had the occasional good day.

As with most things in life, with the slightly smooth came

the remarkably rough. Most of the glimmers of happiness in our home came when we were alone or in the company of our immediate family members. Otherwise, Jackson's behaviour suddenly became antisocial. For some parents in different circumstances it might have been 'just a phase'. For me it was much more serious. He was acting antisocially because he didn't want to be sociable. He was sick of all of the replacement attention and affection being poured upon him from anyone and everyone except his mum. And the problem was predominantly female. It's hard to imagine a two-year-old boy already experiencing problems with the opposite sex, but we started having some serious woman trouble. My son, who had always been fiercely loyal to his mother, took a dislike to girls. To be more specific, he was on a mission to alienate and attack any woman in her early to mid-thirties who came within ten yards of me.

Once again this presented me with questions that he was as yet unable to answer. Had he lost trust in the fairer sex because his mummy had gone away and couldn't come back? Was he wearing his metaphorical Team Desreen onesie to prevent any significant female influence infiltrating our home? Had I forgotten to teach him that it's not right for a boy to raise his hand or bare his teeth to a girl? Or was I simply overanalysing his every move?

I didn't think I was, so it was at this point I started to expect the worst and plan accordingly. That way disappointment was less likely to be the outcome.

Jackson put on a number of performances that told me I needed to get antisocial, too. I thought about the amount of time I had spent allowing friends to comfort me and realised that perhaps I should have spent more of it comforting him. His mum had totally vanished but his dad's attention was also split between dozens of faces, some of which were part of his intimate life, some vaguely familiar and some completely unknown.

It might have been easy for me to conclude that his distaste for the female sex came about because women tend to show themselves more in times of bereavement, but that just wasn't the case. Perhaps I chose my friends well, perhaps these things are just moving with the times, but there were definitely as many men as women offering us their support.

One Saturday afternoon in January, three months after Desreen was killed, Jackson and I met a lovely couple through my friends Gareth and Leigh. The husband – a father – was a really nice guy who immediately started playing with my son despite never having met him before. They took to each other straight away. His wife was equally warm. A mother, she knew the right buttons to press.

Only my son didn't want his touched. When a 'Go away!' wouldn't suffice he decided that the only way to show her how he felt was to crawl under the table and attack her foot. Naturally I pulled him away before he drew blood, but he looked enraged. On other occasions there were snarls, growls, smacks and attempted bites. He reacted badly to female strangers on the bus, my friends, Desreen's friends, my mum's friends – age, or even a degree of familiarity, made little difference in the end: it was gender that offended him.

He used to pour affection over his mother and blame me for anything that went wrong. 'No, Daddy!' he would shout if one of his trains broke, accusing me of responsibility for the incident even if I wasn't in the room at the time. I was the one who received a whack when something on his plate didn't meet with his approval, even if his mummy was there holding the spoon to his mouth. But that all quickly changed. I could suddenly do little wrong. He stopped yelling at me and started worshipping me. My name would be delivered through a song rather than a shout.

His maternal grandmother, Bev, was out of luck though. While I was gradually becoming 'Mummy' she was quickly replacing Daddy. We would find ourselves both laughing and crying about this at the same time. How heartbreaking that a child needs the love of his mother so badly that he will look to replace it so quickly with the next best thing. Yet how fortunate that he had enough people around who loved him to be able to pick and choose where the appropriate affection came from.

Jackson needed time away from the crowds and in the company of only those whom he knew and trusted. My phone was ringing incessantly with calls from people who wanted to be there to show they cared. So many invitations to meet or visit came, via text messages, emails and social media channels, but they only really met one response. 'I'd love to see you but sadly Jackson doesn't really feel the same right now and he comes first.' Who could argue with that? I listened to what he wanted and let him lead me and that was the best thing I could have done. He knew it was time to keep only the closest people close and he appealed to me to do the same.

On the odd occasion when I did meet up with someone outside my immediate circle of friends and family, I tended to walk away feeling that I had been dishonest about my feelings, that I had acted as if I were more positive than I felt, just to make them feel less miserable about having taken an hour out of their day to see me. Ironically, I realised that I was often meeting people to make *them* feel better rather than the other way round.

Shutting the world out was a decision that I made consciously, one that I suspect will, ultimately, separate friends from acquaintances. It's hard to imagine that the people I haven't seen for over a year, but who have tried to make arrangements to see me, won't one day think, 'Well, I've tried and tried but he's just not interested so I'm not going to try anymore.' Deep down I know that those who really care would wait a decade to see us if that's how long it takes for us to feel ready. Frankly, I don't care about the rest. I've simply got too much on my plate, too much pain in my heart and too many plaguing thoughts in my head to make room for any other problems or concerns.

Closing down was the right thing to do for both of our sakes. Ridding myself of all other distractions allowed me to interpret and understand my son's needs. And having time – or rather *making* time – to play was crucial to this. I learned that children can communicate extremely effectively through play, but as with any form of communication, it's wasted if it's not two-way. I would learn nothing by sticking Jackson in one corner and letting him play with trains, while I sat in the other drinking gin. I had to become a trusted playmate if he were going to open up to me.

And so we played together every day. It sounds like such a simple thing, a parent's duty perhaps, but I remember feeling exhausted and broken not just from playing games but also from *playing happy*. 'I can't believe how something I used to love can take so much out of me and make me feel so bad,' I remember telling Bev as I followed Jackson round the living room floor with a toy train. 'At least you're doing it,' she reassured me, hinting that I shouldn't be beating myself up about the pain I was feeling inside.

Yet in those earlier days it often hurt so much to see my son happy. Of course that's what any parent would want for their child, under normal circumstances, but I felt guilty about being the one to witness the smile of which his mother had been deprived. I never resented his apparent contentment in any way,

I just felt so sad for Desreen that he was still able to be happy. I was always on the edge of tears when I heard him laugh, too. It was as if I didn't deserve to indulge in enjoying his happiness when my heart was so badly broken. But I knew that I had to put his feelings and progress before mine. To me that was simply my responsibility as a father. And so we continued to play.

The professional 'weekend dad' in me told me that play started out of the home. It had to be an occasion rather than an impromptu or improvised game in our own living room. So, for example, I took my friend Olly up on his offer to take his daughter, Annalise, and Jackson to football training one Sunday morning. Unlike some fathers present, I really didn't care if he kicked the ball or climbed the bars on the gymnasium wall as long as he seemed comfortable being there. Either way I would play with him.

In his own typical style, Jackson shouted orders at the man who shouted the orders at him and quickly swapped his toy of choice from a football to a train. The markings on the gym's floor became a never-ending network of tracks and he was the Small Controller, commanding every shunt and signal. But while the football still had his attention, I noticed it take on a new purpose. Jackson got angry. He picked up the ball and threw it at the wall over and over. He was in a mini-rage. I joined in and we took out our pent-up aggression on an innocent pile of bricks and released some of our at-the-surface grief-induced anger. Then we carried on playing with the trains as if nothing had happened.

Later that day it was time to get busy with the Play-Doh. We covered the dining table with newspaper, took out some pots of nostalgia-inducing goo and went to work at turning the different primary colours into a clump of browny-purple mess. Chatting as we went, I brought up Mummy and explained once more what had happened. 'Mummy gone!' he confirmed. 'Not come back!' he went on. 'Mummy!' he shouted towards the hall, a direction that would once have been met with certain reply. 'Not coming!' he reaffirmed with a shrug. And so we continued to play and chat.

But then trouble struck. He asked for something I kind of knew he didn't want – his now cold lunch, which was still sitting on the table from an hour earlier. 'YUCK!' he exclaimed, as he tasted a stony morsel. Then it got thrown on the floor. I became nervous about the future of the living room furnishings when I looked at the mountain of colourful gunk in front of him. Faster than I could pull it away, it was launched across the room. For a two-year-old, he was already showing exceptional promise for cricket.

Some would say he had simply got bored and was throwing a tantrum. But that word temporarily went out of use in our home; it was replaced with 'toddler grief'. This meant that I always gave him the benefit of the doubt and tried to offer him comfort rather than punishment. On this occasion we left the living room and went to his bedroom for a tear-fuelled chat. Like my counsellor, I asked him what he wanted to happen next and he indicated that a nice lie-down and a cuddle would do.

Lying on the bed he, rather confusingly, gave me a little smile, which quickly dissolved into a huge angry roar – a kind of shout that suggested that I had done something wrong. Then the smile came back, then another angry roar. I realised this was Jackson's own kind of primal scream, and so I joined in on what would be the first of many, many more on many, many different occasions. We both found this to be an immediate outlet for frustration, one which allowed us to get on peacefully with our day faster than I would ever previously have thought possible after such a forceful expression of upset.

But it wasn't all anger, violence, and shouting and screaming;

we had softer and more joyous times, too. Just as a spontaneous roar could take the edge off our fury, we found dancing could also bring a smile. We would dance around the living room and the kitchen, and I jumped around the flat with Jackson on my shoulders singing along to 'We Found Love' by Rihanna and 'Locked Out of Heaven' by Bruno Mars, just to bring a little laughter and happiness into our home.

And when we grew tired from the mixed emotions of our days we would go to bed. My son, a child who has always slept in a bed because he flatly refused to sleep anywhere else, would only sleep on his mummy's side. But that night, after our attempt to play football and mould Play-Doh, he insisted on sleeping on my side. Something about swapping sides, and me being on hers, made me so upset. Jackson saw me cry.

'Want dummy, Daddy?' he asked offering his favourite form of comfort to me freely. 'Take Thomas, Daddy,' he also commanded, thrusting his beloved toy into my hands. 'Take it!' he insisted, shoving the dummy into my mouth.

I was watching out for my son's behaviour, in order to help me understand how best to care for him. But that evening I was so moved to learn that he was doing exactly the same for me. It was around this time that 'Jackson' wrote his second post for the blog, as a way to help me to understand what was going on in his head.

I've just been to one of my favourite places, Peckham Pulse soft play, with a little mate and three old dudes. It's off the hook, this place. Ball pool, big slide, shaky bridge, tunnels, the lot. There's usually some fella in the corner who thinks he's the shizzle, too, dishing out all these rules that none of us listens to. It must have been his day off today so we let rip and proper had it.

Anyway, I'm gonna rewind a bit otherwise you just ain't gonna get it. I've been having some serious woman trouble lately. Like, I'm handsome and that and I've got all these girls putting their names down already, but it ain't that kind of trouble. I just don't like them much right now, especially when they go anywhere near my dad. I'm like: *Back off! Mummy would slap you down if you came anywhere near her man*. I'm kind of just doing her work for her now that she's gone.

And here's the thing. This is why I need to get some of this stuff off my chest today. I think I know she's gone. I haven't seen her for ages and I keep repeating what my daddy says to me about how she didn't want to leave me but that she can't ever come back, but something is still confusing me. I keep thinking she's still here, that I've just seen her in the street or in the park or wherever.

As I was saying, at the moment most chicks get a big fat 'whatever' from me: a filthy look, a massive raspberry or some repartee that sounds elegant and articulate in my head but usually comes out more like, 'Ubbubbubbaabah, Thomas, Percy, Henry, Raaaaar!' But then I see a lady who looks a bit like my mum and I'm charm personified. I'm thrown.

So I'm down the Pulse today and this woman goes to give me a hand over an obstacle that was just too high for me. She had black skin, just like Mummy's. She wore her hair the same way as Mummy did around July of last year. I think she was French and maybe a bit taller than my mum but it's always hard to tell from down here. She was daft and funny, too, not scared to make a fool of herself to make kids laugh. The only real striking difference was that this lady seemed a lot more comfortable showing her legs. Weird, because I always thought my mum's were lovely.

So there we were playing and I was holding her hand, happy in unfamiliar female company for the first time in months and I felt like what I've been missing so much was back. But I only felt like that for a minute. I might be small but I'm not stupid. I know my mum when I see her but grief can really mess with your head. It was like happiness one minute then crushing sadness the next. I've got stuff to play with everywhere, free run of the place and yet there I am floored, in tears, confused.

'What's wrong, Jackson?' asked Daddy, although he obviously already knew – I could tell by the look on his face. 'Do you want to talk about it?'

'No, Daddy!' I shouted, lying face down on the floor in tears.

He gave me some space for a minute or two and then came back and asked me again. Now, give me an online forum like Daddy's blog, a MacBook Pro and the time to think my thoughts through and I can really hold my own. But ask me on the spot and I fall to pieces.

'Want some raisins, Daddy,' I replied mid-sob.

He didn't buy that response any more than I meant it. Like he's dumb enough to think that dried grapes are going to make me feel better when I've barely eaten a piece of fruit since I was born.

CONFLICTED AUDIENCE

One of the magazines that contacted me in the wake of the *BBC Breakfast* appearance, *Men's Health*, wanted a piece that was less focussed on my family's story and more about male grief in general. I put a status update out to the blog's rapidly growing Facebook and Twitter communities to ask if anyone knew of any grief experts I could speak to.

'There's no such thing as a grief expert,' one commentator replied, 'not unless they've been through it themselves.'

This statement got me thinking; perhaps this person was right. But even if someone has grieved, how could they, or anyone, be a true expert on something that affects everyone so differently? After just three months I had already found myself disagreeing with at least half of what I read about the so-called stages of grief. I had also grown weary of people telling me how I was going to feel and when. After all, how could anyone know anything about how I would feel in the future if they knew so little about my past, about who I was before this hideous thing happened to my life?

This was a real eye-opener for me. I had a blog about grief that loads of people were reading and following – and perhaps even looking to for answers – but I realised that, actually, it was little other than a collection of real-life stories. It was not a guidebook to grief and nor was I any sort of expert. I was just *me* facing *my* life as a widower, sharing how it felt to be widowed young and to care for a grieving toddler. I promised myself that I would never condescend to or patronise another bereaved person by trying to impart advice that might be completely inappropriate for anyone apart from me.

As usual, though, there was a contradiction here. I could vividly remember what it was like to sit up in bed, staring at a computer screen and praying, naïvely, that I would find answers, solutions or remedies that would somehow magically fix my broken heart. After all, how can you know what to do or where to turn when nothing like this has ever happened to you before and when people are generally so uncomfortable talking about it? To make things extra-specially complex, I wanted advice but when I found it, I tended to reject it outright. It always seemed to come from people who had been able to begin to rebuild their lives and I couldn't imagine mine ever being anything but broken.

It's often said that no two people grieve in the same way. I've heard stories about how grief can create tension between even the closest of families and friends, simply because some feel others aren't grieving the way they should. I only had to look around at my wife's funeral to understand how differently people respond to bereavement. My eyes were dry while others sobbed uncontrollably. With so much conflict, and emotions running so deep, there will always be those who feel they are entitled to their say; I had to get used to that. But I question whether anyone is qualified to tell another person how they truly feel inside or how they should wear their grief.

'What the hell do you know about death?' read one comment on my blog. 'You're a sad man and all you care about is your blog,' another opined. 'Stop going on about your dead wife, you'll be married again in a year,' another predicted. 'Strikes me, if you keep dwelling on something, you will never get over it,' somebody else suggested on the *BBC Breakfast* Facebook page, soon after I'd appeared on the show.

At this point my wife had been dead just two months and I had never professed to know anything about bereavement except how *I* felt while trying to come to terms with my wife's sudden death. And I didn't actually care about the act of blogging, but what I had started to care about was campaigning and fund-raising to help bereaved adults and children get the support they might need to work through such difficult times. I didn't feel it was unreasonable to still be talking about my wife only weeks after her death and I certainly had no plans to remarry. I also had no idea how I was ever supposed to get over her death so quickly, whether I chose to talk about it or not.

These comments, and some worse still, hurt like hell. As a thirty-three-year-old man – who had been through school, sixth-form college, university and held around ten different jobs – I had accepted some years ago that you can't like everyone you meet and that not everyone will like you. That's just the reality of the world we live in. Having been through the inevitable anxieties of adolescence, these days I care very little for seeking the approval of everyone whose path I cross, because I understand that different personalities, different morals, and different values, make it impossible for us all to get along. But I lost much of my rational side when I was crushed by my wife's death; trolls ruled. I could be sent a thousand kind messages of support but just one cruel comment would leave me in pieces for days. I became an easy target for those who prey on people's insecurities and get satisfaction from causing a person already in agony yet more pain.

In my heart, however, I knew that I needed to go on. Not because I felt I owed anyone anything, and not because I believed

I had the answers, but because I wanted to create a legacy for my son and because I was determined that my wife's death would not be completely in vain. I told myself that while it was going to be tough I must listen to the positive comments that people shared. And whenever I'm in doubt (which still happens) I remember just one type of message that I have received from several different people, which keeps me on track.

Ironically, given that I originally set up the blog to help reach other young widowed fathers, it was the messages from young mums whose husbands or partners were still alive that moved me most. 'I just hope that if anything ever happens to me, my husband finds you and your blog.' I suppose that was the closest thing I could now get to my own wife's approval – other young mothers telling me that they saw value in what I had to share. But I knew my wife well enough to understand that the only thing I needed to do to honour her memory was to raise our son the way she would have.

Lots of people told me that I should be proud of myself for speaking out about the social taboo of death and grief, which is so often marginalised and swept under the carpet. But I found it impossible to feel anything remotely positive or to indulge in any sense of achievement when I felt so terribly negative in myself. The only thing that really made me feel at all moved was hearing other people's stories about how the act of opening up about my own grief had helped them through theirs.

Simon Hancox was widowed in December 2012 when his wife, Annabel, died of breast cancer

When I think back to the dark days and nights of January 2013, I shudder. It leaves me cold, afraid and feeling blank. My wife and best friend of nineteen years, Annabel, died on 28 December 2012 after an eight-month battle with secondary breast cancer. Our two young sons, daughter and I were left devastated and numb.

In January a friend told me about Ben's appearance on *BBC Breakfast*. Like me, he'd experienced the death of his wife recently, albeit in very different and tragic circumstances. I watched the interview, read the blog and felt the need to make contact. I emailed Ben and we started to talk. What was immediately clear to me was the feeling of no longer being alone. I didn't know anyone else in my circle who had experienced what I'd been through. I didn't know what to say, what to do, how to behave. How can you when the world has been ripped apart from you and your loved ones?

Ben came up with the idea of creating a secure online group, through which widowers could connect with each other, share their fears and thoughts, and generally give and receive some emotional and practical support. And so, the online forum was born in January 2013. We jokingly referred to it as 'Fight Club for Widowers'.

I found 2.00a.m. a lonely time: my friends and family had gone home and my children were tucked away upstairs in bed. I turned to Ben and the online group of fellow widowers – who were often also awake from grief-fuelled insomnia – and they turned to me. We listened, nurtured, pushed, challenged, cried, empathised and conversed with one another.

Ben and I have struck up a close relationship even though we've never actually met. I hold him dear, I smile and cry with him, and I thank him with all my heart for opening up and sharing his journey. Connecting with Ben and my fellow widower friends in this way has enabled me to do something productive to cope with my bereavement. With the support of loving family and friends, I've formed a charity in the name of my late wife. Annabel's Angels was launched in May 2013.

Emilie Adams, a mum of three, was widowed in March 2012 when her husband, Rob, was killed in a road traffic accident

When I read about Ben's story I could not help but draw a parallel with the tragedy that had befallen my own life. I checked his website and immersed myself in his posts and the comments by fellow grievers. What I discovered that night was much more than I expected. I found solace in the fact that I was not on my own. *Life as a Widower* has become a friendly community of grieving people, all in the same boat, speaking the same language, understanding each other and offering comfort in times of need.

My husband, Rob, died in March 2012 just a few months before Desreen was killed and until I stumbled across Ben's blog I had not met or spoken to anyone going through a similar phase of bereavement. I had not discussed or read about how other people in my situation might deal with their feelings. I had a lot of support from a wide network of neighbours, friends and family but crucially no one who had been through it. Finding the blog made me feel as if I had turned a corner.

Bill Wright lost his daughter Anni, a twin, in January 2013 when she died of a brain tumour

In mid January 2013, a week and a half after the shocking, quick and unexpected death of my two-year-old daughter, Anni, I attempted to lift my head from my zombie-like haze and read something other than the eulogy I had written for her funeral, which I would be delivering in two days time. I began to scan articles in the *Guardian*. But it was hopeless; I had no interest in reading anything. All I wanted to think about was Anni; nothing else mattered.

Then I stumbled upon a feature that Ben had written. The subject spoke to me, especially the fact that Ben had a confused two-year-old son who was grieving and upset. Anni left behind a two-year-old twin brother, Ed, and a big sister, Bella.

It would be a couple of weeks before I felt strong enough to read Ben's blog but very soon I found myself actively looking forward to each new post. The blog provided me with room to articulate thoughts that I might have otherwise only processed internally, through fear of making others feel uncomfortable.

It also played a crucial role in my grief journey. Ben invited me to contribute a guest post. I was grateful to be given the opportunity to engage with the bereaved community that he had created. Initially I had no plans to share my post with anyone outside of that community, bar immediate family and close friends. But I gave it some consideration and realised that one of the biggest successes of Ben's blog was getting people to talk about one of society's great taboos: death and grief. I decided to share my post on my Facebook wall.

It was a very good decision. When my piece was published, I was four months into my grief and had only managed sporadic attendance at work for the previous two months. It had never felt quite right going in, keeping my head down, trying to act normal, when inside my heart and nerves were ripped to shreds. By posting my piece on my Facebook wall I was able to give colleagues a glimpse of what my family and me were going through and I felt so much better for it, as if a weight had been lifted from my shoulders. I no longer cared about putting on a brave front.

I've since managed to go from strength to strength at work and have been back full time for months. This has been so vital in improving my state of mind; it's one less thing to worry about. It's given me back my confidence, to know that I can still fulfill my self-appointed role as protector of Anni's mummy, brother and sister. I'll always be grateful to Ben, his blog and his readers for the part they have played in this.

Tracey Brailsford manages a bereavement and family support team at a charitable hospice in Chesterfield

I came across Ben's blog quite soon after it launched and started to use some of his blog posts in the support group that I run, which is for younger people whose husbands, wives or partners have died. We started the group in recognition of the distinct set of issues that arise from this particular type of bereavement: younger people face the challenge of grieving while trying to work, pay a mortgage, becoming a sole parent, socialising and maybe finding new love.

The power of the group is the group itself and I believe this is the power of Ben's ability to share his story. Grief really does mimic madness and it's reassuring to know you are not alone. Bereaved people often feel relieved to know that they are not the only one who has made it through their partner's birthday and coped, and then had a meltdown in Tesco when they saw their partner's favourite yoghurt.

People like Ben are helping to break a taboo and teach people how to be open about death, dying and grief.

Another response came from a woman who had lost her mum when she was just fifteen months old

It's nearly thirty years since my mum died. I was fifteen months old when she left the house to buy me a pair of shoes and crashed her car into a lorry. Knowing why she left the house has given me an enormous sense of guilt for years, no matter how ridiculous I know it is to feel this way.

I don't actually know much about what happened. I know roughly where it was, because at some point I managed to muster the courage to ask. I know that years later my dad met a taxi driver who was behind the lorry but I don't know what he told him about that day. I was told that my mum died instantly, though I suspected it was a lie made up to protect my feelings. But I was told very little, or at least, not enough. I was never encouraged to talk about it and so asking about her was always a little bit scary, like something I wasn't meant to do. It was only when I was six, and was taken to see a psychologist for the first time, that the adults around me realised that I had convinced myself that she died because she accidentally turned on the indicator. As a child I used to think that once you did that, the car just turned on its own.

My relationship with my dad is still a bit strained. I love him, and when I see him there are tender moments that are very precious to me. When I was younger I was so proud of him for looking after me on his own for two years, and for the fact that my hair is done perfectly in all of the pictures of me as a child, to a standard that would put other mums to shame. I know it must have hurt him when, at the age of two-and-a-half, I went through a phase of calling a few of the women in our village 'mum'. But those are all things that I could never talk to him about. Nor could I ever get him to acknowledge how horrible my relationship with my stepmother has been.

Ben's blog made it a little bit easier for me. Although I can't help but envy the fact that Jackson has a dad who is from a different world and era to mine, it cheers me up to see that he is getting it right. Ben doesn't look like my dad, but in many of the pictures of him and Jackson, he has the same look in his eyes, and somehow I can convince myself that my dad was feeling all of the same emotions as Ben, even though he never talked about them. And it eases my pain.

RUNNING AWAY

Fitness played a massive role in my attempt to bring myself back to life after my wife's death. For weeks I seemed to survive on little more than various different types of stimulants to keep me going and sedatives to help me stop. I had to take pills that inhibit reflux just to be able to even stomach food and drink, and then once settled, I went on to abuse my system with a diet that consisted largely of sugar, caffeine, alcohol, Valium and Nytol.

I grew too thin, my complexion was grey, my eyes were bloodshot and the skin around them was scaly and red raw. I read a comment someone had made about me on a local forum that described me as 'a shell of a man'. It already hurt enough to actually *be* me but it also really stung to realise that people saw me that way. I didn't want to be seen as a victim and I hated the thought of people pitying me. I didn't even really like the idea of people taking care of me that much. So when I caught a glimpse of myself in the mirror one day – looking gaunt, pale, unshaven and hollow-eyed – I knew that the only person who could really do anything to make me feel any better, physically at least, was the man looking back.

I started running again in preparation for the half marathon that Desreen and I had signed up for the year before. We had planned to run it with over a dozen of my colleagues. Suddenly alone, without my training partner and with little more than synthetic stimulants in my system to keep me going, I could barely muster the energy to run a bath.

I don't think many people really expected me to do it. Some told me that everyone would understand if I wasn't up to it; that maybe it would be too hard on my system and too difficult without Desreen by my side. It's strange that more people encouraged me to curb the running than they did the drinking – there always seemed to be a good excuse for that.

I quickly found that fitness fuelled fitness. The more I ran, the better I felt and the better I felt, the less inclined I was to treat my body so badly. The better my body felt, the more clearly my mind could process my thoughts. And the more clarity I had about what was going around in my head, the less I constantly tortured myself by going over everything that was happening time and time again: the police investigation, the looming court case, raising Jackson as a sole parent, being alone, going back to work.

When the day of the run came around on 17 February I felt ready. I was well trained, in pretty good shape and I had one of my two best men by my side – Woody would play Desreen for the day. Despite an injury and his distaste for distance running, he decided to step in to provide some best-mate moral support.

Desreen adored him. We used to spend Saturday afternoons together, she and I praying that Jackson would have a nap so the three grown-ups could properly catch up. I rarely got a word in edgeways, though. Woody was one of our few close friends to not yet have had a child, and I think Dessie liked to live vicariously through his stories of late-night adventures. It's pretty safe to say that she exaggerated his exploits in her own head for her own delectation, reaching conclusions about his tales that were somewhat detached from the reality.

As Woody and I stood there at the start line I could tell he was expecting me not to be okay. Desreen should have been there, not him, and I imagine he thought I would be a mess, daunted by the physical and emotional challenge. Only, it wasn't the half marathon distance that I was nervous about – it was the fact it was the *Brighton* Half Marathon.

Brighton was a special place for Desreen and me; it held great memories. A few weeks after we met, we both realised that all we had done was hang out at bars, clubs and gigs, always with other people around, and that we hadn't really spent much time alone together. I grew worried that we hadn't had the opportunity to actually decide how well we got on. So, with very little money in my bank account as a still emerging young PR professional, I booked us into a hotel in Brighton for a low-key weekend. We made a promise to each other that we would politely decline any offers to go out the night before.

'That is, unless Jay Kay from Jamiroquai calls,' Desreen said. 'I quite fancy him.'

I thought we had a pretty watertight agreement. I was wrong. On the bus journey back to her place from an afternoon spent wandering the grounds of the Tower of London, like a new couple that didn't really know what to do with each other, she received a call from her friend Emma. Simon, Emma's then boyfriend and the guitarist from the Brand New Heavies, had four tickets to a private Jamiroquai gig in Holborn.

'Sorry, Benji, it looks like we're going out tonight after all,' she informed me as my eyes rolled into the back of my head.

The gig was a total washout because the venue's electrics blew and the mostly drunk audience was far too rowdy to indulge the band in their attempt at an unplugged acoustic set. But Desreen looked amazing and, having made the effort to get dressed up and go out, we agreed to spend the rest of the evening at a private members' club, Soho House, at Simon's invitation.

'What's happened to Des?' Simon asked. 'I've never seen her look so good.'

Maybe she was just happy. And perhaps happiness makes people look as well as sadness can make them look ill.

We were having such a good laugh that it wasn't until around midnight that we decided to turn in, so that we could get up early the next morning to head to Brighton.

After a pretty plush night out drinking champagne, we went from one extreme to the other and took the night bus home from the West End to Desreen's place in Dalston – and this was before Dalston was either up or coming. Desreen slept all the way there. She's the only person I've ever known who can nod off and reach full snore between bus stops, but tonight was different. She seemed more *unconscious* than asleep – totally out for the count. I let her snuggle into me, thinking that the forty-five-minute journey would be enough to replenish her, at least to the point of being able to walk the very short distance home from her nearest bus stop. I was wrong again.

I manhandled her to the then still always-open end of the Routemaster bus and she kind of fell off the bus and into the street, her slumberous state not even slightly roused by her descent. And there she was, dressed elegantly but nuzzling up to a dirty east London pavement, completely unmovable.

I would find out later that Desreen was the Queen of Self-Diagnosis. Before going out that night she'd taken a beta blocker for her most recent 'condition' – imminent heart failure. It would appear she had misread the label, though. She seemed to think that you were actually *meant* to take them with copious amounts of alcohol.

It didn't take long for someone to pull over and ask what the hell was going on and what I'd done to her, probably assuming Rohypnol was involved. While I tried to explain to this rather intimidating man that she'd drunk too much and had been given to falling asleep at even the slightest motion since birth, she woke up, tugged on the stranger's sleeve, pointed at me and said, 'He pushed me!'

Needless to say, Brighton did not go to plan. We arrived and Desreen crawled straight into bed, called room service and went to sleep. I guess it was at this point that I began to appreciate exactly the kind of girl she was – fun-loving, entertaining, naughty and absolutely no use to anyone when tired. She had a thousand character traits that I would come to love and I was lucky enough to see many of them unfold that weekend. Brighton was so special to me as a consequence that I returned four years later to buy her an engagement ring from a beautiful and tiny vintage jewellery shop in the Lanes.

Standing at the start line I suspected that, given our history there, my mind would focus on the affairs of my heart rather than the strength of my legs during the 13.1-mile run that day. But instead my head seemed to almost empty as my feet started to hit the streets.

Thousands of people packed the route with numbers, trainers, sweat and Lucozade. The sun made a rare guest appearance and spectators and runners alike braved the February elements in shorts and T-shirts. Cheers, seagulls and the English Channel provided the soundtrack to the coastal run and I picked up a medal for the one hour, fifty-six minutes and fifty-three seconds of effort I put in. My work colleagues, Woody and I raised thousands to help a charity to build homes and shelter for child-headed families living in extreme poverty in South Africa. It felt pretty fitting and extremely poignant that we should help raise funds for a charity for black kids who have lost their parents too soon.

Strangely, none of my memories of Desreen and me together

at the seaside particularly played on my mind as I ran. I passed numerous landmarks that had provided the backdrop to moments in our relationship, but somehow I didn't feel plagued by them. I simply didn't encounter the overwhelming sense of sadness that I'd anticipated enough to carry a handkerchief in my back pocket. I just set out, thanked Desreen for the sunshine, kissed her wedding ring that now sits next to mine on my left hand and began to make my way towards the finish line.

I had anticipated dramatic emotions when I got there. My imagination had seen me complete the final leg of the race in slow motion, Vangelis's theme tune to *Chariots of Fire* playing, with Olympic-winner-style tears streaming down my face as I collapsed in a heap and cried for the love of my late wife. Instead I got a medal, a bad case of cramp and a goody bag that contained a Mars bar and a bag of ready-salted crisps, which I washed down with a sugary drink to help fix the pain. And then I sat there on the pavement waiting for my physical pain to turn emotional – but it just didn't happen.

This was one of the first of many episodes of what has become predictably unpredictable grief, where emotions don't always happen the way I'd expected – the way they do in the movies. In a film of my life, the crowds would have been cheering me over the line, applauding the bravery of a newly widowed man being able to put one foot in front of another so soon after his wife died. A stirring song would be playing, crooned by a power balladeer. The tears would have started streaming down my face at mile twelve. Others around me would have been so moved that the sea level on the coast would have risen from the added saline. I would have ripped off my shirt, kissed our little family's initials tattooed on my chest and then been carried off on a stretcher as I recovered from the ache in my heart and the pain in my legs.

In reality, I just sat there throwing salt and sugar down my throat while I chatted to some guy who didn't know me from Adam. And, after saying goodbye to Woody, who had to go straight to Manchester after the run, I then had quite a nice day drinking Guinness and coffee-flavoured stout with my workmates. We ate lunch, discussed the run, drank too much and then made our way back to London on a delayed and sluggish train. I walked through the door with a medal, a smile and Dan, who had kindly picked me up from the station, and immediately heard the most beautiful sound in the world – my son screaming my name, delighted to have me back.

The film wouldn't have shown the less dramatic, yet real, emotions that did come. I hadn't envisaged them myself. But at 4.00a.m. I awoke with Jackson pretty much asleep on my head; the king-sized bed did nothing to prevent him wanting to invade my personal space. So I flipped sides to the left, the side that used to be occupied by my wife, and *then* the tears came.

I thought about how she should have been there with me. I thought about how there should be two medals hanging on the wall. I thought about how she would have been multitasking – running February's London Fashion Week and running the half marathon simultaneously. I thought about how I should have been hugging her at the finish line rather than chatting to a stranger on a pavement while my calves cramped. And I couldn't help but think about how much my son was going to miss out on the mum who had missed out not only on the run, but also on seeing her beloved child grow up.

It wasn't how it would have been in the movies, but then, in my experience, neither is grief. The real version would simply be too hard for anyone to watch.

CANCELLED FUTURE

I've never once thought that I should try to be positive in light of my wife's death. Playing a mind trick of that magnitude on myself would have required an enormous amount of energy, energy I didn't have; but even more than that, it simply never occurred to me. I'm not that big on the power of positive thinking: some people can get on the London Underground when there's a heatwave blazing on the street above and *think* themselves cold. I tend to be covered in sweat in a train that's so viciously hot, like it or not. I found it impossible to run away from the crushing reality of life after Des.

I had taken fun for granted my whole life because it was always something that came naturally. All of a sudden it became forced – something that could touch me momentarily but not without emotional consequences such as shame, sorrow and sadness. My life had always been blessed and happy and then one night it became tragic and melancholy. I sometimes see people willing me to be the person I used to be once again – wanting me to re-engage my social life or laugh as freely as I did before – but I'm not convinced I ever will. If we are the people we are because of what has happened in our lives, how could something so significant ever truly be erased from me? And why would I want it to be?

I can only imagine that trying to stay high on the positivity and the adrenaline I'd created for myself via my running regime, my blog and my media and campaigning work, would have been like never letting a good night out end. You can go on and on and on but the longer you leave it before calling time, the worse you are likely to feel the next day. And when my grief hangover eventually came, it hit me hard. I knew that I needed to go through it; numbing the pain would only prolong it. Things needed to calm down: I needed to be kinder on my system, which had, once again, been hit by eating and drinking all the wrong things; I needed to stop saying yes to everything I was being asked to write, appear or comment on by the media; I suspected I needed to take a break from other people's grief, which I was increasingly living through via the blog; and I needed to give myself the time and space to truly feel my feelings and really think my thoughts.

Inconveniently, this realisation coincided with my return to work after four months off. I was in the unfortunate-fortunate position of having been able to take extended leave. My employers invited me to simply do what felt right. That said, even if they hadn't I'm sure I wouldn't have returned any sooner. As far as I'm concerned these days, some things – most things, perhaps – are more important than a career.

My preferred option would have been not to go back to work for a good long time yet. My little boy had been lucky enough to spend ten months with his mummy after he was born, creating a bond and relationship that, typically, only a child and its mother get the chance to share. Now that she was gone it felt as if he and I needed that same opportunity. But it was time for me to get back behind my desk. I had promised I would return after four months simply because, as with the holiday three months after Desreen died, it had sounded so far off when it was first agreed.

When I was made the company's managing director six months previously, around the same time that Desreen started her own fashion agency, it felt as if we were on our way up. Then, suddenly, demoted by choice and deflated by circumstance, *we* was now just *me* and I knew that my career was on its way back down. And I didn't give a shit. I had decided what I wanted to do with my life by the age of sixteen, started working in the industry at eighteen and fifteen years later I was at the top of my game. But I couldn't have cared less if my employer had changed my role from managing director to traffic director. The only title that interested me at this point was Daddy. I no longer cared enough about the money to care anything about the work. All I required was enough to get by and to live a loving life with Jackson.

In my heart I knew that I needed to concentrate on rebuilding our lives, but then I found myself at a desk and in a job that would ultimately give me no emotional reward. I was working for others at a time when I most needed to be working on my son and myself.

Lots of people told me that they thought work would be a good distraction for me; that it would give me something else to think about. The only thing was, I didn't want to think about anything else. And even if I had wanted to, my brain simply isn't wired like that.

We're all different in this respect. Zac lost his sister, Zoë, to suicide when he was still at university. When we talked about his grief for her and Desreen, he told me that he was able to compartmentalise them both and that he would perhaps try to grieve for them later. Now, in some ways Zac and I are very alike: we work in the same industry, we mostly enjoy the same things, we find the same jokes funny and some have commented that we even look like one another, but the way the two of us deal with grief is so different. Observing this difference in two such similar people really showed me how difficult it is for anyone to judge another person's response to loss, whether they are a close friend or an outsider. Personally, I find my mind usually thinks about more than one thing at a time. And one of those things is *always* Desreen. So it didn't matter if I was at my desk in Fitzrovia or on a sun lounger in the South of France, my grief was always going to be there with me.

When I did return to work, all the trappings of normality – my commute, my desk, the meetings, seeing friends and colleagues – made me feel distinctly abnormal. It only took me a few days to realise that it was way too soon for me to attempt some kind of metamorphosis of my mental state. I just wanted to crawl back into my cocoon and shut myself off from the outside world. I was slipping back into my 'normal' life when nothing about my life felt normal anymore. I thought about nothing but Jackson and Desreen all day. I was entirely disengaged from my professional responsibilities.

I felt myself slipping into a depression of sorts; nothing clinical, it was more situational – like I was sliding into a depressed or sunken place that was going to be difficult to crawl back out from. Trying to return to life made me realise just how much I had lost. Falling back into my old habits – my favourite seat on the bus, reading a copy of *Metro* every day – tricked my brain into thinking things hadn't changed. I found myself reaching for my phone to call Desreen ever more frequently.

One morning I saw a picture of Romeo Beckham modelling for Burberry in a newspaper I was reading on the way to work. Desreen would just love this little fashion scoop. The phone was out of my pocket and at my ear before I even realised what I was doing. And there I was, the only person on the bus

– perhaps in the world – who cried at a cute gap-toothed little boy wearing an expensive designer jacket.

Tears on my way to and from work became a regular thing. Some commuters probably saw me cry over my wife more than they saw their own partners during the working week. I suppose it was because the only time I really got to be alone with my feelings, albeit surrounded by strangers, was on public transport. Crying in front of my son became increasingly rare, perhaps because he made me happy and perhaps also because he kept me on my toes with his completely unpredictable temper. There was a time when I would get so upset at him mentioning his mum, but then all of a sudden I would look forward to the two of us speaking about her. I would will him to bring her into the conversation so that I knew that he hadn't started to forget her. Now I pray he never will. I suppose when I was with Jackson I was thinking about his loss; it was only when I was alone that I thought about mine. Perhaps having such a young child to look after didn't allow me much time to really miss Desreen. I don't mean that I didn't have time to miss my wife, nor my child's mother, nor the woman I lived with, but perhaps I didn't have the headspace to really miss *Desreen* – the girl I met on a night out at Christmas in 2004. But I would be sitting on the bus, indulging in my own thoughts, and that would be when that particular Desreen would come to mind. And then the tears would come, barely hidden by the sunglasses I wore even on a grey day. I imagine some people thought I was pretentious while others thought I was mentally unstable.

Funny memories would come to me that would, for just an instant, make me smile before the smiles turned to sadness. I remembered how I would vacuum the living room only for Desreen to get the Dyson back out and do it all over again because I 'never did it properly'. I remembered how she hard-boiled her eggs until the whites went grey and then covered them in so much pepper they turned black: 'Me special peppered eggs, Benji!' And I remembered the time when we were on a train going to visit her parents in Hampshire and an elderly lady practically died from a coughing fit right in front of us. Once recovered – at least temporarily – she took off her jacket to reveal a hot pink sweater fighting against the bright orange of her skirt. I saw an old woman who I assumed would soon be dead. As usual Desreen saw something else – she looked the woman up and down, nodded her head in approval, turned to me and said, 'Fierce colour-blocking.' Being alone made me miss the personality and not just the person.

Stepping back into a portion of my old life made me miss it all the more but my old life was something I could never get back. History. The irony was that in trying to move forwards, I felt as if I were moving backwards. Previously, backwards would have been fine by me because my old life was so much fun, but backwards without Desreen was just too tough to handle. Everything I did seemed to hurt.

Sitting back at my familiar desk, talking shop and drinking tea, might have made me feel normal but actually it left me feeling completely displaced. I missed the toy trains that drove me crazy when I was home, and I missed their adorably bossy little controller. Some told me that the company of friends and colleagues might help, but the more normal they tried to behave around me, the weirder I felt. I wondered whether new friends, or even strangers, might be the answer. But when I talked rubbish about nothing with people who didn't know about my situation, all I really wanted to talk about was how much I miss my wife and love my son. I just wanted the three of us to be together again as a family, planning everything or doing nothing.

The life I loved was in the past and there I was trying to live in the present, surrounded by people motivated by their future, while mine had been abruptly cancelled. People told me that time would heal, but time was only making me feel more confused. And the more time passed the harder it was for me to believe in and to accept my wife's death.

When I looked at photographs of Desreen they didn't make me upset. I would lose myself in the pictures, take a trip back to the three dimensional world in which they were taken. They made me happy. I remembered our conversations and heard us both laughing. In video footage that focussed on our son dancing and so only captured my wife's legs, I could picture her upper body too, her face smiling and her head bouncing from side to side to the beat. I would be back in the moment and we were a family again. And I felt blessed. She was still here. She never left. I would imagine that I was going to see her again because our future was simply incomprehensible without her. When my son told me that he wanted his mummy, I would explain that she had gone and that she couldn't ever come back but I was like a record on repeat; I was just a scripted message read by a man who didn't believe the words he spoke.

Then reality kicked in. I started to think less about what I once had and more about what would never again be mine. I was not just widowed but companionless, too. I had lost my best friend. I would stare in the mirror and see the person I saw nearly a decade before, except now I had a child, a furrowed brow and I never slept. I felt as if my life had taken a huge step backwards to when I was single and loveless and yet I'd been catapulted into a daunting *new* life all in one go – one that might conceivably see happiness again but that, I suspected, would never again allow me the true unsullied joy of innocence.

Perhaps none of us truly controls our future but, having spent so much time planning mine, ours, it became impossible not to grieve its loss. I started to grieve something that had never existed. I felt a great sense of loss for someone I'd never met. For someone I never *would* meet; for someone who was never created. Out of nowhere I started to think about the second child we didn't have and I started to grieve *her* loss, too.

We talked about our next child the afternoon of the day Desreen was killed.

'Dessie, I know this is a really immature thing to say but since I met Lucia last week' – Desreen's best friend's brand-new baby daughter – 'I really want another baby. It'd just be really nice to have some baby cuddles again.'

She laughed at me for being willing to throw away all the previous financial and professional reservations she had scolded me for, all for the sake of a hug.

They say you can't miss something you never had. Perhaps technically you can't. But I now know that you can feel the pain of loss for never having something that you wanted so badly.

SPRING

PARENTAL GUIDANCE

Despite finding myself suddenly grieving the second child I wouldn't ever have, I never stopped counting my blessings for the son my wife and I created. It hurt to think of people pitying him, a child growing up without his mum, but then I would catch myself doing it. Some months after Desreen died I found myself staring at a mother and her teenage son walking down the beach in Ibiza simply chatting as the sea lapped against their feet. I thought about my close relationship with my own mum and shed a tear for that amazing bond, which my son would grow up without.

'Jackson's going to have such an amazing life, you know?' I remember Desreen saying to me when he was about one. With a well-connected mother who loathed negativity, pessimism and limits imposed on ambition, I knew exactly what she meant. But how was I going to stand in for her as his role model when that shared positivity had been so abruptly drained from my life? Only time would tell.

In the meantime Mother's Day was just around the corner. After the pain of a Christmas Day without my child's mother, I decided that I would at least try to approach meaningful dates more positively. Every day has its heartache, I told myself, so why torture yourself simply because it's Valentine's Day? When 14 February did come around, I focussed on it as the day we found out that we were expecting Jackson – the day the pregnancy test turned blue. It became *Blue Day* – a kind of unofficial second birthday for my son, when I would treat him rather than dragging myself down about being the only man in the room without a date. There were enough miserable days in the year without me accentuating holidays and key events with even more doom and gloom.

When a fellow widower with whom I'd become friends online asked what I had planned for Mother's Day, I told him about this approach. But it turned out that I had underestimated just how tough it was going to be. I suspected it wouldn't be so bad because, at the time, I still had a mother, a mother-in-law and grandmother whom I adored.

When the day itself arrived I was crushed. All I had to do was take one look at our little boy and my mind started to race with all of the significant, and for that matter insignificant, moments that he and his mother would no longer be able to share. To make it harder still, Desreen's mum Bev was with us. One look at *her* was enough to show me how it must feel to lose the daughter who grew inside her, whom she raised from child to adult and who, ultimately, became her best friend.

That day the pain was not so much for me but for those around me, including Desreen's brother, Anthony. It seemed that the only answer was to talk about Dessie all day and drink our way through the pain. We bought her flowers although she wasn't there to enjoy them and I opened a bottle of champagne before midday to toast her just because I didn't know what else to do.

The concept of Mother's Day didn't register with Jackson at all, but we talked about her throughout the day and drew pictures for her. I decided to write to Desreen on behalf of Jackson. This would be the first of a number of letters that I intended to write and place in a memory box dedicated to his mum – something Winston's Wish had suggested – until Jackson was old enough to continue for himself, if that's what he chose to do.

Dear Mummy,

I just wanted to say hello. I want to say it to you in person but I know that I can't. I miss you lots and I think about you every day. I know you used to write letters and cards to people all the time so I'm going to start doing the same.

Things have been pretty busy here; lots of guests have been round. Nanny is looking after me more than ever. I sometimes give her a little whack or one of those looks that only you and I know how to give, because she keeps that cloth you hate hanging in the shower. She does lots of cooking and cleaning but someone still needs to keep her in check now that you're not around.

Granddad comes over every week. He's as chatty as ever. He knows a lot about trains and he's bought me a track that we play with at his house. Uncle Ant is watching out for me, too. Not sure what's going on there though because he comes round with toothbrushes as gifts and then eats all my sweets. I've got my eye on him. Grandma and Keef have been staying, too. Keef keeps calling himself *Granddad* but I like *Keef* best. They both looked after me while Daddy went off on his run. Keef makes bathtime fun and I like squeezing Grandma's nose.

All of your friends are looking after me, too. Maz is fun at soft play and Olly gives me ice cream and helps me count motor-bikes. Caz makes chocolate cake and is having twins and Lee has got cool trains. Annie makes us our dinner and Paul gives me fun stuff to play with. Cathy has introduced me to dinosaurs. Zac and Laura bought me my first remote-control car the other day, which is yellow. I know all my colours now and I can count to ten in Spanish. My favourite numbers are *finco, ocho* and *deeee-ef*!

We've been on holiday as well. I wasn't well but I had a nice time with Albie. Olive, Lee, Woody (silly Woody) and Katy helped look after me while I was poorly and we all missed you being there. Olive dyed my pyjamas pink in the wash. You'd probably like them because you like boys in pink but I'm pretty sure you would have said that she wasn't allowed near my clothes again.

Uncle Mat, Auntie Michelle, Sophie and Lucy have also been here. We had a nice time in the park and I ate more ice cream. Uncle Nick came too, and we played with my trains. Lots of other people have brought presents and cards and flowers. There have been almost as many deliveries as when you still lived here!

Nursery is going well. It's nice to get out of the house and play with all my friends. I've got my review in a couple of weeks. I hope I get a pay rise! I need a new spring/summer wardrobe, Mummy!

I'm faster than ever at scooting and I've got more trains than I know what to do with. James is my new favourite, I've gone off Thomas a bit and I can't decide if I like the old TV series more than the new, but I'm two years old so I can change my mind as often as I like.

Daddy and I went to the aquarium the other day to see some fish. I wanted to get in the tank with the big ones with fins but Daddy wouldn't let me, so I went to sleep soon after we got there. He made me walk over this thing where we could see big fish swimming underneath. There was no other way in and it was a bit scary — we would never have got you into the building!

I went to Annalise's birthday party yesterday and played all day. I still don't like fruit or veg unless they come in squeezy pouches so I just ate chocolate buttons, chips and cake. Arlo's birthday is coming up soon too and I think it's fancy dress.

Anyway, Mummy, I love you. I wish you could be here with us today. I wish you could be with us every day.

Big kisses and cuddles from your favourite boy.

Love, Jack-Jack xx

Father's Day, some four months later, was an entirely different affair. Something inside me, perhaps Desreen's voice, told me that it was a day to consider my fortune rather than my hardship. I was father to a wonderful child and the child of a wonderful father, too. I also had a father-in-law I'm close to and who has always liked me, despite the fact I married his little princess. I reckon any guy should count that as one of life's great achievements. I was still alive, I was still a dad, and when I walked into the room I could see my son loved me with all of his heart. With a touch of a cold making him want to stay close, we did little else but cuddle on the sofa all day.

That day I was lucky man. Lucky to spend another day with my boy and grateful enough for that fact to thank my lucky stars that my beautiful wife made me a dad to such a wonderful child.

BITTERSWEET HOME

I seem to have met a lot of grief specialists and fortune-tellers since my wife died, none of them professional but each has spoken with the authority of an expert. Many people have been able to tell me not only how I'm going to feel but also *when* I'm going to feel that way. 'Year two is *always* the hardest,' apparently. I guess I'll just have to get back to everyone on that, because, as I write, I'm busy having a hard enough time getting through year one.

What has become clear to me, though, is that however misguided or unwelcome some comments are, generally speaking, people care. They want the bereaved to get better or, at the very least, to get real. Unfortunately, that good intention isn't always enough to prevent severe annoyance setting in.

I've found that most people fall into two camps when it comes to grief support: those who offer platitudes in the hope that their words might be of some comfort, and those who offer personal insights in the hope that they might not be one of those people who can only offer platitudes. The people I tend to get most from emotionally fall into neither camp. These people *do* more than they say: dinner left on the doorstep, the ability to recognise when to reach out for a hug and when to leave well alone, playing with my son while I clean the kitchen, cleaning the kitchen while I play with my son. I've found that it's too easy for the talking bit to sound trite, especially when it comes from people who don't know me that well. I think maybe it's because some people want to somehow *solve* grief rather than help others through it.

I sometimes imagine this dialogue between two people in my head.

'Have you seen Ben since Desreen died?' asks one.

'Yes, I saw him on Tuesday,' replies the other.

'Oh my God, you're brave! I just couldn't face it. What the hell did you say to him?'

'I told him I couldn't imagine what he was going through but that I was positive he'd find happiness again some day.'

'Oh, well done! I would never have thought of that. I'm sure you're right. He's only young. Well, at least you've got that out of the way. Drink?'

The platitudes came thick and fast immediately after Desreen died and I actually welcomed them at first. In fact, I joined in: 'She had a good life, though,' I remember saying about my thirty-three-year-old wife who had just had her 'good life' with her two-year-old son ripped away from her. *She had a fucking shocking death, too,* I tell myself now. It wasn't until I could take a step back from it all a couple of months later that I started to realise just how ludicrous some of the grief-fuelled piffle we so often spout actually is.

When I went back to work my life grew ever busier and my tolerance for platitudes dipped ever lower. I was close to the edge and I found myself wondering if a person knows when they are nearing a nervous breakdown. I suspected that I wouldn't begin to beep like a fire alarm in need of its batteries replacing, so I would have to listen out for my own warning signals. They were telling me it was time to slow down. Everything just became way too hard.

Leaving home for work each morning became too hard because my son would sob not only over the infinite loss of his mummy but also over the daily departure of his daddy. Writing the blog every day became too hard because of the emotional repercussions not just of my own grief shared online but of others who shared their own tragic stories in reply. Not sleeping became too hard because the energy I lacked to play with my son made me hate myself and feel ashamed. And thinking about the incident became too hard because it made the whole thing feel too real. I knew that one day I would need to sit in a court of law and face the driver of the car that killed my wife, but months went by without any obvious developments. I suspected it would be way over a year before we had a conclusion about exactly what, or perhaps even who, had caused Desreen's death.

In many ways, the easiest thing I did was one of normal life's most stressful tasks – I bought a house. Moving was inevitable. The flat Desreen and I rented before she died was nothing more than a stopgap. We took a gamble on making her new business successful enough to afford us our future home and it didn't pay off. What did, however, was the life cover we took out as a result of her professional endeavours.

'I can't afford this yet, Benji. Why don't you get cover now and I'll do it later when the money starts coming in?' Desreen suggested as we sat in a meeting with our financial advisor.

'Okay, great idea. So if I die you're sitting pretty with my personal life insurance *and* death in service through work, but if anything happens to you, I'm fucked?'

She giggled naughtily behind her hands, pretended to start spending the money in her head, then conceded and signed the papers, both of us assuming we were throwing our money down the drain either way.

Just a couple of months after she died, Desreen's legacy

afforded Jackson and me our own home in East Dulwich, an area in southeast London where we had already lived happily together as a family of three. I was almost certain that she would have chosen the new house herself if she were still alive. A striking red brick building with period features and infinite potential for spending money on soft furnishings – it ticked every box on her list. It should have felt like a dream fulfilled but with my passion for life and its material trappings sapped from my soul, it was merely transactional – nothing more than money changing hands for a pile of bricks.

I can't imagine that there have been many other people either so unhappy to have finally bought their first home or so totally exhausted before they'd even started packing.

HAPPY RAIN

Any happiness I felt after Desreen's death was entirely thanks to Jackson. I experienced comfort and love from others but no one else was able to ignite a sense of joy like him. I suffered agonies not only because he had lost such a devoted mum but also because of his subsequent loss of a happy dad. But looking back, I wonder just how much of my unhappiness he actually registered because we still laughed, smiled and loved one another almost as if she were still there. Even at a time when I felt so utterly broken, I could feel the potential Jackson had to patch up my shattered heart. I would never be the same again but I knew that I could let happiness back in if I only allowed myself to open up to all he had to offer as a delightful, funny, entertaining and completely unpredictable child.

Taking time out to properly play with Jackson every day was therapeutic for us both. I could lose myself in the monotony of pushing trains around tracks at his command. Being the leader in our games allowed my son to more freely express his own feelings. Sometimes this meant he got angry and I would have to duck when carriages flew at my head. Other times, however, he would show nothing but love.

'They're nice butterflies, Jackson,' I told him one morning as he showed me the fruits of his Play-Doh labour.

'Mummy would be very proud of me,' he replied with no hint of sadness in his voice.

There's no doubt about that, I thought.

A melodramatic screenplay of our lives would perhaps describe a father unable even to gaze upon the son who looked and behaved so much like the wife he had lost. In real life, however, her really rather remarkable reflections shone through him every day, bringing her into the family home in which she never lived. The impossible was made possible through the miracle of a child.

The problem with miracles, though, is that they never seem to come when you need them the most. Sitting at my desk trying to hide the tears because I had just found a note from my late wife in my drawer, might have been the time to draw a little happiness from my son. Except my office had neither a crèche nor a bring-your-kids-to-work policy. I couldn't be with Jackson all the time. He spent time at nursery or with Desreen's mum and I travelled at least two hours per day and worked around nine. I had to spend most of my day away from the only person who could make me happy while doing a job that suddenly left me so miserable. If it were true that all you need in this world is love then I wouldn't have bothered leaving our loving home in the mornings.

The commute still made me cry every single day. I would write for my blog, I would think about Desreen or I would do nothing at all other than sit and be transported from home to work. Often it was the doing nothing that hurt the most. I would pass a park where we once strolled with the pushchair when our son was a baby and think about the conversation we had that day. I would see a flock of pigeons and remember just how much she hated them. One day, when I was just staring out of the window, I saw an accident that brought back the night my wife was killed. A man lying still in the street; ambulances blocking the flow of traffic; distress written across people's faces, tears running down mine; relief that this man appeared to have been luckier than some, as I saw him gesture to the paramedics. I am someone whose mind is naturally at its most active early in the day and I found the mornings almost unbearably hard. I lost count of the number of times I got to the entrance of my office block and turned away, unready to face colleagues and clients with a face that couldn't hide its pain.

I came to expect to feel upset every single day during the commute, but my emotions were entirely unpredictable and inconsistent once I was in the office. I would sometimes feel a sense of relief. I knew that my colleagues were a fantastic group of people and that they genuinely did care. But often, after a few short minutes I would find myself wondering what I was doing there; I would feel guilty for leaving my son. I would chat to my colleagues about Jackson, about Des, about weekends, the weather, sometimes I might even talk to them, albeit half-heartedly, about the work itself. This, however, was where the problems lay. I would drift off into space, my concentration evaporating; I just couldn't focus my mind enough to make myself care any more.

Public relations can make a person a little light on perspective at the best of times. There's often a drama, there's usually a crisis, and the typical PR professional tends to be quick to use words like 'disaster' and 'nightmare' about entirely fixable issues. Not being able to find a guest book in the same precise shade of powder blue as a client's company logo, for an event that same day, can instigate a nervous breakdown. Being habitually 'like, totally manic' can cloud a PR person's sense of reason. I sometimes picture my ex-colleague Matt rolling his eyes at the tears and tantrums all too often shown in the PR workplace and hear his Australian voice barking his favourite less-than-pastoral quip: 'Get a fucking grip. It's PR not ER.'

I felt no urge to shout or swear, I simply had no sense of gusto anymore. The spark that once made me pretty good at my job had been all but extinguished. If I'd had a PR epitaph at the peak of my career it might have read: *He tried to cut the crap*. Suddenly I just couldn't find a knife big enough. And not because the work didn't matter anymore; it just didn't matter to me. I felt entirely indifferent about the industry I once loved. And so I felt guilty again: guilty because I knew others deserved the job more; guilty because, having been the company's managing director, I understood how my apathy could affect my colleagues' careers and the success of the business. I would go to work in tears and return home miserable, dejected, deflated and without the one person who would always listen to me.

Although I should probably say, without the one person who *used* to listen. At this point I hadn't yet realised that there was someone I could talk to. I hadn't realised because, to my own shame, I had underestimated the potential of a two-year-old boy's counselling skills. That was until a day in March when I picked Jackson up from nursery after a particularly emotionally draining and difficult day at work. His first nursery review since Desreen died was taking place the following day.

I can picture myself perfectly that day, as if I were somehow outside looking in. I can see everything about the moment itself, too. It was pouring with rain. My mood was heavy. I wasn't feeling angry; I was sad to the point of absolute misery. I was blocking out everyone around me. I pretended I hadn't seen any of the mums I usually stopped to chat to and I brushed over the feedback Jackson's carers gave me about how his day had gone. I just wanted to grab him and go home. I skulked around the nursery's heavy wooden door and peered inside. My son and I locked eyes and he changed my mood in an instant.

'Daddy!' he shouted with so much glee in his voice as he ran across the room to greet me. 'Daddy!' he repeated breathlessly, unsuccessfully searching for other words to express his excitement.

I stepped in to help his conversation flow. 'Let's go home, Jack-Jack. You're going to need to put your hood up, it's raining outside.'

Jackson laughed. 'It's not raining, Daddy, it's *happy*.'

And with those six words, neither of us needed anything more. His joyous outlook on what was otherwise an all-round miserable day immediately uplifted my soul. And he was happy to see me smile.

'Not raining,' he continued cheerfully. 'Silly Daddy!'

And who was I to argue? Just a silly daddy to a two-year-old boy who apparently already had it all figured out.

After Desreen was killed I thought I would never smile again. I couldn't imagine how anything would be able to take away the hurt. And yet with a happy and healthy toddler around, moments of pleasure frequently shone through the dull, heavy and debilitating fog of grief. They were quite simply irresistible. They brought with them so much relief and respite that they would imprint themselves on my memory and act as a medicine for the pain.

As we grow up and lose the innocence of infants, I think we begin to accept limitations. We're told not to run before we can walk. But have you ever actually seen a toddler walk? They only ever move at speed. My child wasn't old enough to fully understand the gravity of the situation when his mummy died. He didn't understand that he would never ever see her again. And so, despite the tough times and the confusion, he let himself keep smiling; he let himself keep being a child and I let him keep running. After all, if we had both just meandered through our grief without at least one of us getting ahead, I don't think we could have achieved the smiles that I had thought would never cross our faces again.

Perhaps one day he will fall behind and I'll pick up some pace. And when that day comes it'll be my turn to wipe his tears, to make him smile and to tell him that it won't always be raining. As long as we have each other, sometimes it will also be happy.

Dear Daddy,
I had my review at nursery yesterday. I got lots of feedback, which I'd like to take you through because I think some of it applies to you, too. Mummy taught us both the importance of open and honest critique, whether in the home or the workplace. In fact, Daddy, Mummy also demonstrated how it's possible to let anyone we come into contact with know how they are getting on in their roles — that no one is too big or too clever to be subject to an impromptu appraisal. That's why I told that man in the off-licence I didn't like him the other day. Well I didn't, Daddy! It's his job to be nice to you, not mine to be nice to him. Mummy would have put him back in his crate, too. Remember how she would always make you sweat when dealing with frustrating bar, restaurant and shop staff, but then flash her beautiful big smile, politely thank them for pretending to see things from her unbending point of view and leave with a handful of free sweets left on the cash desk for paying customers, having not bought anything? I really miss that now, Daddy. Shopping just isn't as much fun anymore.

So I've had my first progress review since Mummy died — the first since I moved to the big boys' room at nursery, too — and I'm sure you've been eager to know how I'm doing.

Only, deep down, I think you already know. Thing is, Daddy, I'm not all that different to you and Mummy.

I could go on all day about what I get up to, who I play with, how my communication skills are coming on (like *hello*, have you seen my blog posts?), my social, personal and physical development, but we all know you should only really focus on 'things to work on' in a review. Everything else is just vanity and if you don't know that by now then there's something really wrong.

Naturally you're concerned about how I've responded to Mummy dying four months ago. You want to know if I've regressed, if I have difficulty in responding positively to the female staff, if I act differently at nursery to how I act at home. Well, Daddy, you can analyse things until the cows come home but I think we should measure my feedback against two criteria: 1) was I already like this before we lost Mummy and 2) am I just really similar to the two of you?

So here are a few things that stuck out for me.

1. Sometimes I get cross and want time alone.

Don't even go there, dude! This is you and Mummy all over so I don't even want to hear you ask me if I'm okay. Just give me some space, yeah?

Mummy used to disappear into the bathroom for hours to get a break from everything and everyone. You sometimes disappear into your own head or retreat to your laptop when you're sick of all the tea and small talk. BTW, that computer thing of yours is so boring when it's not playing the Mickey Mouse Clubhouse! What do you see in it?

Nanny told me that when Mummy was small she hated it when there were too many guests in the house and that she would often take herself off to her room. I know for a fact that you do that same thing yourself now. You pretend to be on the phone and retreat upstairs when there are too many people round at ours. You might play the Mr Social role well but I know big gatherings make your teeth itch. So before you start on the whole 'you need to try to be more sociable' nonsense, take a long hard look in the mirror, boy. Sure, we're all friendly and outgoing when we need to be, but what's wrong with a little privacy and space now and again? You guys turned out okay and I'm not acting any differently to you. So review that one, Daddy!

2. I don't like being told what to do.

So this one's simple. Just stop telling me what to do! I mean, if you even bring this up with me I'm gonna open a can of whoopass on you. It was Mummy's least favourite thing in the whole wide world, too. She hated rules. Well, I'll correct myself, she hated other people's rules. She loved making them. Remember the family newsletters she would create for you, me and Nanny that outlined her latest thoughts on how we could make things run more smoothly around the house? They were fun. I've never seen such a pretty dictator as Mummy.

3. I don't always allow people to look after me.

Do you not think I'm old enough to look after myself, or something? Well, actually, of course you don't, I'm two. But you haven't got a leg to stand on with this one, Daddy. You're the worst at it. I've seen you carrying a suitcase and three big bags while pushing my buggy uphill and still refuse help. I know it drives you crazy when people treat you like you're ill at the moment. You hate it when people try to do the jobs you're perfectly capable of doing yourself. You don't want people to encroach on your independence any more than I do. So quit smothering me!

4. I'll be more likely to participate in cooperative play from the age of three.

Well, that gives me another seven months to enjoy telling others to get out of my frickin' space then. Just over half a year before someone starts saying there's something wrong with me if I won't participate in group activities. It looks like a long time on paper, but the four months since Mummy died have passed so quickly and I'll be three before you know it.

Maybe this is one for you too though, Daddy. You're thirty-three and I don't see you participating in cooperative play right now. Perhaps you also need a little more time. That's fine though, stay and hang out with me. I might not want to play with others yet, but you're not others. You're my peoples. You're my brethren. You and I can just chill, fam. Let's just put each other first and the rest will sort itself out, blud.

Oh yeah, and one last thing. Good review but no pay rise. They're putting them off until after the audit. Same shit, different room, Daddy!

Love, J-Bo x

POETIC LICENCE

Running away from life's challenges is always an option. I did it once when I was about nine but I was back home before my parents even noticed I'd left the house. I've never really been one for roughing it, so rather than hitting the streets and taking up home in the discarded packaging of my parents' new analogue TV, I returned home an hour later and suffered in silence on the sofa while watching it in the comfort of their living room. I must have really hated whatever was planned for dinner that night to have seriously contemplated leaving home before my age had even hit double digits.

For a while I considered treating my grief with the distractions and diversions of abandonment and escape and, briefly, it seemed like an attractive option. I pictured Jackson and me trying, or pretending, to be happy on holiday at Disneyland. I even wondered whether it might be a good idea to make a clean break and move to somewhere like Miami or LA so that I wasn't surrounded by everyone else's grief at home.

But I figured that the problem with attempting to run away from grief is that it is likely to come running back after you. Deep down, I knew that fleeing would be like putting a flimsy plaster over a septic wound – just an ineffective delaying tactic. Eventually, reason told me that our injuries needed nursing. And yet, in my experience, reason doesn't always seem to win through when you're grieving – the temptation to up sticks and try to leave the pain behind can remain strong.

Perhaps this wouldn't be so hard if everything and everyone around us didn't constantly remind us of our loss. Surely this would be easier if Jackson and I lived in the sun. Maybe we just need a new start. When these thoughts crossed my mind, pros and cons lists simultaneously dropped into my head – and the cons outweighed the pros, every time. I imagined living in a place where we didn't know anyone, where no one offered support and where there were no familiar faces. Even if lately I had spent most of my time at home pushing those faces away, at least I still knew they were there to call upon in our hour of need. I figured that grief over Skype would lack that essential personal touch.

And yet the appeal of recreating – rather than just rebuilding – my life after Des was often still strong. New hobbies and interests that didn't constantly stir memories of the wife I'd lost, suddenly seemed attractive. But nothing I did would make my thoughts stray very far from Desreen.

I suppose I could have tried any number of things to distract myself: rock climbing would have concentrated my mind and taken its focus off my loss; training for a marathon might have thrown me together with new people with shared motivations; finally taking that photography course I'd been talking about for over a decade might have helped me to channel a new form of self-expression. Yet it was writing that became my focus. It was cathartic; it was something entirely new to me that somehow brought out my pain and then began to ease it, if only just a little at a time.

It also made me realise that it was okay to embrace new experiences that I wouldn't get the chance to share with my wife. She was determined that the three of us would always try different things and continue to expand our minds, so I can only imagine that she would be happy not to see me sitting still for too long.

Trying new things brought me in front of new people, too, people who never had the chance to meet Desreen. I had thought I would hate spending time with people who didn't know her and couldn't relate to my pain. But I just loved hearing how much they liked her anyway – how much admiration they felt for and amusement they drew from the person I wrote. She continued to make me proud.

Some months after Desreen died I realised that new friends can be a tonic for the pain. Basic manners dictate that you can only talk about yourself and your own life for so long with someone you don't know that well. Closest friends and family will indulge you forever, or at least you will indulge yourself in them, like it or not.

I decided to meet up with an acquaintance of mine, also called Ben, after he had surprised me by showing up at Desreen's funeral. Although in theory we had known each other for years, we really only knew *of* each other. That was until Zac's stag weekend during the summer of 2012. We immediately hit it off, and a couple of weeks later at Zac and Laura's wedding, Desreen could be heard telling Ben, in no uncertain terms, that he was not allowed to be friends with me.

Then she turned to me. 'He's bad news, Benji,' she told me, right in front of him, her tongue firmly in her cheek. 'You don't need any more friends, anyway, because you've got me.'

In short, she knew that he was good fun. As a purveyor of good times herself, she knew trouble when she saw it and trouble was standing next to her husband, smiling faux-innocently.

'I'm watching you, Ben,' she told him.

I suspect the three of us would have become great friends.

Desreen and Ben shared a mischievous nature that made them people-magnets in a social circle.

At Desreen's committal I looked up from the hollowed earth to the sun-filled sky in an attempt to catch my breath and dry my eyes. When I looked back down I saw Ben there in front of me. He just smiled, and I took comfort from knowing that people who I didn't know cared, in fact did.

Over lunch some months later, Ben, like Desreen, suggested that I push myself a little further still.

'You should write poetry,' he said, after listening to the lyrics of a song I wrote in memory of Desreen with my friend Paul.

It had never crossed my mind and, frankly, I was embarrassed to even try. My English qualifications hadn't extended beyond GCSE level and I really had no idea how to express myself in that way. And yet something in my head told me that being scared of trying was ludicrous. As I am often forced to remind myself, what's the worst thing that can happen when the worst thing that can happen has already happened?

I went home late from a long lunch, which was light on food and heavy on alcohol, slept terribly – my mind racing with thoughts and espresso martinis – and suffered my worst hangover since the day after Desreen's funeral. And then a few days later, completely unplanned or unsolicited, the words to my first poem filled my head. Two days later the same thing happened. Before I knew it, writing poetry was a regular thing. It became a coping mechanism and another way to explore my feelings, so that one day my son might understand what we went through when we lost the woman we both love, far too soon.

I found that poetry helped me to express things that I otherwise might have kept hidden inside. Negative thoughts that I found difficult to convey as long-winded prose finally spilled out and articulated the darkness in my mind. Love, which I so badly wanted to share, seemed less indulgent and sickly-sweet when kept succinct. And explaining what had happened to my son began to make more sense when expressed through language simple enough to appear in a children's storybook.

HALF MAN

Half the patience,
Half the fuse,
Half the parent,
Half enthused.

Half a man,
Half a boy,
Half the home,
Half the joy.

Half the time,
Twice the toil.
Twice the effort,
Half the spoil.

Half the father,
Half the son,
Half the future,
Half the fun.

Half the memory,
Half the drive.
Half dead,
Half alive.

Glass half empty,
Glass half full,
Sometimes vibrant,
Mostly dull.

Wholly wanting to feel whole again.
Wholly living with a hole within.

MOVING ON

I felt extremely displaced after Desreen died. Arranging and holding a funeral in her hometown of Havant, eighty miles from our flat in London, meant there was a lot of toing and froing between the two locations. Add in a Christmas that was split between our two family homes, 270 miles apart, and Jackson and I didn't really stop for breath. This was up there with the most excruciatingly painful aspects of the already agonising situation. While friends kindly invited us to stay with them, to 'get away from it all', I could think of nothing worse than spending any more time away from our home. And how can you hope to get away from 'it' when 'it' never leaves you?

It wasn't so much not being at home that filled me with torment and dread, more the getting ready to leave. The once simple act of packing a bag became one of the most stressful, upsetting and anxiety-inducing experiences imaginable. With no actual Desreen there to have and to hold, being in our home felt like the closest I could actually get to her; standing by a headstone in a cemetery will never make me feel close to her life – only her death. Packing our bags made me feel I was leaving her behind, as if I were removing my son from all the things he held dear. And, perhaps worst of all, I never really wanted us to go to the places we had to visit, so it didn't even feel worthwhile.

I've often wished it were possible to simply *get a grip*. But the problem, I've found, with grief, is that it takes your grip away; you can't grip it because it's got too tight a hold on you. In the midst of the much-dreaded departures from home I wrote a post on my blog to help explain why the process of placing things into a case stirred up such dramatic and distressing feelings.

Because my short-term memory seems to have been buried with my wife and I can never remember where I've left the things that I need. Because not being able to remember where I've left the things that I need is my least favourite experience at the best of times and instantaneously turns me from Dr Jekyll to Mr Hyde. Because when I'm Mr Hyde I turn the house upside down and find things that I wasn't looking for. Because when I find things that I wasn't looking for I discover mementos of our marriage that make me upset. Because when I'm upset I do things in a rush. Because when I do things in a rush I pack my wife's bag instead of my own. Because when I pack my wife's bag instead of my own and I'm standing at the door ready to leave, my son tells me that I'm not allowed to touch Mummy's things. Because when I touch Mummy's things and Mummy isn't there he gets upset. Because when he's upset he's difficult to travel with. Because when he's difficult to travel with I get stressed out. Because when I get stressed out I can lose my rag. Because when I lose my rag I hate myself. Because when I hate myself I feel like I've got nothing left.

I could have just hunkered down and refused to move. In the end, that's pretty much exactly what I did. After the stressful Christmas travels, the disastrous holiday, and my return to work, life was just feeling too fragile. I followed Jackson's lead and closed down my social life, and with that I stopped moving about as much as I had been doing before. But at times, that felt selfish. And it's hard to be selfish when there's been a bereavement in not just one but two families – when so many people love, cherish and admire the person who has gone. Sometimes, one of the hardest parts was feeling that I needed to split myself into multiple people when I didn't even feel like an entire version of myself. I felt a kind of pressure to be there for others – to comfort, rather than be comforted by, the people who had also lost Desreen. Jackson and I were now the closest thing to her they had. I just hoped that one day, the pressure I felt would seem worth the pain.

What I couldn't have realised so soon after my wife died was that the agony of moving around hadn't even really begun. After Christmas I decided that it was time to move house. Given my feelings about travelling eighty miles down the A3, I can appreciate why some people might have thought I had lost my mind. But I knew that it was the right thing to do. And I knew it was what Desreen would have done had things gone the other way.

We lived in a functional flat in southeast London that we moved into in a hurry. The week after we got back from honeymoon we decided not to undertake any more big projects for at least a year. Although we were living in a one-bedroom flat in Camberwell with a baby who would soon reach his first birthday, we decided there was little point. After all, the only place he would sleep without screaming the place down was next to his treasured mummy. And I know that she loved it as much as he did, even if she sometimes pretended to agree that it was time for him to have his own room.

But then, out of the blue, a small but dramatic spanner hit the works. We found ourselves with an extremely unwelcome new tenant. Without so much as asking if it was okay to stay the night, a mouse decided to move in permanently. This was not good. Desreen hated practically everything that moved. Pigeons, spiders and rodents were the stuff of her worst nightmares. So as soon the mouse moved in, it was time for us to move out. An hour after the first sighting I had found our next flat online.

'Do you not think this is a little dramatic, given what we agreed about not taking anything else on?' Desreen queried. She was due to return to work the following week, after ten months' maternity leave. She had been the one to take on the lion's share of our wedding arrangements at the same time as caring for a newborn. Now I was asking her to move house. Perhaps she could deal with one little mouse after all, she seemed to be implying. But I insisted.

'No, I don't actually, darling. There is no way I can live with both you and a mouse. We've only just got married and I won't have a little creature like that tear us apart so soon. I know you well enough to understand that this is not going to work.'

Frankly I didn't care about finding the perfect place. It just needed to be modern and clean and have no signs of holes anywhere – the complete opposite of the place we were living at the time. The flat I found ticked every box and we moved in a month later. But we never liked it. Everything about it fought with our own tastes and it was only ever intended as a creature-free stopgap before we bought our first family home. Every detail of that eventual purchase had been planned – from the lighting to the furnishings – all I had to do was pick up the baton that Desreen had always gripped too tightly for me to carry.

'Benji, please don't get involved in things that don't concern you,' she would inevitably have told me had I tried to have a say in buying anything other than the house that *she* deemed perfect.

With her gone, only I could make that decision and perfect no longer came into it. I doubt perfect ever will again. I needed something that would allow us to comfortably live our new lives: a place with a kitchen that I could cook and entertain in, but with enough room for Jackson to play without being reprimanded for just wanting to be a child; a house with enough space for the people who wanted to help raise Jackson to spend time comfortably; somewhere that Desreen would have approved of and that would hold all of the beautiful things she had collected to make our eventual house our home.

I didn't need to look very hard. After about eight viewings I found it, put in an offer and moved in two months later. The fairly painless property purchase and, eventually, moving in, was a walk in the park compared to the piercing process of *moving on*.

One day in March, five months after Desreen's death, the agony of my grief grew too intense for me to make it into work. The pressure to carry on had just become too strong and I was desperately missing my wife. Waiting in vain at the kitchen window for her face to look back at mine as she returned home from her morning run was crushing me. I had showered, shaved, dressed and got myself ready for the day ahead before my son had even woken up, but then I sat with my head in my hands, sobbing uncontrollably.

Bev walked into the room and in her own unique manner instructed me to phone my boss, Mitch ('boss' alone does a great disservice to my good friend), and tell him that it wasn't possible for me to come in that day. Most people who know her would do as they were told, so five minutes later I was in jogging bottoms and an old T-shirt and looked ready for a duvet day. But I've never really been one for sitting around doing nothing. So I announced my plans.

'This place isn't going to pack itself up,' I declared, to the assembled crowd in the living room: Bev, Kelson, Jackson, Marianne and her baby daughter, Lucia. 'I'm going to sort Desreen's stuff out.'

When I was a child I heard an adult – maybe a friend of my parents – say something that stuck with me for life. She refused a seat and sat on the floor instead. 'That way I can't fall any further,' she said. It was a sentiment that resonated with me that day. I already felt so terrible that I assumed it would be impossible to feel any worse, so I took on the job that scared me most.

Bev has always come across as a tower of strength. Everyone who knows her marvelled at her resilience and so-called strength in the wake of Desreen's death. I'll never know quite how she is the way she is – or what she is in fact feeling behind her facade of fortitude. I suspect it is thanks to a combination of her Jamaican heritage and stoicism, her faith and her resolute love for Dessie that made her so determined never to falter in her support for her daughter's husband and son.

Ever since Desreen's death, Bev has been able to read my mood like a book. One morning I walked downstairs in tears and she simply raised an eyebrow and asked me, 'Have you written anything today?' I shook my head, turned around, crawled under the covers and indulged in a little catharsis in the form of a blog post. Sometime later I emerged a little less heavy-hearted.

That day she knew that the task ahead had the potential to bring me to my knees. I barely noticed when she had skulked into my room with a large glass of Chardonnay and half a Valium. It wasn't even lunchtime but then, who gives a shit what time it is when the job in hand involves packing up your dead wife's one-and-a-half-year-old wedding dress along with all her other belongings? It didn't take me long to finish the bottle.

Once I've started, I tend to like to throw myself into a task. I suppose grief was no exception. I put on one of Desreen's baggy sweaters and turned on her favourite radio station. Neither the alcohol nor the drugs were enough to suppress the hurt of listening to tunes she would have chosen herself – songs from acts and artists including TLC, De La Soul, Soul II Soul and Azealia Banks – while vacuum-packing clothes that she hadn't even had the chance to wear.

I folded a dress that she wore for my mum's sixtieth birthday and another that she looked so amazing in on our honeymoon. I found numerous pairs of similar high-heeled boots that she wore to cover the ankles that she hated. Countless designers and pattern cutters had contributed to a beautiful wardrobe that now served no purpose. We had no daughter to appreciate the clothes; no friends who could wear them so well. Frivolous garments of linen, silk and cashmere once filled by a beautiful lady now filled ugly, functional, plastic shrink-wrap bags. Things that brought her so much pleasure in life would now rest in pointless peace. I packed them all away to worry about another day, maybe even another year. I knew that at some point I would want to dig out the clothes Desreen was wearing in photographs taken with Jackson and put them aside as keepsakes and memories for his future.

The stabbing memories were everywhere. I could still smell her body in her nightclothes. Not her perfume, just her scent. One of the most frustrating things, however, was just how few things carried her smell. She washed her clothes immediately after wearing them and so nearly everything emitted the scent of detergent, or nothing at all. And it felt impossible to simply throw her things into bags without inspecting each and every one – without taking time to recall the times that she, that item and I had spent together. The intensity of it all – of so many memories flooding over me – left me almost winded. Each of her belongings delivered a different emotional blow.

How the hell had such a horrendous situation come to pass? How could my young wife have lost her life long before the use-by date on her cosmetics? And what the hell was I supposed to do with them? How could a husband who had bought his wife *this* compact in Manhattan and *that* makeup bag in Soho, ever part with such treasures? But what is a man with only a son to do with them?

Suddenly I was grieving not only the loss of my wife and my son's mum, but the intense female presence in our lives – something that I have always valued so much, thanks to my close relationship with my mum and my grandmother, and then later with my mother-in-law.

This absence revealed itself in the unworn jewellery, stray hairpins and lacy lingerie that I found all around our room. There's something almost ugly about precious metals and stones shoved in a box rather than worn. They seem to radiate an emptiness and lack of purpose, which somehow takes off their shine.

I tried my very best to pack up the house when Jackson was asleep, out with his grandparents or at nursery. He was far too playful not to think it funny to unpack as I made progress with the boxes, and far too sensitive about me touching his mummy's things for me to be able to get the job done with him there. I tried to explain that we were moving to a new house but I knew that he wouldn't understand until we were there.

When the day to move out arrived, Woody came over to help. I'd had the keys to our new house for over a week and both my parents and Desreen's had come to stay to help decorate. I had a firm plan and together we got loads done: my father, my father-in-law and I painted all the rooms that needed attention and my mother and mother-in-law helped take care of Jackson.

We stayed at the old flat each night but brought Jackson to the new house for an hour or two each day so he could slowly adapt to it being his new home. I thought that letting him play hide and seek in all the different rooms and putting a paintbrush in his hands would make him see it as a fun place to be.

As Woody and I stood in my old living room, now completely emptied of all Desreen's, Jackson's and my belongings, it finally hit. I would never share a home with my wife again. I sat on the floor and sobbed.

A new beginning, and yet our dream home felt like nothing short of a full stop and the continuation of a living nightmare. When we moved I wrote:

> Just one small thing occurred to me as I unpacked our pictures and began to contemplate where to place them. For now this is simply a house and it's going to take a long time before it feels like a home. I could lie to myself and hang the old cross-stitch *Home Sweet Home* picture but, right now, a truer tapestry from my heart would read *Home Bittersweet Home*. A sweet dream we had as a family but only realised in the bitter absence of the woman we love.

The house was simply bricks and mortar, the things in it little more than stuff. Perhaps it would take years for it to feel like a home. Perhaps *home* would never hold the same meanings or connotations for me again.

Nevertheless I took solace in the fact that I finally felt as if I had done something right. The first time I picked Jackson up from nursery after we moved into our new home, instead of turning right out of the building to head for our old flat he turned left. 'New house, Daddy!' he instructed, pointing in the direction of the street he had only lived in for three days. And that night, when

I tucked him into bed, he squeezed me tightly and, completely unprompted, told me, 'I love the new house, Daddy.' After he fell asleep I found myself laughing for the first time in a while. Just like his mum and dad, I thought, the boy loves an upgrade.

Dear Daddy,
It's been a while. I haven't felt much like writing because I've been so busy moving house, and hanging out with my grand-parents.

I love the new house though, Daddy. I know that you took a risk on us moving and that you were worried that I'd totally freak out about leaving the last home we lived in with Mummy, but I really love it.

Thankfully you've chilled out now. Wise move giving up half the kitchen to me and my stuff too, it'll keep me away from all your precious stuff in the living room. I mean frankly I don't care if Mummy's Missoni throw acquires a little extra pattern; from where I'm standing everything looks better with a touch of Play-Doh or Crayola on it. I really enjoyed it when you left me in the living room with the sofa, your laptop and a tube of Carmex, too. The couch looks amazing now, Daddy. I tried to tell you that it could do with a little pattern too. I loved what you tried to do with that wall in the kitchen as well. 'Sea Urchin' I think you said the colour was. Well it's 'Seabiscuit' now, dude! Funny how all those paints Grandma bought me ended up being a horsey brown colour after five minutes. Why you didn't choose an equine shade for the kitchen in the first place is beyond me, but you can chill now, Pops, I've got the walls covered. You've done enough, just leave it to me. I mean, you've seen me after nursery twice this week looking more like Jackson Pollock than Jackson Brooks-Dutton, haven't you? I've got the skills to pay the bills!

If I think about it I probably only paint the sofa, the walls and myself to get a laugh or some attention. Mummy would have spent £400 buying a candle or something on your card much to the same effect, but seeing as you won't trust me with your wallet since I hid your work pass in an attempt to keep you at home with me, I've had to get creative. I love making you laugh, too. Someone needs to and it's not as easy as it used to be. That's probably why I act like I do.

I reckon you've worked me out though.

'How's Jackson?' I hear them all say.

'I almost hate to say it but he's doing remarkably well. Generally he seems to be a really happy child. But sometimes I wonder if he's playing me. Oh, and don't try to tell me he's only two, because I know him best,' I hear you reply.

Busted! I'll give you this though, for an old git you're quite down with the kids. Of course I'm not a hundred per cent happy. I mean, who is? My mind strays, I wonder what the hell's going on and, to be quite honest, I find it hard to express myself at times. Perhaps I don't want to talk about it either. Maybe I need a bit of time to take it all in. Some days I want to hide behind that fake smile I pull. And yeah, sometimes I ask you if you're sad, I indulge you, I counsel you (for free, too, but I'll be back with the bill one day, you cheap mofo) and I listen to what you have to say, but that doesn't mean *I* want to talk about my feelings. Remember, we all have to face this stuff in our own way. Sometimes it's easier to grin uncomfortably like Victoria Beckham on the red carpet, and spit the words 'I'm fine, Daddy, I'm happy' through gritted teeth. Truth is we all have our highs and our lows. I might only stand 91.5cm tall, but I'm not that different to you. In fact, let's face it, Daddy, I'm not that much smaller than you!

I guess what we have to remember, though, is I'm doing pretty well now but I reckon my hardest days are yet to come. I'm two, everything's a game, it's always playtime and I've got loads of people round me who I love. One day when I'm too cool to play and too adolescent to talk, I'm sure things will be different. If you think about it, it's a shame you can't act more like me now, living in the moment and all that, then face the bad times with me when I'm ready. Perhaps we're yinging and yanging, though. I suppose we'll balance one another out eventually. I guess we'd be screwed if we were both as miserable as you at the same time. I swear though, you'll pay your dues. This little stand-up ain't dishing the jokes out for free forever. One day I'm coming back to sit in the audience and listen to you cracking the gags. They better be good too because I'm propping this double act up right now.

Anyway, laters. Time for me to go and start colouring in the white bits on that monochrome sofa you just bought. I mean, come on, Daddy, what were you thinking? It's like a moth to the flame. And this moth has got a lot of felt tips.

Love you, Daddy.
J-Bo xx

ACCEPTING HELP

One of my many dreads about my life as a widower and my new role as sole parent was the perhaps unavoidable loss of independence. It would be easy to assume that a man who is married and a father by definition already lacks freedom, but it just wasn't like that with Desreen and me. We both loved to get out and do our own things, both alone and with friends. We both enjoyed keeping fit, and while it's easy, if not a little embarrassing, to take a baby out in a running buggy while they sleep, it's more difficult with a toddler who constantly wants to escape. So as well as wanting to grow together as a family we also respected one another's space. We wanted one another to continue to be the person we met and fell in love with.

We hadn't planned on having too much help in raising our son, either. We tried out a part-time child minder for a few weeks. We soon realised, however, that we were really only sacrificing our hard-earned wages to enable ourselves to give our employers even more of our time for no extra reward – a cruel paradox of life for today's hungry young professionals. That said, we were in the fortunate position of being able to call on my mother-in-law, who has been there to offer an extra pair of hands every week since the day Jackson was born.

Bev met Jackson minutes after he breathed his first breath. She was so sure our baby would be a boy – and so determined that he wouldn't take the other name that Desreen had in mind – that she wrote a greetings card to the three of us, each addressed by name, before he was even born.

After four days in labour, ending in a C-section, my exhausted wife wasn't going anywhere in a hurry. I, on the other hand, ran the halls of the maternity ward and found her mum. 'It's a boy! It's a boy!' I yelled. She told me later that she's never seen anyone more excited.

Jackson was born soon after 9.00p.m. and it wasn't too long before Bev and I would have to leave the hospital. The two of us sauntered home, thrilled and dazed, and raised a glass to both Jackson and his courageous mother. I could never have imagined quite how many times Bev and I would find ourselves in that same scenario in the future – toasting Desreen but in sorrow rather than celebration.

Jackson and his Nanny, his name for Bev, fell for each other immediately. Desreen used to joke about how her mum should move in with us and act as our au pair. She would pay her terribly, ask her to do everything and offer no thanks in return – perhaps you could say it would be the typical child-parent relationship. But we didn't need to take any such extreme measures. Bev arrived each Wednesday and stayed until Friday, for the love of her grandson and for the love of her daughter.

Des and I would sneak off into our bedroom and giggle at how we had it made.

'We've got our own live-in housekeeper now,' she joked.

'I know,' I replied, 'but let's just make sure she doesn't get any ideas above her station. It'll never work if she starts answering back.'

At first Des and I planned date nights – the appeal of a free babysitter seemed too strong to simply stay at home. But that quickly changed. We loved having Bev there. The three of us would sit together and eat Desreen's favourite childhood foods – chicken and rice, slow-cooked ribs, fried plantain and dumplings, macaroni and cheese. I was exempt from cooking if Ma was in the house. We would have a drink and laugh at Jackson's filthy temper as we attempted to get him to eat some fruit and vegetables, much to his disgust.

'Don't look at me!' Desreen would bark, as Bev and I debated which parent he had inherited his irritability from. They were happy days; just three friends, who also happened to be a mother, a daughter and a son-in-law, hanging out, having fun and raising a little boy we all adored, together. And thanks be to God for that special time: the time when Desreen and Bev became the best of friends; the time when I grew close to the woman who I would come to need so badly in my life; the time when Jackson bonded with the grandmother who he would need so badly in his.

As I've said, there has never been any appeal in trying to be a hero in all this mess. I could have chosen to soldier on, to *man up* and to raise my child alone. Only, I knew that wasn't what my wife would have wanted. And I knew because she told me. Although she worried about the potential of absolutely anything killing her – throat cancer was her most frequently self-diagnosed illness, while the implausible prostate cancer was my personal favourite – she only expressed true concern for her untimely death twice. The first time was to explain to friends just how scared she was that something might happen to her and that I would be left to raise Jackson alone. The second was to make provision against that eventuality by telling me that she would want her mum to step into her shoes, should her worst fears be realised. Like any good husband who knows his place, I was just following my orders in accepting Bev's help. And, like any good mother who respects her beloved daughter's wishes, she was just following hers.

When Desreen died I was scared that the independence we both enjoyed would disappear. No longer in a relationship of equals, where each partner owed the other nothing but love, I worried that I would forever be in debt for any help I received. I also knew that I would feel guilty every time I left my son in anyone else's care, as if I were leaving him feeling fatherless when he had already lost his mum.

But that became something that I had to work through in my own head. I see families with two healthy, happy parents who get to spend far less time with their children than I do, through no fault or due to extreme circumstances of their own. I also try to remember all the other parents out there who are raising their children alone and I picture them taking all the help they can get. And I thank God that Jackson always had another maternal figure in his life who was more willing than ever to be there for him after his mother was killed. Although perfect family status is out of reach, I'm grateful that when he and I reach out we still have a wonderful family there reaching back to us.

TIME STEALS

•••••••••••••••••••••••••••

I have come to realise that the way a person perceives the passage of time is heavily dictated by their state of mind. Some say time flies when you're having fun but, in my experience, it can also go way too fast when you're not. The winter that Desreen died was cold, wet and dark. The only time I remember the sun shining was on the day of her funeral. Weeks went by with gloomy grey skies and I barely remember day breaking the night. Had I not been widowed, I would have expected that time would pass by torturously slowly for the bereaved. But then suddenly it was spring, the days grew lighter, the nights grew shorter and six months had already passed. How could it have been that long since I last saw my wife?

I started my blog as a way of capturing raw, live grief. As painful as every word was to type, I suspected that if I didn't document it in the moment, it would soften and lack the intensity of the pain – the intensity of *my* pain. I was told repeatedly that time would heal me. I was led to believe that someday I'd be fixed. I thought I had to start when I did because once I was somehow cured of my grief I would no longer remember the agony on which to base my writing. But I don't believe I was ever told the truth about time.

'Time heals' is one of the most overused clichés in grief's book but I think it's bollocks. I can't tell anyone, with any degree of credibility, how I will feel ten or twenty years from now and no one can tell me (though they may often try). What I can do is apply a little judgment based on facts about myself to reach a reasonable conclusion.

When I was about nine years old I broke my right arm in three places. I had a cast on for weeks while it 'healed' and when the bones were looking better and the NHS budget dried up, time dictated that it was appropriate for my arm to *move on*. This was medicalised time; it was a target. My arm is a mess now. If I'm wearing a T-shirt and I stretch both arms out at the same time, people can't hide their horror. I've never heard anyone say, 'I can't see the difference' or 'I think it's lovely – much nicer than the other one.' I've got arthritis in it, too, which I've had since my twenties.

So I reasoned that time didn't heal my arm; it just changed it. I began to wonder how anyone could expect my head and my heart to be healed by time when my arm still causes me pain from something that happened when I was at junior school. I concluded that time cannot be the great grief fix-all that it's made out to be. It's more like a convenient verbal medicine for an inconvenient all-too-often unspoken pain that can't be healed.

Yet as I fought this concept of time as a remedy to my grief, I also found it controlling me. I was a slave to the time dominatrix and she would inevitably have her way with me. I came to realise that only by documenting *my* grief – against a traditional timeline of weeks, months and possibly eventually years – could I explain to those who have never been bereaved, just how endless the process and pain of grief can be. Only this way could I help people to understand how time might soften emotions, how it might change the way a person feels, but that it can probably never entirely heal.

A poem I wrote on the five-month anniversary of Desreen's death explained how I felt at that point.

SO-NOT 5

Set not my life on your watch,
Measure me not in time I pray,
My heart has moved on not a notch,
Not five months, no, one long painful day.
Hold not your breath for progress,
Your lungs will not survive the test,
See not my smile as success,
Not five months, no, just empty time bereft.
Forget me not if you don't see me,
I flower not, I'm but a seed,
A new season it will not be,
Not five months, no, a harsh winter, indeed.
Set not my life on your watch, expect time to neither take nor give,
Put not my heart before your own, I beg, make time to love and live.

Six months was perhaps just long enough for some people to expect me to be feeling okay. For me, it was just an opportunity to reflect on how far I had or hadn't come and how the passage of time left me feeling.

Next week is the six-month anniversary of my wife's untimely death. It simultaneously means both everything and nothing to me. Everything because I can't believe how much our families and friends have been through in that time; nothing because I suspect that what we're going through has barely started.

Everything because it's been the longest six months of my life and I've never felt so many emotions so intensely; nothing because, looking back, I can't believe six months have passed so quickly and so much of it feels like a blur. Everything because my whole outlook on life has changed; nothing because I feel so powerless now that I understand that I have no real control over the future. Everything because it's twenty-five times longer than the previous longest period of time (seven days) that I hadn't seen my wife in eight years; nothing because I've started to understand that time is a measure that holds little value in grief.

And so, as we approach the six-month anniversary I can imagine that there are people out there who'll assume that's long enough for a person to have begun to heal. In my experience it's not. Time is simply a medicine dished out by untrained practitioners. But for me it's a placebo and I'm familiar enough with the taste of the real thing to know when I'm being taken for a ride. The truth is I feel every ounce of sadness and loss I felt six months ago.

I would be lying if I said that my feelings nearly six months on were exactly the same though. I know this because I've been keeping a diary in the form of a blog and when I look back I can compare. I wrote a piece called *Imagining It* back in January, very soon after Desreen died, which aimed to explain how it felt to lose her so suddenly. I covered elements of confusion, guilt and physical pain that I no longer feel with the same intensity. If I still had the same physical symptoms, for example, I'm sure I would be extremely ill by now. And if you had seen me as the shell of a man I was back in November and saw me again now, I'm sure you could assume that time was indeed healing. Yet it's not. I guess I'm just on a journey towards slowly learning to survive with an open wound. And I guess there's little other choice than to survive when there's a young child there who needs you more than ever before.

Although I don't believe that time heals, I'm starting to face the reality that it does change things, so I'm going to tell you what it feels like for me some six months on. The most important part of that sentence is not the measure of time but the part that says 'for me'. I understand how natural it is for human beings to compare themselves to others. I know how it feels to get cross at people for pushing their beliefs on me. I appreciate that one person's six months might be another's six years. And above all, I know myself and I know that all I'm doing is documenting how I feel at any given moment in time. Perhaps after seven months I'll change again. Maybe I'll regress. Who knows if my feelings will be closer to month-one than month-six? I'm only certain of one thing: I'll be the only one feeling my exact feelings. You'll be the only one feeling yours. We'll share common ground but we all grieve in our own way and in our own time.

I mention this because I've felt some upset and discomfort recently for being criticised for *my* grief: *I'm not angry enough, I'm too positive, I'm just out for myself.*

Perhaps, given my current fragile state, I could hear a thousand positive comments and concentrate only on a handful of negatives. But that's *my* grief. When my wife died I was more preoccupied with who hadn't got in touch than who had. These days I can't even remember who did and who didn't.

But the struggle I'm experiencing with my grief is also telling me to grow a thicker skin. That struggle is telling me that all that matters now is the approval and the wellbeing of the people I love or respect. It's telling me that I set out to help people and if there are still those who can find solace or empathy in what I write, then it's worth carrying on. It's telling me to be the gauge of what's right and what's wrong. It's telling me to face the reality that you can't please all of the people all the time. And it's telling me not to waste my increasingly precious energy trying.

So this is what grief feels like for me six months on: it feels like sadness. Sadness because the person I shared my life with is no longer here and never will be again. Sadness because any precious moment of happiness I feel, however brief, is followed by a crippling sense of foreboding and loss. Sadness because it tears me to pieces to think of my son not being raised by the mother who adored him and who was planning to make his life so special. Sadness because I fixate not just on my own loss, but that of my wife's family and friends and I feels theirs, too.

It feels empty. Empty because whatever I do, however much I occupy myself, however much I try to honour the memory of my wife, I feel nothing. No pride. No sense of achievement. No progress. Just nothing. Empty because a part of me died with my wife. She was part of me. We were part of each other. The physical part has gone and it's taken so many of the positive emotions that I always held so dear.

It feels endless. Endless because I know I'll never be healed. Endless because I'll never see her again. Endless because I'll never see the old me again. Endless because there's no conclusion, just an unknown expanse of time ahead of me in which I will always miss her. Endless because a huge part of me doesn't want the pain to stop because it would feel as if I were doing my wife a disservice in death. Endless because I have both my feelings and my son's to worry about for as long as I'm lucky enough to be alive. Endless because it never leaves my mind for a moment and I find it hard to concentrate on anything else. Endless because I rarely sleep and so there are now more hours in the day, yet I don't have the energy to fill them with the things I used to love or the things that made me a healthier person.

It feels like disbelief. Disbelief because when anyone talks about my wife's grave I shut down. Disbelief because I don't think I'll ever truly be able to get my head round what's happened. Disbelief because, well fuck it, I just can't fucking believe it has fucking well happened.

It feels lonely. Lonely because my days never come to a natural close with a 'goodnight', a kiss or a cuddle from the person who always told me when it was time to go to bed. Lonely because however much company I'm in, I still feel alone. Lonely because intimacy has gone. Lonely because I've lost my wife, my best friend, my co-parent and my partner in fun and mischief, all in one go.

It feels disappointing. Disappointing because people I bump into often assume that they don't need to mention what happened because it happened six months ago. Disappointing because some people avoid talking about my wife, as if she never existed.

It feels shared. Shared because I understand now that I feel some comfort when I comfort others. Shared because I believe that if we pass kindness on it will come back to us. Shared because so many people are looking out for my son and me.

Shared because I've let the people who I initially pushed away back in. Shared because I stopped trying to be a hero and started to accept and truly appreciate help.

It feels hopeful. Hopeful because I have let moments of happiness back into my life and I have said *to hell with the consequences and the hangover that they might create*. Hopeful because I'm exposed to my son's sunny disposition and his beautiful outlook on life. Hopeful because he tells me, 'It's not raining, Daddy, it's happy', when all I see are dark clouds ahead. Hopeful because he can answer for himself at two-and-a-half when people ask where his mummy's gone. Hopeful because when the other kids at nursery discuss the bracelets that they are making for their mummies, my son doesn't get upset. He just says he's making his for his daddy.

So today my grief is not the Gollum I spoke about in the beginning. But it still feels ugly, isolated, wretched and schizophrenic enough to be Sméagol.

BEARING SCARS

After more than six months of more or less caging ourselves in the safety and security of our home, with little interaction with most of the outside world, the time came to emancipate ourselves, throw ourselves to the lions and attend a wedding in Cornwall.

'We'd really like you to be there but we totally understand if you don't want to come.' This is something I've got used to people saying. It's a comment I interpret in various different ways depending on my state of mind: *we really do want you there but we expect it's going to be incredibly hard on you, so don't feel that you have to come; we would like you there but we don't want you to ruin a happy occasion with your miserable face;* or, from my own point of view, *I've got the perfect excuse not to go because the very people who invited me have handed me a get out of jail free card.*

I wasn't so scared of attending social occasions if I had my close friends around me, and there would be plenty of them at the wedding. Of course it was likely to be difficult to sit through a marriage ceremony, to hear a happy couple take the same vows that Desreen and I had just a couple of years before, and to listen to heartfelt speeches about love, marriage, friendship and the future, but these people were my mates. And when I married Desreen I made a vow 'for better or for worse'. Things had certainly got worse since that day, but I felt I owed it to myself to at least try to have some better in my life, too.

Desreen and I had known the groom for years. A mild-mannered, funny, warm and kind man with an exceptionally well-groomed moustache, Julian was a friend of Zac's. It was at Zac's annual house party, better known as Zacfest, that we were introduced to the bride, Charlotte, years before Julian had even thought about asking for her hand. She's a confident and attractive firecracker of a girl who only ever tells it the way it is, and Desreen loved her straight away.

'I wouldn't cross her,' Desreen informed me with a chuckle the next day – a very big statement of approval from my wife, a woman who loved a strong personality and wouldn't usually have a problem crossing anyone.

One weekend some months later, Charlotte introduced us to her beautiful, playful and incredibly polite daughter, Madison, whom she had talked about a lot when we first met. Two-and-a-half years old at the time, she joined six adults for a weekend away in Devon and was the star of the show. Des commented that she wanted our future child to be just like her. Little did she know just how similar Jackson and Madison would be: confident, funny, charming, wise beyond their years, hair and eyes that turned heads and the ability to cut a killer look at anyone who didn't see things from their point of view.

When the invitation for Julian and Charlotte's wedding arrived, Desreen talked about how much she was looking forward to attending. For once it read 'kids allowed'. Neither of us could wait to see Jackson racing around with the other children and muddying up the type of clothes for which Desreen would doubtless have to hide the receipt.

The wedding was set for 4 May 2013, a date that my wife would never get to see. Her chance to watch her son playing with her friends' children was gone forever. But I steeled myself. I convinced myself that I was ready and that I would be in the right company for what my wife would have called my 'relaunch'. Using the words of her eulogy to guide me, I headed to Liberty to spend an obscene amount of money on new clothes, the irony being that I wanted to dress down a bit so I wouldn't mind getting a bit grubby with Jackson in the wedding venue's grounds. The truth is, I didn't want to wear the suit that I both married and buried my wife in and I was absolutely planning on spending the day avoiding adult conversations and hiding behind my son.

Children can be an amazing shield against anyone or anything you fear in a social situation. When Jackson's around I'm Perseus, he's my aegis and I can take on the gorgon Medusa or any other monsters or monstrosities without fear. On the few occasions when he has misinterpreted someone's proximity to me as aggression they have suffered a tiny punch, a bite or a lion-like roar and a ferocious dressing down. I know I should teach him not to show such hostility towards others (and I often do) but sometimes his fierce loyalty is just too irresistible to quash. Des would always have shielded me in exactly the same way. She was a 'don't fuck with my man' kind of girl and consequently Jackson's a 'don't fuck with my daddy' kind of boy.

With our wedding wardrobes sorted and my party perma-smile rehearsed, the day came to head down to Cornwall. We met our friends Zac, Laura, Oggie and Emily and their two border terriers and picked up a hire car in King's Cross. All of us were there the night that Des was killed and so I felt at ease and comfortable in the group – after what we had all experienced there seemed to be nothing we couldn't discuss.

Jackson, however, was less at ease. After just forty-five minutes the immaculately clean car was freshly reupholstered with the contents of his small but suddenly mighty stomach. This was a sign of things to come. After our disastrous holiday earlier in the year I immediately felt defeated. While I tried to clean and change my distraught son on a roadside in Notting Hill and watched my friends' dogs feasting on his regurgitated lunch, I so badly wanted to tell everyone that I'd tried but that I couldn't take it anymore and that I was just going to take the two of us home. But I said nothing, urged myself not to be so easily defeated and told myself Jackson's affliction was just a touch of carsickness. I was so wrong.

After a seven-hour journey, a number of junky on-the-go meals and a night's broken sleep, I woke up to discover that Jackson's temperature was through the roof and his skin had started to break out in spots. It was the beginning of our two-week journey into chickenpox, which hit us both, Jackson gently and me with full force. Having spent hundreds of pounds on a weekend that we wouldn't get to enjoy and, far worse, having worked myself into a state of anxiety about whether or not to attend, I couldn't even be bothered to be bothered. I simply shrugged the situation off as yet another shit on my shoe and got the two of us back home to London as quickly as I possibly could.

I called in support from both sides of the family to help take care of my perky little sufferer, while I ended up bedridden for a fortnight.

'Oh, God! You don't want to get chickenpox as an adult,' I was told. No, it wasn't that high up on my bucket list, I thought. As I stood looking in the mirror at the blisters erupting all over my body, the idea of feeling and looking even worse than I had for the last six months terrified me. And the thought that I might have to be alone with nothing but my own grief to keep me company made me genuinely fear for my own mental health.

So I self-prescribed strong painkillers, sleep, damp flannels to cool the intense burning pain of the blisters and a promise not to allow myself to sink into a deep depression from being forced to be on my own in my bed with my thoughts.

That promise was going to require an alternative remedy – distraction. I watched every episode of everything I'd ever wanted to see on television but had never taken the time to sit through. Looking back I have to laugh that my media medicine of choice would be the fatality-filled WWII series *Band of Brothers* and the confusing, violent and really rather depressing *Game of Thrones*. Was I trying to make myself feel worse?

Actually, worse was almost impossible. I was already wretchedly miserable: the unexpectedly excruciating pain made me break down in the middle of the night and curse the heavens for testing me so harshly over the months; I was terrified when I read that my latest symptoms might be the start of the worst-case scenario side-effects of chickenpox – tightness in the chest leading to the onset of pneumonia – which could ultimately orphan my only child.

But, you know what? I'm glad I got ill and I'm glad it hit me so hard emotionally and physically. Because when I recovered I felt alive, I felt grateful and I felt more positive. I had gone so low that it felt as if I had turned a corner when I stepped back up. I had been forced to take more time off from being a full-time parent than I felt Jackson deserved and I wanted to be more present for him than ever before. I was covered in scabs and now I'm covered in scars, but they will always remind me that I got the chance to recover; that, unlike my wife, I got the opportunity to live for my son.

And if ever I find myself being quite so melodramatic about an illness that children are able to brush off as easily as a common cold, all I need to do is remind myself of the words

Bev said to me as she popped her head around my bedroom door to check that I was still alive. 'Desreen would say, "Get up, lazybones! You've only got chickenpox. Just remember, I had to have a Caesarean."'

If my darling wife had lived until she was 100 years old, she would never have let this one go.

GRIEF GAUGE

Perhaps because I had never expected time to be a magical medicine that would mysteriously heal me of the devastation of losing my wife or lessen the pain of grief, the passage of time simply wasn't a useful measuring tool for me. I found myself gauging how I felt in a different and completely unplanned way.

Before Desreen died, she and I had planned to take our little boy on a trip to Crystal Palace Park – just a couple of miles down the road from where we lived. I had heard that the park housed a series of sculptures of dinosaurs and extinct animals and thought Jackson would love to check it out. The weather got the better of us each time we intended to go, though, so we never made it as a family of three.

After she was killed parks became my enemy – just a necessary evil to keep my son entertained for a short time while I mourned her constantly. I couldn't bear the sight of happy parents; I couldn't stomach the miserable ones who were arguing with one another either. I felt sick with anxiety waiting for Jackson's increasingly volatile behaviour to suddenly turn. He would be aggressive towards children whose only aggravation was playing happily and innocently with their living mothers. I couldn't blame him, I felt the same, and I had to at least half-laugh when he turned his hostility towards grandmothers, too.

One pensioner even got a little kick just for the crime of being in the wrong place at the wrong time with her little grandson. But while I knew we had the perfect excuse – a line that would floor anyone who challenged my son's antisocial behaviour – I hated the thought of him showing anger towards people who had no reason to understand what we were going through. Our story had been all over the news, too, and so, conversely, I was also worried that I might break down if anyone so much as looked at me with a sympathetic eye or a tilted head.

Back then the sky was always grey. I had to get us out of the house so that we didn't go out of our minds, but when we did venture out it was often too cold to be anything like fun. So when I finally felt well enough in the aftermath of the chickenpox and when, at last, the sun started to shine, I felt my mood's dark clouds begin to dissipate – if just a little. It was time to get out and to try to have some fun with my son.

I wanted to take him somewhere he had never been before, where I was unlikely to see anyone I knew, so we headed to the park that we had planned to visit as a family. I couldn't have known at the time but this place would become what I labelled my 'grief gauge' – every time we visited I would sit in the same spot and reflect on how I felt compared to the time before.

Our inaugural visit was a day of firsts for Jackson: soft ice cream in a cone from an old-school ice cream van; building sandcastles despite not being on a beach; sculptures of prehistoric creatures; and his first joyous jump on a bouncy castle. Seeing his face when he discovered that particular pleasure made up for two miserable weeks in just two seconds. Yet just moments after I felt a smile stretch across my face, the tears welled up. Sadness that my eyes could see his happiness while my wife's remained forever closed.

My son's smile was there to stay, though, and as I watched

him play I thought about how innocence breeds contentment. Unlike me, he was living in the moment. If he was having a nice time, why would he do anything other than laugh and smile? What could possibly make a child cry when there was sunshine, swings, slides, scooters and soft-scoop ice cream?

Unfortunately, along with grief there often come conflicted emotions. And, for me, my son's happiness was often accompanied by more pain.

Hearing him laugh reminded me that we would never see Desreen again; that I felt guilty and regretful that he was missing out on his mother, and that his mother was missing out on her son; and that I felt ashamed when I realised that I didn't want to be sad forever.

Seeing him happy made me realise that I felt lonely all the time; that I no longer ever felt truly fulfilled either in company or alone; and that I had started to detach myself from every social scenario in which I found myself.

Watching him play made me believe that I would never be able to escape our loss; that I wouldn't ever be able to stop going over *that night* in my head; and that I would spend more time worrying about the rest of my life than actually living it.

Until that day I hadn't realised that it was possible for a parent to be made sad by seeing their child happy. Perhaps it's that constant conflict of emotions that makes grief so powerful, so heartbreaking and so often intensely crippling.

Six weeks later we returned to the park. I suppose it would have been easy for me to dread it, to focus on how Jackson's first jubilant experience of a bouncy castle made me feel so acutely aware of his loss. But rather than concentrate on how bad it made me feel, I turned my attention to how happy it made him. And this time he was even happier than the time before, the sun was stronger, the weather hotter and there were even more happy families enjoying the day. Only, on this occasion, I didn't find them unbearable. In fact, I realised that we were a happy family, too. Diminished but somehow managing to smile, to laugh and to show how much we love one another. Unexpectedly, I felt that I had begun to appreciate what we still had together on any particular day rather than worrying too much about what we might or might not have the next.

This time Jackson played with children he didn't know, too. There was no glimmer of aggression when he helped one up onto a slide because they were too small to do it on their own, and another to get down because they were too scared to do it alone. Neither did he show any signs of anger or frustration towards mums, dads or even grandparents for that matter. Once again he had fun, and I smiled, just a touch more than the time before.

Another six weeks passed by before we went again. This time he was on familiar ground. He knew where he was heading and he knew what he wanted to do and in what order: ice cream, sandpit, playground and then dinosaurs. He was a joy, he was settled and I was relaxed enough to enjoy the day without torturing myself or letting his happiness weigh heavy on my heart.

A month later we visited the park again and this time I felt more ready than ever to join in and play. I ate half of his ice cream when he told me he'd had enough, we played football, chased squirrels and pretended to couple up like his two favourite trains: he played Thomas and I pretended to be Percy. Bev was with us and she had to assume the role of Jackson's favourite girl-train, Emily. This was the most fun I had seen him have in weeks and the most relaxed I'd felt in ages.

As he scooted round the lake and threw stale bread to angry geese and dirty pigeons, I looked at him playing happily and realised that something had been eating me up for months. I had been feeling not only as if I didn't deserve to be the one who was left raising him, but that Desreen would somehow be displeased with the manner in which I was doing it.

That car killed my wife and my confidence in myself, but to some degree it also robbed me of the love I knew she felt for me – the love that I never questioned when she was alive. At that moment I realised that I had been left so insecure that I had forgotten just how proud of me she was in life. And I questioned why on earth she would be anything less in death. She never wanted to leave me and we had never fought over how to raise our son. At last I could feel her unfaltering adoration touch me again. I could sense her telling me that I was doing okay. I smiled as I imagined her saying, *'I think we both know I could do better, but you are doing your best. You're only a man after all. Keep going, Benji.'*

It took eleven months for me to 'hear' my wife's voice in my head in this way and to feel some sense of ease in my own efforts as a post-Desreen father. I suppose you could label it progress, you could tag it acclimatisation, or you could simply say it was a case of gradually adjusting to the terrible hand that life has dealt us. But whatever you call it, I don't think my wife would want me to feel ashamed of letting my son make me feel happy again. I think she would be disappointed if I didn't.

NURTURING NATURE

No one has ever told me that Jackson looks or behaves like me with any degree of conviction in their voice or in their eyes. Once, when Jackson and I were out shopping for cufflinks for my wedding to his mum, I was actually stopped in a jewellery shop and asked whose he was. The lady behind the counter took offence to the customer's comment and started shouting at him, telling him we looked exactly the same and that it was obvious that he was my child. I, on the other hand, was unoffended. I'm delighted that he so resembles his mother because she had much more to offer in the looks stakes than I do.

'Well, we've got very strong genes, Benji,' she explained to me.

By 'we' she meant black people. Her generalisations on this matter were truly something. 'Black people don't like their meat with any pink in it; black people don't eat rice pudding; black people don't like skiing.' There was really no end to the manipulation of facts to ensure she got what she wanted, or perhaps rather to ensure that she *didn't* get what she *didn't* want.

When she died I prayed that our son would remain just like her – that his looks would continue to be all Desreen and that he wouldn't lose the character traits that made his personality so remarkably similar to hers. He not only looks nothing like me, his behaviour is almost entirely inherited from his mother, too.

As the months after her death rapidly rolled on, the, perhaps inevitable, argument of nature versus nurture frequently came into conversation. Friends who hadn't seen Jackson for a while were struck by how much more like his mum he was becoming as time passed and as his language skills continued to develop. Cutting his eyes to glare in disapproval, the flat refusal ever to say the word sorry, laughing hardest at things that would usually be labelled *naughty*, never leaving a person uncertain about how he felt towards them – he seemed to exhibit more of her trademark traits by the day.

Desreen was notoriously grumpy in the morning. Her ever-chirpy friend, business partner and ex-housemate, Cathy, told me that Des would answer the question 'How are you this morning?' with nothing more than a filthy stare and a slow shunt down the corridor from her bedroom to the bathroom. I had also seen it a thousand times. Yet in the last two or three years of her life, Desreen's early-morning etiquette grew more refined. I think motherhood made her more of a morning person. She often leaped out of bed and ran the six-mile route to work or went to boot-camp classes in a freezing cold park with her friends. In fact, Jackson had rarely witnessed the often mean morning mood of his pre-mummy mummy.

That's why my breath was taken away some months after her death, when he suddenly adopted her disagreeable daybreak disposition.

'Morning, Jackson!' I said perkily, as he awoke.

He simply glared back with heavy eyes and said nothing – aggressively. Knowing my way around this particular temperament all too well, I understood that it was best ignored. I'd learned the hard way.

'Morning, Daddy, I'm awake now,' he would reply after a half-hour delay.

One morning Bev was there to witness this too and we found ourselves staring at each other, really quite speechless. It was as if Desreen had never left.

In a softer mood, Jackson would also mirror Desreen's wonderfully affectionate side. While minding my own business on the sofa, I would feel him nuzzle up, uninvited, and get comfortable in what his mum would call her 'nook' – a space wedged between my arm and my chest. Like her, he continued to eat soap suds in the bath despite my pleas to go cold turkey. And even his use of language reflected hers: his reply to the question 'What's wrong?' was always either 'Nuffin' or 'Just everyfin.' From everything I saw in him every single day his sense of humour, mischief and fun seemed entirely inherent.

Naturally, most people would indulge me as I consistently leaned towards nature as the dominant force. After all, how could someone who was no longer around nurture his phraseology?

An intelligent cynic was quick to offer a counter-argument. 'That's a very one-dimensional view of it,' Zac's mum Dot remarked one day, as we nattered in her kitchen. We were having a grief chat. She had gone through its mill when her daughter, Zoë, who suffered from manic depression, took her own life in 2000. 'You might not realise it but you probably positively reinforce his behaviour when he acts like Desreen.'

As a person who appreciates sentiment over sentimentality, that made a lot of sense to me. I thought about one morning over Christmas, just a few weeks after Desreen's funeral, when Jackson wouldn't stop throwing his breakfast from his high chair in Bev and Kelson's living room. I asked him to stop but he did it even more. I removed him from the room and suggested that he apologise otherwise he wouldn't be allowed back in.

'No!' he shrieked. 'I don't!'

At the time he hadn't yet learned the word 'won't', but I

speculated that he knew exactly what he was saying – that he used the word 'don't' because he meant it. His mother never said sorry, either. If she were ever in the wrong she would just stay silent. It could last hours, even days. Invariably I would have to apologise, just to get her to speak again. It drove me insane but at the same time it kind of made me laugh.

Just as I would have done with Desreen, I turned my back to Jackson to hide the smile on my face. I was telling him to say sorry but I was willing him not to. If he gave in to me I would be losing another piece of Desreen, and too many of them were already slipping away. I may have hidden my pleasure at his misbehaviour that time, but he was smart enough to be able to tell the difference between being in trouble for bad behaviour and being just troublesome enough to be behaving like his mum.

SUMMER

THAT'S LIFE

I learned a lot about myself in my first few months as a widower. Although I was under no pressure to be positive about life – in fact I had decided to let myself just be – I felt that there was one big thing that I could feel fortunate about. I'd finally figured out what life, in my eyes, was all about.

'What then?' my friend and colleague Daniella asked during a train journey from London to Nottingham as we headed to a work meeting in June 2013.

'Relationships,' I replied.

She looked down to the floor, slightly forlorn; she'd recently broken up from her long-term boyfriend.

'I don't mean two-people-together relationships. If I did then it would be game over for me already. I mean relationships with the people you love and who love you back. What I'm really trying to say,' I went on, 'is that we spend so much time planning to be happy in the future but what so many of us often mean when we say "happy", is wealthy. Our future is dictated by the prospect of some day having more: more material things to make ourselves, and maybe our kids if we have them, happier in the future – but not now, never now.

'Then we get there – we hit forty, fifty, sixty – and we're more comfortable than we were at twenty or thirty, but it's still not enough. The goalposts move. So "happiness" gets pushed further down the line – and then what? We retire and look back at our lives and realise we've never let ourselves achieve true happiness because we were too busy looking for it in all the wrong places.'

For years I had been a striver myself, but I had never felt much pain from losing the material things I coveted. I once lost a house I was trying to buy and got over it in a few days. And I can't even remember most of the things I once obsessed about having. If I did buy them they just became stuff and if I didn't, then it's telling that now I can't even think what they were.

Two days before that train journey I met another young widower for breakfast. We had never met in person before but we had chatted online through a private forum I'd set up for men who were suffering the way we were. All of a sudden two guys in their thirties were sitting opposite one another talking about our two-and-a-half-year-old sons, born just sixteen days apart, who, as yet, had no concept of materialism. And although naturally we were both devastated, we agreed that the one thing we were grateful for was that we finally had some sense of what life was all about.

Since we had both lost our wives, in equally sudden and tragic circumstances, neither of us was fortunate enough to be able to say we were happy anymore. But we agreed that we were more contented with what we had left than we would be if we were still aiming to 'have it all'. We were finally able to genuinely appreciate what we had in life. What each of us still has. And we agreed that neither of us would ever take for granted what might become of our lives.

As Daniella and I chatted on the train, I found myself talking about Jackson and what he had taught me about materialism.

'Kids don't want stuff,' I stated, aware of the sweeping nature of what I was saying. 'We make them want stuff. Kids want love. They want time. I've heard my son ask me to play with him so many times but not once have I ever heard him ask me for a pony. Perhaps the pony request only comes when our kids are craving love, affection and attention, but they've suddenly realised that it's not going to come from the parent who's too busy planning a happy future – just not a happy *now*, never a happy now.'

Before Desreen died, I was one of the lucky ones in life. I was happy the whole time. Together we aimed high, we too wanted more than we already had, but we would also have been happy settling for less so long as we were all together. Maybe I will be happy again one day, because I know that I will find that happiness in my family, my friends and my child. I understand that the pain of losing Dessie will never go away and I also understand that neither money nor material things could ever fill the gap her loss has left.

From here on in, relationships with the people I love will be my life's only measure of success. Everything else is just buyable, disposable, losable and highly replaceable stuff. And stuff, in my experience, rarely makes anyone very happy for very long. I'd choose love every time.

WHAT IF

What if we'd never left home that day,
What if we'd travelled a different way.
What if we'd gone by taxi not train,
What if we'd only had starter not main.
What if I'd worn pink and you'd worn blue,
Would I have been taken instead of you?

What if you and I had fought that day,
What if we'd both had cross words to say.
What if we'd spoken in anger not love,
What if I'd prayed harder to God above.
What if His attention were on me and you,
Would a different three now just be two?

What if you'd drunk red and I'd drunk white,
What if we'd played different music that night.
What if I'd been ill the day before,
What if we'd never walked out that door.
What if the street had a different name,
Would things have worked out just the same?

What if our horoscopes had said 'take care',
What if they'd told us 'don't go there'.
What if we'd both known something was wrong,
What if we'd both known all along.
What if we'd known we had just eight years,
Would four have been laughter and four have been tears?

What if the skies were yellow not blue,
What if you were me and I were you.
What if a butterfly hadn't fluttered its wings,
What if 'what ifs' could change these things.
What if 'what ifs' could make things right,
Would 'what ifs' have been there that night?

What if you and I had one more day,
What if I could do anything to make you stay.
What if our son could hold your hand,
What if we could help him understand.
What if the three of us could be back together,
Would I ever leave your sides? Not I. Not ever.

SAYING GOODBYE

In June 2013 I got a call from my mum telling me that her mum, my grandma, was really ill and didn't have a lot of life left in her. My mum was never going to say the words 'you need to come home immediately' because she appreciated that I had a choice. By this time I had been grieving intensely for seven months and, quite frankly, I wasn't sure if I could take any more. That was probably partly why I'd been home so little since Desreen died. Although I had known my grandma was becoming increasingly frail, my heart wouldn't allow the reality to sink in. It would cause me too much pain and I suppose we all have our limits.

When the call came, however, I knew what had to be done. I didn't get a chance to say goodbye to Desreen – one minute she was there the next she was gone – but that opportunity existed with my grandma. I just needed to muster the courage to make it happen before it was too late. I booked the train, and Jackson and I embarked on the journey from our new home in London to my family home in Southport.

My grandma had been suffering from pulmonary fibrosis, a scarring of the lung, which made it increasingly difficult for her to breathe. In her last few weeks she was well cared for and made as comfortable as possible in the incredible hospice where my mum had worked as a nurse for more than twenty years.

I was told to expect to see her looking very thin and fragile, but I just saw my grandma. Jackson and I arrived by surprise. We poked our heads around her room's curtain and casually said hello even though we hadn't seen her for months. She beamed from ear to ear. I beamed back. I had worshipped her from the moment I was born and Desreen adored her from the moment they first met. She made no bones about telling me that my grandma was her favourite member of my family. That was no surprise, because she was everyone's.

She was the woman who allowed me my first taste of gin and sneaked me a cheeky puff on a cigarette when I was much too young to know what to do with either. When my granddad went into hospital – where he would eventually die – in 1983, I hadn't yet started school. My grandma and I became really close. She would pick me up from nursery and ask me what I would like to do before my brothers finished school. Invariably I would ask her to take me to the pub for a steak and kidney pie; I was only four. As a child I loved spending time with her, talking, cooking, playing cards and board games and making up songs. And as an adult I loved to chat to her while indulging in our shared love for whisky, gin or sherry. I had always seen her not only as my grandmother but also as my friend.

When I leaned in to kiss her, Jackson, who was usually territorial about my affections, seemed confused. He sat on my knee and stared at his great-grandma lying in her hospice bed. Her conversation was met with raspberries, a terrible tongue-blowing habit that my son had learned from a Plasticine penguin called Pingu, and his favourite retort, 'You silly old bird,' which he picked up from a pet parrot in *Peppa Pig*. My grandma thought both were hilarious.

I was less sure. I tend to watch my son's behaviour obsessively for signs of distress or upset – I don't like to put him in situations that make him uncomfortable if they can be avoided. But this was different somehow. He seemed less troubled than he did puzzled. He just stared at my grandma with a heavy brow.

And then I realised that he had never before seen a person ill in bed. His stare turned to something like a look of empathy and he let out a huge sigh and lifted his T-shirt to reveal red spots on his stomach. 'I've had chickenpox,' he exclaimed glumly, in an attempt to trump her terminal illness with the faded souvenirs of his virus. We laughed so hard at my now healthy child seeking sympathy from a dying pensioner who was barely able to breathe through her chuckles.

It's hard to hold a heartfelt conversation with a person in other company. My parents were there and Jackson was busy trying to charm the hospice staff out of cakes and sweets usually reserved for the patients. So the next day I showed up alone.

'Hi, Grandma,' I said with a kiss. 'I've been thinking, we haven't had a moment alone to talk since Desreen died. In fact, we haven't had a moment entirely alone to talk in years.'

As an adult I only ever saw my grandma in the company of her husband, John (the man she married after my granddad died), Desreen and our family. Suddenly, knowing that she was dying, I wanted to get back to the times we had together when I was a child. I wanted my grandma to myself. We might not have been able to get to the pub for a pie and a pint, but we could catch up over cake and tea.

When Desreen died my grandma couldn't call me straight away. She was quite simply too devastated. Although she knew my wife the least well of her three granddaughters-in-law, they bonded immediately. Each had a keen eye for style and a strong taste for gin. They both loved me, too, which made it easy for them to get along. Des never called her anything but Grandma because that's who she was to her.

'Why did she have to die?' she cried down the phone. 'Why couldn't it be me instead? I've had my life and my body's broken. Why couldn't it just be me?'

Still in shock and still *being strong* I simply replied, 'Because it doesn't work like that, Grandma.'

Finally, seven months later, we were able to talk without the traumatic tears and without distractions. It wasn't until this moment that I realised that there had been someone close who could relate to my situation all along. My grandma was widowed in her late fifties. My granddad was a charming man who adored his ever-growing family. I'm unsure whether I remember him or whether my memories have been acquired from the stories shared by my family over the years, but it doesn't matter to me because when he comes to mind I feel as if I know him, I see his face and I hear his voice. And from everything I know about him, I've always admired the traits that made him the man he was: a sociable but discreet man who was talented and yet humble; generous and great fun; a loving husband, father and grandfather – all qualities that I consider worth aspiring to in life. My grandma and I spoke about him and Desreen and, for once, there were no apologies about drawing comparisons over our respective losses.

I told her how much Desreen loved her and we talked about our family. She was reflective, as you would expect from an eighty-seven-year-old woman who knew she didn't have long left, but she spoke of only one regret in her life.

'When you're a close family,' she began, 'you'll drop everything for one another. I regret that I couldn't have been there for you more.'

Given the quality of the conversation and the genuine

empathy and understanding she offered, I suddenly regretted not letting her, too. I imagine her words and insight could have helped me a great deal, but I was just too scared of watching her fade before me. She had been unable to travel for some time and I'd been unwilling.

'There's no point regretting,' I replied. 'You've always been there for me and I know you would have been even more if your body and I had let you. So let's agree to no regrets.'

As my grandma gasped for breath she told me about her favourite pair of slingbacks, which she bought when she was just a girl; how she was proud of the family she had created with my granddad; her views on death and grief; and she asked me what my plans were for the future. I realised something that had never really hit me before. She sounded just like me. Or rather, I sounded just like her. Listening to her outlook on life was like listening to the thoughts in my own head. But then I suppose she put many of them there; sowing the seeds that made me grow into me.

I remember her explaining to me how she saw life and death when I was probably no more than ten. She beckoned me over and asked me to take a good look at a pot plant on the window-sill in my parents' living room. It was in flower and a few of its leaves had fallen onto the soil and dried up. She pointed to the body of the plant itself and asked me to imagine it was her. She then explained that the flowers in bloom were the families she had created through her daughter and her son: my mum and my uncle. She turned the plant around and showed me a number of little buds that hadn't yet fully flowered. She told me that they represented my brothers, my cousins and me and that the reason they hadn't opened yet was because we had our entire lives ahead of us. She pointed to the dried leaves on the soil and explained that, one day, they would represent her. Her days as the roots and the stem of the plant would come to an end but she would live on through us by being taken back into the soil and feeding us through her old life.

She never once mentioned God or heaven. I think she simply believed that *she* was creation. That she had helped create our family and that the family that she had created would continue to procreate because of her creation.

It's hard not to think about what happens after someone you love so much dies. It's natural to look towards the spiritual because it's often too hard to accept that such important questions can't be answered. Maybe it's just too much for a person to accept that a loved one's end could be *the* end.

But when I look at my son there is one thing that I am clear on, thanks to that conversation with my grandma. His mum lives on in him. He is both her and me *because* we created him. I hope one day, when Jackson is desperate to have her back, he can take some form of comfort from this. When those days come around, thanks to my grandma, this is what I'm going to say:

YOU'RE HER

You're her,
You're me,
We're us,
We're we.
When three,
Then we,
Now two,
Still three.
I go,
No me,
You're here,

Still three.
In you,
Still we,
You're her,
You're me,
You're you,
All three.

For now, though, there was no need for such serious conversations with my son.

I nipped in to see my grandma one last time before Jackson and I returned to London. My mum had already warned me that it would be our final goodbye so I wanted to make sure that I cherished every moment with her. After briefly saying hello to his great-grandma, my son pulled me by the hand to a family room he had discovered, which was full of toys. As I set up a play kitchen and pretended to bake a cake, he lay down on the floor and kicked his legs into the air.

'Change me, Daddy,' he instructed.

'No, Jackson!' I exclaimed. 'Tell me you haven't.'

But I could already smell that he had, and I'd been caught out. For the first time ever I had left the house without the nappy bag. I knew that there was a supermarket a five-minute walk away but I also knew that I could neither leave a toddler smelling so bad in a hospice full of dying patients nor take him to a shop where people were buying food. I swept him up and took him to the toilet, hoping that the offending matter would be in a solid enough state to gently remove and flush.

Jackson didn't want to cooperate. He was more interested in pulling toilet roll from the holder on the wall than standing still. I tried to prevent him from wriggling but the more I tried the more he writhed.

'Oh bugger!' I said under my breath as my hand slipped into what had been his dinner the night before. He heard me.

'I'm not a bugger,' he replied.

'No, Jackson, you're not, and Daddy is very naughty for saying that word.'

'But I'm not a bugger, Daddy,' he went on. 'You're a bugger!'

I was mortified. Not only had I taught him his first swearword but I could imagine him leaving the little cubicle and telling my grandma that she was a bugger, too. Then I started to panic that he would also call the entire hospice staff the same name. And they all still worked with my mum. *Bugger!* I thought.

My grandma died on 8 July, two weeks after Jackson and I last saw her. For me this meant that, in a family dominated by men, I had lost two of the three most significant women in my life in less than nine months. This time was different, however, because I had the chance to say goodbye. I got to spend some really special time with her before she went, I saw her comfortable, perky, laughing and pulling her charming, gap-toothed smile, which she always asserted with such force that her nose would visibly move. She told me that she had never wanted to get the space in between her teeth fixed because it would remove all the personality from her face. She made the right choice. She was personality personified.

I had known my grandma was dying. I'd had weeks to process this and to come to terms with how I *thought* I felt. But then I suddenly didn't feel how I thought I felt. I had forgotten to heed my own words from the blog posts that I had been writing for months. I'd started to marginalise my grief, possibly because of my grandma's age and because she'd 'had a good life'.

The fact is, she had. She raised a wonderful family and I've never met a single person who didn't fall for her charms, her amazing sense of fun, her warmth and her outstanding dress sense (there was never a time I saw her out of pearls and heels). Having thought I had known how I would feel – that the worst possible thing that could happen to my life had already happened and that nothing could ever break my heart so badly again – I suddenly saw things from a different angle. I put myself in my son's little shoes.

The word 'grandma' conjures up an image for people, but sometimes that picture doesn't do these women justice. For Jackson, his grandmothers are now the key living maternal figures in his life. Desreen's mum is raising him every bit as much as I am. She is completely indispensable to the two of us. We both need her and we both need my mum, too. I started to think about that day in the future when Jackson has to tell his friends that his grandma or his nanny has gone. Sure enough, someone will offer him a platitude about her innings. But that won't be a day when Jackson feels that he has lost a grandmother; it'll be a day when he loses the closest thing he has had to a living mum since he turned two. And that's why I don't believe in making assumptions about how bereaved people, young or old, should feel or cope with loss.

Having considered my son's feelings, however, I did something that I'd been fighting against all year. I hid the pain I was in over my grandma's death and buried it deep inside. I decided to pretend it wasn't happening because I couldn't take any more upset. I told myself that I didn't have it in me to deal with the death of two women I love so much, at the same time. I suppose sometimes there's only so much one man can take.

Jackson, on the other hand, was much more open to facing what had happened to his great-grandma than me.

'Are we going to see Great-Grandma later?' he enquired out of the blue the day after she died.

'No, darling, we can't,' I replied. 'You see, she died and so she's gone away and can't ever come back.'

'Is she with Mummy in the sky?' he immediately asked.

'I do hope so, baby. I really do.'

PATERNITY LEAVE

The night Desreen was killed, I stopped crying for a moment, turned to Zac and said, 'Well that's my career in PR over.' I was in such a state of shock that my mind switched between rational and emotional thoughts with absolutely no sense of pattern. Although I wasn't really in control of my own faculties at that point, either physically or mentally, I suppose I just knew that it wouldn't be long before work lost its worth.

For two such busy working parents, I think we did a pretty good job. Desreen was big on equality and would reprimand me any time she thought that things weren't completely fairly split in the parenting stakes. I took a new job when Jackson was still a baby and negotiated flexible hours that would allow us to share all of our nursery drop-off and collection responsibilities. I was delighted with this arrangement. It meant that I actually got to spend time during the week with the son I adored so much, rather than just at weekends.

Desreen's expectations of an equal approach to raising our child also meant that I was as prepared as I could be to care for him after she died. It was my worst nightmare realised, but I definitely knew I could do the job because there was nothing she had learned that she hadn't taught me or that I hadn't taken the trouble to teach myself. Being my son's father after his mother's death was never what daunted me. Being a sole parent who worked too hard and who rarely had time for his now one-parent child, was.

Returning to my job had demonstrated that work no longer held any value whatsoever for me. Life insurance had afforded us the house that I otherwise would have been paying off for the rest of my life. I had some savings, enough to give me the freedom not to work for a couple of years, and besides, I needed much less money than ever before. Material things didn't mean anything to me without having Desreen there to share in them. Staying in a job that paid well financially but drained the only resource that now mattered to Jackson and me – time – seemed not only pointless but also wasteful and unfair to my son. I looked at our life ahead and realised that Jackson would start school in just over two years. At that point I would have no say in the matter: it would be a legal requirement for him to spend time away from me five days a week. I would never get the chance to spend all of my time with him again.

I remembered a brief argument Desreen and I had the night before she died. I had left work early that Friday afternoon to buy Jackson some new toy trains and Des had dashed home to see his face as he opened them. The two of them sat on the sofa playing as I reached for my laptop to send an email, which my company's finance team needed to receive before the end of the working day. I only had a few minutes left to get it out.

Desreen tried to strike up a conversation about something that I knew could wait.

'I'll be right with you, darling. I just have to send this email and I need to check the figures because it's late and so it can't be wrong.'

'Same old story,' she said. 'I want to talk to you now. That can wait.'

'It can't, but I'll be finished in five minutes so just hold that thought,' I replied as I finished what I was doing. 'Right, go on, I'm done,' I said a few minutes later.

'I don't want to talk to you now,' she insisted stubbornly.

'Don't be silly.'

'I'm serious; it's always the same. The only thing you care about is work.'

'That is ridiculous and you know it,' I snapped. 'The only reason I work so hard is to help secure our future. I would give it all up tomorrow if I could, it's not like I get any buzz from this, you know? Everything I really care about is in this room.'

She went quiet the way she always did when she knew I was right. Even if she were in the wrong, though, she always managed to make me think that every argument we ever had must have been my fault. It's a skill I have never witnessed in any other person before or since Desreen.

With the memory of that discussion ringing in my ears, I gave leaving work some thought, took financial advice and spoke to my family about my decision.

The same day that I decided I was going to resign, Bev arrived at our home to stay with Jackson and me. She had been considering her future too, and had some news she wanted to share.

'I've got something I need to tell you,' she began. 'I've decided I'm going retire early. I've been thinking about my life and I realise that, God willing, my place is now with Jackson. So I'm going to leave work to help you take care of him.'

'Same here,' I said. 'I'm jacking it all in for the next couple of years. It's my time he needs and not the stuff my salary can buy. So let's both do it together, because I'm sure he's going to need as much support as we can offer him. I'm sure we are, too.'

I think some people were quite horrified initially; it's not really the norm for a young guy to leave a successful career to care for a child, especially when he doesn't have a wife bringing in an even larger salary. I suppose the typical expectation of a father's role is to be a provider, even now. I decided it was more important for Jackson's father to provide the kind of care, attention and emotional support only a parent can offer, no matter how many other family members and friends are also around to help. I made the decision that felt right, emotionally, both for my son and for me.

I made up my mind for certain on the return journey to London after seeing my grandma for the very last time. Jackson played happily on my knee throughout the two-and-a-half-hour train journey home. Three middle-aged women sat next to us and chatted all the way. I was braced for them to ask Jackson where his mummy was, convinced they were wondering why I wasn't at work.

Jackson beat them to it. He picked up my iPhone and showed them the picture of Desreen I had as my screensaver.

'That's my mummy!' he shrieked adoringly, out of nowhere.

And that's my boy, I thought, my breath taken away by the pride he confidently showed in the parent he had not seen for seven and a half months, the parent he was starting to understand that he would never see again. My decision to spend all my time with him until he started school had never felt more right. I got off the train, navigated the pushchair containing my sleeping son plus three large bags through the crowds at Euston station, and walked straight to my office building to resign.

'When would you like to leave, ideally?' Mitch asked.

'Today?' I suggested, less than half joking.

'Perhaps we should give it until the end of the week,' he said, with a smile.

Two days later my phone rang while I was taking my final journey to work on the bus. The blocked number made me nervous because I thought it might be the police with an update about the case, which I'd been warned might take a very long time to resolve. My anxiety soon turned to dark humour, however, as the voice on the other end of the line revealed itself to be that of a call-centre worker from the Child Benefit Office, who suggested I should have made contact with her rather than the other way round, and that I should have done it in November.

Yeah, I thought, I had nothing else on my mind back then. What was I thinking?

I remained polite, answered her questions, thanked her for calling and went back to my journey to work. But I quickly became aware that there was no way that the people sitting around me hadn't heard what I had to say: that I was thirty-three, that I was widowed just a few months earlier and that my child was only two years old when his mother had been killed. I had spoken quietly but that often makes passengers on London buses listen with more intent.

When the chap sitting next to me got off the bus a couple of stops before me he passed me his mobile phone so that I could read a text message he had typed. He could see that I was wearing headphones and perhaps he didn't feel comfortable conveying this message to a stranger verbally. Not having experienced anyone sneaking me a gadget at the back of the bus since a school friend spelled out *BOOBIES* in numbers on his calculator when I was nine, I was unsure what was happening. His message read *Have a good last day at work and good luck*. That's all he wanted to say; ten little words that I thought said so much more about humanity than the sum of their parts.

And I did have a good last day. I had been considering my decision from the first moment I stepped back through the doors, four months after Desreen was killed. And I felt completely at peace with my conclusion when I left the building for the last time that Thursday afternoon at the end of June. But just the day before, Mitch had looked across from his desk to mine and asked me how it felt to be leaving behind the position I'd spent the last twelve years working towards. I surprised myself as I began to cry; I thought I had no reservations whatsoever.

'I've been telling people that I can't wait to get out of here, like a pregnant woman who's waiting to go on maternity leave,' I said through the tears. 'But it's yet another loss, isn't it? I've been in PR for even longer than I was in a relationship with Desreen and it's given us many of the great times we had together. I know I'm doing the right thing for Jackson and me, but if you think about it, it's just something else that has been taken from me in the whole mess.'

Adjusting to no longer going to work was much harder than leaving my job. I suppose the routine of going to the office every day and being accountable to employers and clients will, to some degree, institutionalise a person. I thought about the old guy in *The Shawshank Redemption* who was set free after decades in prison and how he couldn't cope with the outside world. I could empathise with the character's confusion about what came next. After two weeks and a day I realised it was the longest amount of time that I hadn't worked since I was twenty-one. For a while I joked that I was unemployed, but it was just a front for coming to terms with the fact that I was now a full-time father.

Thankfully I wasn't alone; Marianne was still on maternity leave with Lucia and Caroline was just about to give birth to her twins – the time had gone so quickly since she found out she was expecting, the day after Desreen's death.

I imagine many men would have felt deeply uncomfortable hanging out with their late wife's friends eating cake, drinking tea and talking about *The Three-Day Nanny,* but it was no big deal for me. I was already on great terms with Desreen's closest friends. Desreen, Jackson and I had been on holiday to Spain with Marianne, Olly and Annalise just three months before Lucia was born and Desreen died. We had also spent so much time together after she was killed that, at one point, Olly even told Marianne that he wished Jackson and I could move in with them. I had been in Marianne's company so much when I first met Des that it probably wouldn't even have felt all that strange.

Back then, Marianne was the third person in our relationship. She and Desreen were inseparable when I met my future wife. Much like my friends and me at the time, neither of them had been seeing anyone for a while so they spent most weekends together partying. And then suddenly I came along. In fairness to Marianne, she made me feel nothing but welcome. Although she was pretty much always there by Desreen's side, we got along really well. Ultimately, having her blessing was probably vital to keeping Des and me together. There was simply no way I would have lasted otherwise. Desreen and her friends were the 'Spice Girls' after all so I concluded that if I wanted to be her lover, I'd have to get with her friends. Either way, Marianne made it clear that she was here to stay.

'I've been thinking,' I said to Desreen just a few weeks into our relationship, 'that perhaps we could go up north one weekend and you could meet my family.'

'Yeah, I'll be up for that,' Marianne piped up, 'I love parents.'

'Oh, right, sure. You can come too, Maz,' I responded awkwardly, thinking that she must have been confused and heard it as an open invite.

'I ain't asking, Ben! I'm coming. What else would I do if Des wasn't here?'

And that's how it went. I met Desreen's parents for the first time and Marianne was there. I met her brother for the first time and Marianne was there (or at least she was in the next room, which was more appropriate given that I was in bed with Desreen at the time). And when Desreen died, Marianne was there along with all of the rest of my wife's friends and their partners. We supported one another through the pain and heartache and kept one another close.

As I ventured into a long-term paternity leave of sorts, I began to feel more comfortable about my son being exposed to the maternal company of friends, the kind of company he had all but rejected immediately after his mummy died. But I wasn't about to expose him to just any old girls; my son would first learn to trust his mum's best friends again and to eventually understand why she loved them all so much. Those same girls would continue to offer their patience and energy to their friend's only child and, one day, they would be able to help teach him about the incredible woman she was. He needed them to get to know his own mother better. And they needed him to ease the pain of her having gone forever. Desreen had some of the best friends a girl could ever ask for and one thing that she has helped me to understand is that true friendship is unbreakable and survives beyond death.

It wouldn't be long until I learned quite how challenging it is to care for a child full-time. I can only speculate how difficult it must be, even for one half of a happy couple to play this role with a child untouched by tragedy. I, on the other hand, only know the difficulties I suddenly faced in taking on the role while having to contend with a grieving toddler and a broken heart.

SMALL TALK

Sometimes I wonder if it's strange to pay so much attention to what a child of less than three has to say. I can't imagine I would have taken Jackson's comments as seriously had my wife not died so prematurely. In trying to make sense of both the exciting world around them and the new and unfamiliar words circulating in their own little heads, toddlers inevitably speak a lot of nonsense. But I did pay a lot of attention, because I longed to know how Jackson felt and what he was thinking, to find out whether he really understood what was going on.

You might expect that a toddler who had been without his mummy for the latter third of his own lifetime would cry out for his daddy when upset or in pain. After almost a year my son still called out her name first. You might think that her continued absence would make him understand that she was never coming back. After almost a year my son still showed continued signs of hope.

19 July 2013, eight months since Desreen's death: 'Mummy's coming to Grandma's house tonight, Daddy,' Jackson shared with me as I dressed him at my mum's house two day's after my grandma's funeral. 'She's coming in a aeroplane.'

12 August 2013, nine months since Desreen's death: 'Annalise, your mummy's out in the hall,' I told my friend's daughter at nursery one day. 'My mummy?' Jackson asked quickly.

13 August 2013: 'Who's your best friend, Jackson?' his carer asked him at nursery. 'Mummy,' he replied.

18 August 2013: 'Mummy likes this one,' Jackson informed me about a shirt that was bought as a gift *after* her death. 'She's coming to see me later.'

After the first six months I suppose I thought we had got there. As I've said, experts in child grief and psychology had told me that children couldn't truly grasp the concept of death or the finality of 'never' until they were around five or six years old. I, perhaps naïvely, thought that my son understood sooner than most. For once my optimism got the better of me. He was only two but I thought that because he could repeat my words, he had realised what they meant.

Toddlers daydream and play pretend all the time, so it's hard to separate what they really believe from childish fantasy or the delightful drivel they constantly speak. Reason should have told me to apply a little pinch of salt when listening to comments from a child who would tell me that he'd had a Tyrannosaurus rex wearing underpants over for a tea party 'last morning'. But reason isn't always the dominant force in grief. Hope can often be found sparring with it.

I should know: I've often been in the same position myself. I know my wife is dead: I saw it happen; I watched her die; I was handed her belongings in a clear plastic bag and then my confused and tired little boy and I were driven home by the police who were on the scene when it happened; I saw her lying in the chapel of rest at both the coroner's office and the funeral home; I gave her eulogy at her funeral and I committed her body to the ground. Yet hope often still trumps reason to get the better of my senses.

In July 2013, eight months after Desreen's death, I was on London's Regent Street shopping for something I never got round to buying. Hope swiftly stopped me in my tracks, took my breath away and prevented me from seeing straight. My phone rang and the caller ID read: Desreen Brooks. I froze. My body ran hot and cold simultaneously. My feet were rooted to the pavement but my head shook from side to side as I looked for her in the street, or for cameras, like it might be some kind of sick joke. It took me what felt like forever to realise what had happened. I had several telephone numbers for my wife stored in my phone: her mobile, her parents' house, a home landline that she never used and her office. Her business partner, Cathy, had just called me from the office. There was no way I could call back. I found myself standing on one of the country's busiest shopping streets feeling sick, shaking and crying my heart out. How could a death so sudden, so tragic and so pointless ever feel real? And if it was like that for a man of thirty-three, how could a child of two be expected to fully accept and understand his loss?

The week we moved into our new home at the end of May, Anthony, Desreen's brother, went to pick Jackson up from nursery. Rather than shoot straight for the exit when his uncle arrived, Jackson guided him into the room.

'Come,' he instructed Anthony, no doubt bossily.

Jackson wanted to share something with someone in the family but clearly not with me. His nursery had a piece of equipment that enabled toddlers, who couldn't yet fully express themselves in words, to attempt to share their moods in pictures. Jackson picked up an angry face. 'This is Mummy,' he told Anthony. Next he selected a sad face. 'This is Daddy.' Next he chose a happy face. 'And this is Jackson.'

Anthony told me about this shared moment some days later when we were alone in his car.

'That's heartbreaking,' I said. 'Why does he think she's angry?'

'Well, it makes sense, I suppose,' he replied. '"Mummy's gone away and can't ever come back",' he said, repeating the words I had asked everyone to learn for the sake of consistency for Jackson. '"She didn't want to go . . ."' he continued. 'I'm not surprised he thinks she would be angry about that.'

'I guess you're right. But I hate to think of him seeing me as so sad.'

'But you wouldn't want the order shifted in any way, would you? It's amazing that's he's still able to say he's happy, if you think about it.'

Seven or eight months after his mummy died, Jackson reached that age where two things started to happen. He suddenly *needed* things that, personally, I imagined he could quite comfortably have survived without: chocolate, Play-Doh, a new car. He *needed* them. He also started snitching. 'Annalise ran round the tree; Albie touched my train; Arlo's got my pink crayon.' Yawn! No one likes a grass, but they all do it. Little ones can be the best of friends and yet they simply can't wait to inform grown-ups about anything that might get the others in trouble.

The first time I noticed both of these things was the same day Jackson actively brought his mummy into the conversation for the first time in a couple of weeks. We talked about her a lot, every day, but usually I was the one who mentioned her first. As my son had little grasp of the concept of time, it was me who was preoccupied with keeping Desreen present and who kept a mental record of how long it had been since we last chatted about the woman we both love.

There was nothing extraordinary about the setting. We were alone, I was washing the dishes and he was playing with his trains. We had been with friends, mostly male, over the course of the May bank-holiday weekend, but some young mums had also popped up towards the end.

As I rinsed the plates I heard Jackson ask for his dummy. Except that wasn't what he said. His dummy was already hanging loosely in his mouth, like Detective Columbo's omnipresent cigar.

'I want my mummy back,' he said, out of nowhere.

'What did you say, Jackson? Take your dummy out,' I urged.

'Mummy loves me. Mummy's gone away.' Words he had now learned off by heart. 'I want to kiss Mummy. Mummy's far away in the sky. I want to go to the sky and kiss Mummy. Mummy *wanted* to go away.'

'No, Jackson, remember Mummy *didn't* want to go away. She loved you so much and she didn't ever want to leave you. But Mummy can't ever come back.'

'Mummy *wanted* to go away.'

I realised it was time for Jackson to know more. His speech had come on so much since the first time I told him what had happened and so I reasoned that his understanding had, too.

'Jackson, there was a nasty accident and Mummy was hit by a car.' I had decided not to hide the truth of what happened from my son after speaking with child bereavement charities about how to help children understand through sharing consistent messages.

'I don't want to be hit by a car, Daddy.'

'No, Jackson, and I don't want you to be either, which is why we always have to be very careful and look both ways when we cross the road.'

'But I want to kiss Mummy.'

'Well then, we can.'

The week before this conversation I had put a large picture up on the kitchen wall of Desreen and Jackson kissing one another on holiday in Spain just three months before she was killed. I suggested that Jackson kiss that.

'Ah! It's Jackson kissing Mummy!' he exclaimed happily as if he had never seen the photo, with which he was already so familiar.

He leaned in and kissed her picture. Then he kissed his own. Then he kissed me and squeezed me tightly.

The next morning Shelley Gilbert, the founder of child bereavement charity Grief Encounter, called to invite me to an event. I told her what had happened.

'It's interesting that he used the word "want",' she told me.

Her words immediately triggered a thought that made total sense of the confusion I was feeling.

'He didn't say *need*,' I interrupted. 'He's started saying he *needs* everything but last night he *wanted* his mummy – there's a massive difference. I *want* her too but I know that I can't have her. Perhaps I should try to take some comfort in the fact he's no longer saying *need*.'

Whether he said 'want' or 'need', I would still feel like shit because I couldn't give him what he was hoping for. But our situation has forced me to give up on the idea of striving for the impossible. I have gradually come to terms with the idea that I'm just going to do my very best for my child, as the surviving parent. Sometimes that's tough. Sometimes he knows when I'm sad. And sometimes when I'm at my lowest point he is also at his, making life feel almost unbearably testing. Discipline can be hard because I don't want to upset my son, knowing how much happiness he has already been deprived of, but the consequences of running from it entirely would be too trying to take.

I don't think it's possible to be a perfect parent. I think it's even harder when *perfect* has been taken from your life. And I think it's even harder still when your child suddenly starts to articulate his own pain by mixing the language of an adult with the innocence and confusion of a child.

'I'm so worried, Daddy,' my son once told me when he was writhing around my bed tormented, panicked and with a soaring temperature brought on by the chickenpox. 'What about, Jackson?' I asked, flustered more by the sudden maturity of his concerned voice than his controllable body heat. 'Me,' he replied.

'It hurts, Daddy,' he said a few weeks later, without any previous indication that anything was wrong. 'What does, darling?' I probed. 'Jackson,' he responded, repeating the same sentiment.

Each time he took my breath away with how precisely he had articulated how I also felt about myself. And each time he made me wonder if perhaps we were both riddled with the same kind of agony and anguish and were simply unable to express it in the same way.

When my wife died I realised quickly that there would always be pain in our home. It will no doubt come and go in unpredictable and intermittent waves. But as long as there is also love in that home, I suspect the two of us will be okay. However tough it gets I'll remind myself of something Jackson said to me the week my grandma died. After acting out a colossal tantrum in the park by my parents' house, I asked him if he was ready to be friends again. 'Don't be silly, Daddy!' he replied. 'We're always friends.'

HEAVENLY LOVE

It's easy to ask 'Where was God?' or 'How can there be a God?' when the mother of a young child is struck down in their prime. But neither are questions I ever asked myself. In fact I turned *to* God rather than away from Him when my wife was killed. Only I didn't really turn to 'Him'; I've never really bought into the part that says God made man in the image of Himself. I find it too hard to believe that creation came from a Wizard of Oz type controlling us all by pulling levers from behind a celestial emerald curtain. And I find it too incredible to believe that an omnipotent power would simply look like a man. I think that I believe in God as an indescribable force, an incredible power, an almighty energy and the stimulus that leads to creation.

Desreen and I married in a church. Her mum has always had faith and she instilled it in her daughter. Desreen was not devout, she took her religion with a pinch of humour and joy. She loved what she called her 'church songs' and would often walk around the flat in nothing but her knickers cleaning, vacuuming, arranging flowers and rearranging furniture while singing hymns in an mock-operatic tone.

There is a flag flying high from the castle of my heart,
From the castle of my heart,

From the castle of my heart.
There is a flag flying high from the castle of my heart,
For the King is in residence there.

When she died I turned to prayer. I searched my own mind but I couldn't find the words, so I bought a Bible and a book of prayer to help. I sought out churches – I couldn't walk past one without going in. I said prayers at bedtime with Jackson and I often talked about God with Bev. I prayed for guidance on how to best care for my son. I prayed for the courage and fortitude I knew I would need just to keep going. I prayed for my wife to have a soul and for that soul to be at peace. I prayed for her wonderful qualities to be imparted to Jackson and me and not to be squandered into the ether. And I prayed for her memory to live on through us. But I never asked God to bring Desreen back to me in some ghostly form. A lifelong interest in religious history, coupled with a cynicism around miracles and life after death, left me unconvinced that it would be the best use of my almost nonexistent energy.

Despite praying, I was still struggling to make sense of my own beliefs. I felt that in a world full of pain and war – a world where people die unnecessarily all the time – it was too insular to isolate the question about just one death, however significant it was to me. I could find no reason for Desreen to have been taken so young. If I were ever to reach any conclusions I would have to consider a broader question: why do some people die so tragically and so young?

Although I don't imagine that God looks like a man, I had to distil Him into some sort of image in order to be able to process my own thoughts. So I made Him the CEO of a massive corporation. Suddenly that made me think that God, our ultimate boss, may have a big strategic plan for the universe but that He can't be everywhere at the same time. Or that perhaps part of Him can, but that His energy is most concentrated in certain points at certain times. God – or the CEO version of God – has His hands full. Those same hands are perhaps often tied up with His exec and non-exec roles across the whole universe. Maybe He's put us here to help run the company – to take care of the day-to-day stuff. Like all CEOs, he makes mistakes and His staff make some for Him, too. And then shit comes along: earthquakes, fire, disease, even out-of-control cars. Some of it is natural and unavoidable, some of it is planned and evil, and some of it is entirely inexplicable and perhaps the reasons behind it will forever remain unanswered.

While I searched the heavens for answers, Desreen's dad, Kelson, an engineer and keen gardiner, turned to nature for his metaphors.

'Sometimes you have a beautiful sunflower,' he said as he looked from his living room to his own perfect back garden. 'It's stronger than the rest, more beautiful and you show it so much care. But then one day a gust of wind comes and takes it down in its prime. The rest of the garden continues to grow and thrive, but it will never feel the same. It'll never look as complete. And you'll never forget its beauty.'

Few people [illegible] such a simple sentiment that also made so much sense of the why? question. Sadly I believe the answer to that is simply *just because*. Seeking any other resolution is to tackle questions that are possibly bigger than man. And if we found the answers, would we be any happier for it? I'm not sure.

My wife hasn't gone to a better place, because the place she loved the most was right by her son's side with her husband, friends and family looking on. If she is somewhere else, maybe she's struggling even more than us because she's been separated from the people she loves and misses us desperately. And if it's true that she is still with us, then I prefer to think of her living *through* us rather than being behind some sort of glass wall. She gave us so much love, laughter, charisma and personality when alive that I suspect that her energy and legacy will continue long after her death.

That said, sometimes I can practically hear her telling me to 'put that bitch down' when a girl who I haven't seen for a while gives me a hug to say sorry for my loss. Seeing Jackson happy in the company of other women, be they family or friends, can also deliver a crushing blow, leaving me feeling as if I'm cheating on my wife by allowing them to share his affections.

On Sunday 28 July 2013, we held a church service for Jackson. John, the vicar who conducted both our wedding ceremony and my wife's funeral service, also christened our son. The three most monumental events I have ever attended and all in the space of less than two years. Just one week shy of two years in fact, it would be our second wedding anniversary the following week.

In church that day I was confused when I looked around and saw so many people in tears. I was on the front row smiling at my son as he sang the words to 'Old McDonald Had a Farm' along to the hymns sung by the rest of the congregation. I laughed as he stood to interrupt the vicar's sermon with an update about what he had done at nursery the week before. And I felt happy to see a little boy so full of life despite having to deal with such a monumental death so young.

It wasn't really until after the service that I grasped why so many people were so upset. The last time we were in such a setting, we were burying my wife. I have lived with the pain every minute of every day and need no reminders to be easily transported back to that time and place. So while others were perhaps reminded of Desreen's funeral and suddenly distracted by their own grief, I absorbed every moment of my son's special ceremony.

'We can't know what God looks like,' John said, striking a chord with my own belief. 'But we do know one thing – God is love. And whoever does not love does not know God, because God *is* love.'

Suddenly it all became clear. I believe in love. Losing the woman I love is what has hurt me so much. Still loving that same woman and wanting to honour her memory has made me want to carry on. Loving the son whom we created through love is what makes me continue to live with love in my life. And so if God were simply love and love is what I fell to my knees and prayed to when my wife died, then it all makes sense to me.

I believe in love, because love is with me every day through my family, friends and my son and because, although Desreen was taken from us with no warning or explanation, her love lives on in me and always will.

LOVE REIGNS

Lost that bitter winter's night,
Searching balmy summer days for you,
Beams of light from a sunset sky
Illuminate you in his radiant face.

Hope whispers tender words of warmth,
'The light's her kiss upon his cheek.'
Cold comfort makes me shiver,
'Hope's signs are not enough.'
Crashing thunder resounds your loss;
Silent lightning strikes my soul.

The winds of change blow fiercely,
Our landscape shattered beyond control.
This storm's path cannot be stopped,
There's nothing we can do.
There's just one tempest we can power,
And so our love rains down on you.

MISSING DESREEN

It took me months to realise that I had been doing everything in my power to stop myself from truly missing Desreen: going back to work, writing, moving house, exercise – I did it all almost obsessively, as a means of diverting my attention from her physical loss. Perhaps that's why I found it so hard when I tried to talk to her; the one-way conversations made me feel like a fool but they also just hurt too much. I would visit her grave and stand in silence feeling a sense of total disbelief that she had gone. The cemetery where she was buried held no sense of history for us and so I have never been able to feel any sense of her presence there.

In London, however, it's a different matter entirely. Soon after Desreen died, I sent Mitch a text to explain how hard it was to travel back into central London. I suppose I wanted him to understand that it wasn't just going to be a challenge to re-establish myself at work, but that everything around it was going to be difficult too: the commute and the memories it would bring back along the way; not being able to break the habit of reaching for my phone to update my wife on my latest news, achievements or frustrations from the day.

The day I sent Mitch the text I had passed a theatre Desreen and I visited on her birthday to watch the musical *Billy Elliot*, years earlier. I remembered how she laughed a couple of seconds after everyone else because she didn't get the jokes and because she didn't understand the northeastern accents. Something that once made me smile now stabbed at my heart. I passed the big blue door she used to live behind in Bloomsbury and I cried. I drove past a restaurant we both loved and I physically ached.

'There are just too many memories everywhere,' I said to Mitch, 'I don't think I'm going to be able to handle it.'

I found myself avoiding parts of the city we both loved: Brick Lane because it was where Desreen had started her business just months before she was killed; Stoke Newington because it was the first place we moved in together; Barons Court because it's where I lived when we first met. She always loved to come to that flat on Sundays because we had carpets rather than floorboards, which made her feel cosy and helped heal her hangovers from Saturday night.

But as the months flew by I began to feel differently. One day in September, as I found myself back in Barons Court to meet a friend, I noticed an involuntary smile reach my lips and eyes. A little memory of the two of us walking hand-in-hand came to mind and, for once, it made me happy rather than sad. I had finally started to see things differently – I was grateful that we had really lived it up in London and that I was left with wonderful memories absolutely everywhere. I hadn't talked myself into this; I wasn't trying to make myself more positive, it just happened. And so I smiled and enjoyed the moment.

In the weeks that followed her death I thought I would never feel this way. Back then it wasn't clear enough to the whole of my mind that Desreen was in fact gone forever. I knew it was a fact but it hadn't penetrated into every part of my consciousness. This meant that I would often, if only for the briefest of moments, forget that she was dead. This happened to me most whenever I went shopping at her second home, Liberty. Spending money there was Desreen's favourite pastime; she loved buying and receiving gifts that came in the department store's signature purple bags. After she died I occasionally went in to buy someone a present from the homes and interiors departments on the third or fourth floor and ended up inadvertently passing womenswear on the first. I would see something that I knew she would have liked and react by picking it up to check the price. I could imagine how excited she would have been if I surprised her with a Liberty bag left in the hall. And then my heart would sink. It was just a little high caused by a trick of the mind, followed by a crashing low.

Sometimes, however, these feelings of devastating realisation were worth it. At least I had felt a momentary sense of contented togetherness with my wife. It occurred to me just how much I would miss buying things for her. I would always miss seeing the joy on her face as she unwrapped anything tied in pretty ribbon. I would miss the emails she sent me listing some of the 'small things' that I might like to consider buying her for her birthday, which invariably cost a minimum of two or three hundred pounds, even if we were meant to be saving. I would miss having someone who loved my gestures as much as she did.

And so I carried on making them: I kept buying Desreen's favourite flowers and stems – a mixture of roses, eucalyptus, thistles and clematis – for the house, knowing in my heart that I was still buying them for her; I read through a folder she kept, which included her interiors inspirations, and then bought the sofa she wanted for our next home and chose the colours I knew she would have loved for the walls; I even continued to eat fish fingers in her memory, though I had never really liked them when she was alive.

When missing Desreen finally began to feel okay – okay to

start to grieve the wife and not just the life I had lost – I turned to writing once more. I still couldn't bring myself to talk to her, so I decided to try to write her letters and poetry instead.

Dear Desreen,
I'm writing to ask for forgiveness. I've just done something that I can barely excuse. I've closed your loyalty card at Liberty. And the store has seen few customers as loyal as you. I half expected to be escorted back onto Regent Street by security or for the walls around me to creak in despair, fearful for their own future as their biggest fan apparently turned her stylish back on the indulgent emporium of fashion, furniture and fabulous fabrics. Yet in a manner typical of the delightfully professional staff who work in this oasis of calm in London's hectic West End, the assistant simply smiled, actioned my request and took your name off its books.

You see, Jackson and I have just moved house. I've changed our address on all the utility bills and it's now increasingly rare that post shows up in your name. Letters from Liberty have still been coming, but I thought perhaps it was time they stopped.

I went to the store back in December and asked them to change the surname on my account. Jackson and I had just taken your surname and added it to ours. But I couldn't bring myself to end your relationship with the store at that point. You bought stationery in there with no more reserve than a schoolgirl buying protractors, pencil cases and Post-its in WH Smith at the end of August on her mum's credit card. 'Oooh, bargain!' you would say when a greetings card cost £6. 'What are you thinking?' you once said angrily when the sales assistant told you they had only made small Liberty diaries that year. 'What am I supposed to do now?' you continued, enraged as if she were personally responsible.

As vacuous and shallow as it may sound, you're everywhere in there for me. We bought your wedding ring there. You only wore it for a month before you died because it took us the whole year after we married to find the right one. Now it sits on my left hand next to mine, white diamonds next to black making me look a little like an overindulged medieval king. You bought Jackson's nappy bag there. Yes, only you, darling: a Marc Jacobs nappy bag, a designer bag to carry everything necessary to keep your little prince's bottom clean. You dressed him in clothes you bought there, too. You pretended you didn't, but the day your friend told you they were opening a children's department I actually thought you were going to ask to move in. You bought everything there. It was Tesco to you. You would tell me not to be so crass, saying that, but it's such a big part of why everyone loved you so much. It was quite simply your shop.

So when letters addressed to you in Liberty envelopes continued to be delivered to our home, they made me smile. I like to imagine you looking down on us from time to time, just not when the sales are on or when your celestial postman passes you the latest Liberty catalogue through the pearly gates (if you haven't already had them fashioned into a new jewellery line). But I'm scared when I'm there too. I worry about seeing people you knew. I panic about bumping into the guy in menswear who always recognises our little boy and asks, 'Is your lovely wife not with you today?' I wonder how

I'll feel when I have to explain. I wonder how he'll react when he has to hear what I have to say.

I go there nonetheless. I go there to be with you. I see things you would love and feel sad that you've already missed out on two seasons that would have filled you with so much pleasure and joy. I find it hard to imagine anyone looking as good in any of the clothes they sell as you, or any of the candles smelling as nice as they would in the house you always made our home.

So I'm saying sorry, but I had to do this because the fashion seasons have started to make me feel a little sad. Time feels as if it is passing by so quickly. They tell me how long it has been since I saw you last when I don't even need to ask. So I know you would understand but I would still fully expect you to be a little cross.

And it's with that in mind that I took the liberty to purchase something from Liberty while I was there today.

Remember your dad asked for a Ming vase for Christmas and we laughed at the thought of going to Sotheby's to splash £14 million on a gift? Well, I figured two things out: 1) that he must have no idea what a Ming vase actually is and 2) that he would have loved a *minging* vase if you had bought it for him.

You were all about Moroccan ceramics in your final months. In fact you were taking me to Marrakech for my birthday so I could buy some for you (your logic was a strange but beautiful thing). So when I spotted a handmade pot from the country you had fallen for, even though you never actually got the chance to visit, I knew it was for him and I knew it was from you.

So forgive me for the account, but I promise to look after your parents and I promise to keep Liberty open through my custom. Where the hell else would I go to be with you now that we've moved house?

Love, Benji xx

MISS YOU

Miss Confident
Miss Shy
Miss Fun
Miss Hilarious
Miss Loving
Miss Loved
Miss Organised
Miss Inspiring
Miss Strong
Miss Fragile
Miss Generous
Miss Loyal
Miss Fashion
Miss Style
Miss Beautiful
Miss Happy
Miss Naughty
Miss Mischievous
Miss Sleepy
Miss Modest

Miss Passionate
Miss Polite
Miss Abrupt
Miss Inappropriate
Miss Kind
Miss Brilliant
Miss Party
Miss Home
Miss Business
Miss Brave
Miss Considerate
Miss Headstrong
Miss Positive
Miss Successful
Miss Wonderful
Miss World
Miss Mummy
Miss Wife
Miss Brooks until the end
Miss you x

AUTUMN

ANGER MANAGEMENT

Desreen would have loved the summer that followed her death. She was always happier when the sun was shining and I don't remember the last time it shone so brightly or so often in London. It made me sad that she was missing out but the good weather also eased my pain, if just a little. The distinct shift of seasons helped me to separate myself emotionally from what had been a tragic and seemingly endless winter. But regardless of how much the sun shone, I knew that the dark nights, grey days, and the wet and cold weather would return before too long. And when they did I feared they would undo me by evoking the painful memories of losing Des the year before.

The idea that all good things must come to an end was once a cliché that I fought against. I used to refuse to go to bed after a night out because I never knew when to stop enjoying myself (a character trait that I picked up from my dad, often to my mum's irritation). I believed that relationships had the potential to improve with time and I used to look forward to growing old with my wife, at least partly because I knew I would always see her as the most beautiful woman in the room. But I learned the hard way that things do eventually – and sometimes abruptly – come to an end. So as summer faded, my mood grew heavy.

Perhaps Jackson felt the same as me or maybe he was just sensitive enough to notice the change in my disposition. Either way, his temperament fluctuated more abruptly than mine; he grew angry, angrier than I had ever seen a child of his age. Not having the matching lid for one of the pans I had already asked him not to play with, or being unable to find the exact piece of Lego that he insisted he *needed* would leave him incensed and enraged. Once tipped over the edge, his rage would become frenzied – he wanted to hit or bite me and the more I tried to stop him, the more he lashed out. When I tried (and ultimately failed at) the comforting or disciplinary techniques that I learned from TV shows presented by calm and collected nannies (which once left me feeling sorry for the challenging children's parents) he grew incandescent. He would try to push me away, lash out and scream and shout but with so much intensity that, once or twice, I feared that he might fit.

Each time this happened I felt like a complete failure as a father. Sometimes I had to leave the room and just allow Jackson to wear himself out. On certain occasions I could think of nothing else to do but hand him over to Bev, if she was around. I felt beaten and as if I were letting both him and myself down. But I remembered a promise I had made to myself soon after his mum died: I was going to try to see what most people call tantrums as an outlet for his grief. When faced with a toddler who seemed more akin to a Tasmanian devil than a child, this proved to be a challenging commitment to uphold. Had each outburst not ended in him exhaustedly crying out or whimpering for his mummy, I might even have accepted that, as everyone was so keen to reassure me, he was just throwing paddies, like any other kid of his age.

'They all go through this,' 'you just need to be firm with him,' 'it's really nothing to worry about,' 'he's no different to other children' – all things I kept being told, which served no purpose other than to make me cross, too. How could anyone with any degree of sensitivity say that he was no different to any other child? He was the only two-year-old I had ever met who had already lost a parent, and to me it went without saying that his loss had affected his behaviour and ability to feel sure that those around him wouldn't suddenly disappear, too.

Dismissing the platitudes once more, I set about trying to explore what I could do to actually help my son rather than simply brushing the issues under the carpet of grief. The first thing I did was turn to my blog. Ever since I published my first post I had been flooded with information, expertise and empathy from generous-spirited readers. All sorts of people got in touch to offer insight into how I might best support Jackson through his loss: child bereavement charities, play therapists, clinical psychologists, counsellors, teachers, doctors, nurses, the list goes on and on. I suspected that my new cry for help would not go ignored. In an online space that gave people permission to be open and honest about the many issues surrounding bereavement, grief was rarely marginalised. And few of my posts prompted more responses and debate than the one that detailed Jackson's increasingly volatile behaviour.

You are not alone. I lost my husband when my son was two and my daughter nineteen months old. Their tantrums open the door for brief insight into their inner grief and always end in sobs for their daddy – my daughter not as much as my son. We've been going for play therapy to help him to better understand death and grief, but we only started when he was four and a half. Prior to this he was too little to understand, so all I could do was weather his storms. Even his new teacher needed help to understand that he doesn't have anger management and impulse control issues the way other kids do. Well, he may have, but layered on top of that is him having to deal with complexities and sadness that no child should have to face, or can face, alone.

At two years old, who can tell what goes on his head? Unfortunately, though, you will be his punchbag from now on. My eleven-year-old daughter lashes out at me since losing her mother last year. This can be over the simplest of things but when they blow up, boy do they blow up! Jackson will need an outlet for his anger and frustration and that outlet will be you. And not because he is actually angry with you, but because he will know that he is safe to lash out at you without fear of repercussion. If he is anything like my daughter, the tantrums will very quickly turn into moments when all he wants is a good cuddle from his dad, and this will be enough for him to realise that you are not angry in return. Experience has taught me that you need to weather the storm for a while, and you'll come out the other side okay. It won't be nice at times, but I'm sure the pair of you will be fine.

I have heard my shrink give advice on this to others: 'Hold the child tightly, tightly, tightly. Even if he struggles against you, he wants to feel safe and loved and held, even if he can't have his mum. A strong, safe embrace to reassure him that there is something he can count on in the world will go a long way.' I also would guess he'd advise you to validate his feelings: 'I know, Jackson, you're so angry, Mummy can't come back and it makes you so angry. Mummy loves you but she can't come back, and it is so upsetting. It's so sad.' I think the urge of most people is to try to get kids to move past the feelings, when they really need to feel them and be told that feeling them is perfectly fine. The 'cheer up and look on the bright side' crew has a lot to answer for, though they know not what they do.

My husband is a clinical psychologist and I have just picked his brains. He suggested that you should perhaps review the systemic reason for the tantrums, as they are usually an emotional response to an unmet need, whatever that may be.

I let all the comments sink in, but I took the last one on board immediately. I asked myself, what are the triggers? I traced things back to the first time that Jackson really lost control. We were staying at Lee and Olive's house in Leeds for a week and we had already been there for five days by the time their son, Albie, had his fourth birthday party. Jackson had behaved really well all week. Being in the constant company of a child a whole year older than him made him eat better, sleep better and even toilet train better – he could barely wait to show everyone what a 'big boy' he was when it was time for the loo. Sadly for my friends' garden, however, the loo tended to be either their apple tree or their decking – something we only tended to notice mid-flow.

That morning lots of children from Albie's nursery began to arrive. I was watching Jackson from a distance, concerned about how he might respond to being one of the only children attending without his mother. He looked annoyed. He joined the others for a picnic in the garden – hygienically set several metres from both the tree and the decking that Jackson had recently made his latrines – but he ate crossly. And when it came to playtime, he just didn't want to play nicely. A sweet little girl with bunches dared to touch a wooden banana, which, though strictly speaking belonged to Albie, Jackson had claimed as his own due to the fact he had been playing with it for most of the week.

Things were just about to turn ugly when I intervened, took away the carved fruit and removed him from the situation before Jackson attempted to remove a pigtail. This prompted a meltdown of epic proportions. There were screams and convulsions, and four little limbs – which seemed more like eight at the time – each made their way angrily towards my face. And the entire time he shrieked just one word, painfully, over and over: 'Mummy!'

Taking something away that Jackson wanted triggered the next two angry incidents, too. One episode began in our kitchen when I retrieved a glass pan lid that he had removed from a cupboard, and the other when I snatched his scooter away because he was racing dangerously fast and wouldn't stop when asked. Being a parent will often make you paranoid about your child's safety. Being a parent who watched his wife killed by a car and only just managed to avoid his son meeting the same fate has only served to intensify my fears for Jackson's wellbeing. But of course, as a two-year-old, he had no real appreciation for my concerns – only displeasure if my worries interrupted his own will. Both times he went absolutely crazy and I had never felt less in control as a parent.

The triggers for his anger, or 'the systemic reasons for his tantrums' as the blog reader put it, seemed to be seeing other young children with their mums and having something that he wanted removed from him.

A couple of weeks after Albie's party I decided I needed to do more than just worry and speculate over Jackson's behaviour, and so I took him to a weekend retreat for children who had lost a parent, which was organised by Grief Encounter. I suppose, naïvely, I wanted my son to meet older bereaved kids who could tell him that it was all going to be okay one day. It wasn't until after we returned home that it occurred to me that they would probably have had no need to attend if they were feeling fine.

Jackson made an immediate impact. As the youngest attendee by some margin, he was showered with affection. I suppose, on first impression, he was just a cute little bundle of long curly hair and big brown eyes. But then came the introductions. Adults and children alike each had to introduce themselves and state whether or not they were happy to be there.

As the first person tried to speak, Jackson interrupted with a shout. 'No! Just stop it!' The ice in the room was broken as everyone erupted with laughter at this huge angry voice coming from such an angelic-looking child. 'It's not funny!' he responded even more angrily, which made everyone laugh harder still.

Everyone except me; this kind of display of rage was why I was there. What seemed endearing and playful to most of the other people present was one of the main reasons that I felt I was underperforming as a parent.

I came down to his level and sat on the floor. Everyone else was standing, towering above him and I realised that this might be making him feel insecure. I cuddled him and whispered in his ear that he could do anything he wanted while we were there. I told him that he could scream and shout, and do whatever he needed to help show us all exactly how he was feeling. I appreciated that otherwise he, more than most of the other guests there, was going to have trouble articulating himself.

That night we sat around a campfire with other children and parents and Jackson managed to break the ice once more. I'd met a young Jamaican mum who was there with her daughter, who was about six. 'Daddy, I'm tired now,' Jackson told me for the first time in his sleep-resistant life. 'Can I take that girl to bed?' he added, pointing to the little girl four years his senior who looked strikingly like his mother when she was a child. I could picture Desreen's face displaying a confused look of pride and horror as she realised that her son had got his first Caribbean crush and that at only two years old, his pursuits were moving way too fast.

Jackson started to develop a cold and he coughed and fidgeted all night in the bed that we shared. As I lay awake I thought about how it felt to be there. I realised that I had grown so concerned for Jackson that I had almost separated myself from the issue. Although both adults and kids attended the retreat, its primary focus was on the children's bereavement rather than the parents'. Perhaps it would have been nice to spend more time chatting to the other widowed parents on our first night, but that evening I had a completely one-track mind – my only concern was Jackson's wellbeing. I couldn't take my eyes off him; I was monitoring his behaviour at all times and so I found it really difficult to make time to talk to the other adults about what I was going through as a bereaved husband.

The next morning, however, Jackson was put into a group with other young children for therapeutic play. And so I, along with some of the other parents, attended a kind of group counselling session, which would encourage us to think about ourselves and not just our kids. This took me by surprise but I welcomed the chance to share my feelings with people who seemed to understand what I was going through, but it was hard to listen their stories. I draw very little comfort from knowing that others are suffering too and some people appeared to be facing the most unthinkable challenges.

When I returned, Jackson was alone with the charity's founder, Shelley. His cold was getting worse and he just wanted to cuddle up to me; as he did, he fell asleep in my arms.

By this time Shelley and I had met on several occasions and spent a considerable amount of time together discussing some of life's most sensitive issues. Now a mum of four, Shelley set up Grief Encounter after losing her mother at the age of four and her father at nine. More than anyone else I've met, she understands how the loss of a loved one can have profound effects on children. I was relieved finally to have found someone who would cut through all the bullshit and who wouldn't try to reassure me that one day everything would be rosy again.

As Jackson slept I explained to Shelley why I'd brought him

there and I talked her through the triggers I'd identified that made him go mad.

'He was just going so fast,' I explained about Jackson on his scooter that day, 'and he wouldn't listen to me warning him to slow down or stop and so I took it off him. I just cut it dead.'

'Interesting use of words, Ben,' she responded. 'He loves his scooter, doesn't he? And something else he loves was abruptly taken from him, wasn't it?'

I nodded and took it in. Perhaps he was feeling a disproportionate amount of anger about having things taken away from him because of the sudden loss of his mum. I still don't know what the hell a parent in my situation is supposed to do to keep a child like mine safe from physical harm and emotional distress at the same time, but I knew at that moment that I had to accept that I was playing a role in his upset and confusion – that perhaps my response to his behaviour was making it even worse. But I was angry, too. He'd lost his mum and I'd lost my wife and we were both angry together, which no doubt occasionally made us poor company for one another. If he snapped, I snapped and if I did, he would. I guess you could speculate that we were fuelling one another's fire. As the adult in the relationship, however, I knew that I would have to be the one to try to make some adjustments.

I had changed my doctor because the very first time I visited him after my wife was killed I knew that he would never take a child's grief seriously. I explained to the new GP that I wasn't looking for a box of pills to fix my son and that I wasn't expecting him to have all the answers, but that I wanted a referral to someone who might actually know the right questions to ask. Within less than a week I got what I was hoping for: a phone call from my new doctor explaining the research that he had done on our behalf, an explanation about what would happen next and an indication that my son's mental wellbeing would be taken seriously by the relevant clinical bodies.

While seeking advice from those more learned than me, I also tried to find ways to teach myself to be a calmer parent. I thought about the hypocrisy of shouting at a child to tell them not to shout; it didn't make sense that I was asking him not to get annoyed when I was also clearly short-tempered. I started to train myself to spot the signs that indicated his mood was about to turn and then to divert his attention to something else. I began to better understand when to reach out for a cuddle and when to leave him well alone. Some days he would strip himself naked in the kitchen to show just how cross he was with me – a toddlers' habit that simply wouldn't work in the adult world – but I would just pretend that he wasn't there until he decided for himself that it was time to calm down.

But the anger triggered by my son's grief weighed heavily on me as a parent and I grew increasingly conflicted in my response to his moods. On the one hand it caused me great pain to see him so obviously affected by his loss. But on the other I was also suffering and grief had left me feeling an undercurrent of fury, too, so it was hard – and perhaps it always will be – not to feel even further antagonised by his intense and increasingly frequent episodes.

And, so, as we had earlier in the year, when Jackson's anger was directed towards any passing female, we retreated once again. I turned down invitations to other children's birthday parties because I suspected they would stress him out. For his birthday, I invited just two of his closest friends round to our house. I suppose I knew that if my behaviour had been affecting his so much, then I needed a little less stress in my life, too. And there are few things more stress-inducing than holding a party for a large group of three-year-olds.

I don't kid myself that behavioural issues in bereaved children ever really end, especially when their problems began before they could even properly talk, but we slowly managed to create a slightly more harmonious home. I tried to embrace my son's displays of anger because of something Shelley told me the night the sombre party of widows and widowers and their children arrived at the Grief Encounter retreat.

'He's quite something, you know,' she began. 'When some of the adults in the room seemed too afraid to even introduce themselves, he made his feelings quite clear. "I don't want to be here," he was telling us; "I'm angry about what's happened," was his message; "This is not funny!" he shouted at everyone in the room. No one opened up more than him and that's amazing for a child of his age.'

I had seen his emotional turmoil as nothing but negative; perhaps when a child seems as though they might explode with rage it's hard to see things any other way. But when I talked to others who were less close to the situation, and when I thought things through in a calmer state of mind, it all began to make a lot more sense. I had spent the best part of a year trying to encourage people to open up about their grief, yet I hadn't realised just how open a child could be. His transparency of feeling was almost too hard to bear.

But when it almost got too tough, I forced myself to look at things differently. *How much worse might things eventually be if he bottled up all his feelings from such a young age? What if he* were *taking his anger out on other children at nursery instead of on me at home? Wasn't I a hypocrite if I tried to make him suppress his emotions just because they were sometimes too painful to handle? And wasn't it my job as his parent to love him unconditionally and to support him, regardless of how hard things got?*

Just as one of my blog's readers suggested, Jackson had been using me as his punchbag. His obvious sense of anger had to go somewhere and I began to appreciate that it was mostly directed towards me because he loves me and trusts me to be there for him, no matter what.

This insight wasn't just a wake-up call about my relationship with my son, but also my relationship with my parents. Jackson and I had been behaving in exactly the same way, passing on the worst of ourselves to those who loved us most. In his case, me – his only surviving parent. In my case, my mum and dad.

When I started to understand that my behaviour towards my own parents since Desreen's death often mirrored that of my two-year-old son's towards me, I knew that something wasn't right. It was time to take the painful lessons I had learned as the father of a grieving toddler in order to try to become a less painful son to my parents. They had been incredibly supportive since Desreen was killed but I was aware that over the months they had frequently got the worst of me in return. Perhaps it was because I spent more condensed amounts of time with them than most, hence they saw the many mood changes I could experience over the course of just two or three days. I could often wake up in quite a buoyant mood and be in foul temper by the time I'd finished my breakfast. And being so close to my parents made me feel like I shouldn't have to hide or mask how I truly felt.

I knew that I'd been using my parents as my occasional emotional punchbag for nearly a year but being snappy and bad-tempered towards them served no other purpose than to make me feel worse than I already did. I decided to explain exactly how I was feeling to them. I wanted them understand that what grief had done to my behaviour and personality was no reflection of the love I felt for them. And as I began to talk more freely with my parents, Jackson began to do the same.

'Is Mummy in that cloud there?' he asked as he held out his arms for me to pick him up in the park near our house one day in late September. By this time, at least in Jackson's mind, Mummy was in the sky. It's what most people tell children when someone dies, and allowing him to be in the care of others meant that his understanding of where Desreen had gone was influenced by more people than just me. It was something I grew increasing comfortable with, because at least it allowed him to feel some sort of presence, however distant.

'Did Mummy bang her head, Daddy?' he continued.

'Yes she did, Jackson, but she banged everything else too,' I explained softly. 'Remember I told you that she was hit by a car and that we must be very careful when we're by the road?'

'Don't worry, Daddy!' he squealed enthusiastically. 'I'll make it better.'

Although I felt sadness in my heart, a smile came to my lips. In that brief moment in the park as we looked up to the sky and talked about death, I relearned a valuable lesson about family life, one that my grandma and I had talked about as she lay dying. Perhaps it doesn't matter how old you are or which branch you sit on in your family tree, when you love one another you just want to make things right.

'Jackson,' I began, 'you know that Mummy can't talk to you anymore because she's gone and she can't ever come back?' He nodded. 'But that doesn't mean that you can't talk to her,' I told him. 'So if you ever want to speak to Mummy then just do it. She won't be able to answer back but that doesn't necessarily mean she's not listening.'

PAPER ANNIVERSARIES

'The firsts are the worst.' I heard this comment so many times from so many people who had also lost their wife, husband or partner. They were referring to all the significant calendar dates that they had spent without their loved one in the first year after their death. I suppose in some ways I may have been lucky that I had nine months' grace until all the dates that meant something to me rolled around. But that also meant I had more time to dread the potential agony of facing all of my 'firsts' in a concentrated block of eleven weeks: our wedding anniversary on 6 August, my thirty-fourth birthday on the 12th, what would have been Desreen's thirty-fourth birthday on 4 October and then Jackson's third birthday on the 17th. All those so-called milestones would have to be faced before even considering how terrible the first anniversary of my wife's death was likely to feel on 10 November.

I have learned that dread is an interesting emotional state. By its very nature, dread means that whatever you're facing comes with some degree of warning, unlike shock, which comes without any prior notification. Shock is instantaneous and reactive. Dread, on the other hand, is gradual and leaves very little room for surprise. Dread is dreadful but it's not shocking.

Unlike the shock of my wife's death, the dread I felt for the 'firsts' that lay ahead gave me time to prepare for what was to come. And the calendar dates themselves were never the worst days for me; it was the anticipation of them that hurt the most. *How could Desreen be dead before our second wedding anniversary? How could I be turning thirty-four without her? How was it going to feel to know that she would always be younger than me even though our birthdays were only a few weeks apart? What was it going to be like not to celebrate her birthday with her for the first time in eight years? What I would I feel like when I saw my son blowing out the candles on his cake and happily unwrapping gifts that his mummy didn't get the chance to buy?* I tortured myself for weeks with all of the questions competing for space in my head.

Anticipating the dates was agonising but now I think it might have been part of a process of overcoming my shock. When time, which had lost its meaning to me since my wife's death, became more relevant to me through dates that touched my heart, my brain gradually began to tell me that what had happened really had happened. The birthdays and anniversaries individually chipped away at a layer of subconscious denial, which I think, to some degree, had protected me from the depth of pain that came through both the dread and eventual event of my 'firsts'.

I was looking towards the dates in expectation of the pain but also in order to plan how to either face or distract myself from them. The first decision I made was that I had to mark at least some of the occasions with a sense of celebration. Few people toast their wedding anniversaries with anyone other than their husband or wife and so I immediately found myself at a loss. Just a year before we spent the most spectacular day together at the Olympic Village in east London. We had lunch in Soho, dinner in Fitzrovia and then we rolled home to play with our little boy who was having fun being looked after by his Uncle Anthony. What was I to do on my wedding anniversary without my wife? How would I cope spending that day alone and dealing with the idea of ageing beyond my wife's limits within the space of a week?

I found the answer in my best men. I jokingly invited them to accompany me on my 'second honeymoon' back to the place Desreen and I had gone on our first – Ibiza. With my birthday just around the corner – which didn't make me feel that I was getting older, so much as it made me feel how young I was to be already widowed – I felt the need to try to act my age. Grief had made me feel old beyond my years and I wanted to at least try to have some fun again. After Jackson's christening, he and I stayed at Bev and Kelson's house for a week and then he stayed on for four more days as I went away with my friends.

Although I was in desperate need of a break, the thought of leaving him plagued me. Since my resignation from work we had spent so much of our time together that even hours apart were filled with guilt and sadness. It didn't matter if I was filling that time with mundane things or mandatory legal procedures, I felt a constant sense of shame in being separated from him for even the shortest amounts of time.

Leaving him for several days was somehow a different matter entirely. Judging by the way Jackson talked about his mother nine months after her death, I'm convinced that toddlers have a limited grasp on the passage of time. Even if they do understand it to some extent, I'm pretty positive they don't care. And why would they when other people manage their diaries? Being a parent to a preschooler is akin to being a PA. Nonetheless, I wanted Jackson to realise that I hadn't disappeared forever, too, and so I told him every day for a week that I was going away for a few days.

'Jackson, Daddy's going on holiday for a few days next week with Uncle Lee and Uncle Woody. Okay?' I said the first time.

'And me?' he asked. I feared this was going to be even more difficult than I'd anticipated.

'No, not this time, you're staying with Nanny and Granddad.'

'No, silly, I'm coming too.'

I'll try again tomorrow, I thought.

By the time the day came around to leave, he was practically kicking me out the door.

'I'm going now, darling. I'll see you in a few days,' I told him.

'I'm not coming. I'm staying here with Nanny and Granddad. Bye Daddy,' he said with a kiss.

He made it easier on me than I had feared but that didn't stop me from crying all the way from Havant to London on a train almost exclusively filled with mums and children enjoying the summer holidays together. When I met with my friends at the other end, though, they soon made me smile. Woody said something stupid about me having been styled by Gok Wan just because I'd had a haircut and bought some new trainers; Lee hit back with a retort about Woody's new boat shoes and Woody's brother, Anthony, made up a daft song about them on the spot. I could tell straight away that it was going to be the kind of juvenile fun I had hoped for.

The four of us had been to Ibiza together two summers before for my stag weekend, along with ten or so other friends and relatives. This time was different. I don't remember the stag weekend involving any quiet moments of reflection; in fact I don't remember it involving any quiet moments at all. We certainly didn't have any conversations about death. But since that trip, Woody and Anthony's mum had died of cancer, a car had killed my wife and as Lee's dad had died three-and-a-half years earlier, none of us felt uncomfortable or morose discussing loss.

The first two days involved a lot of sunshine, alcohol, conversations, laughter and house music and then my wedding anniversary itself came round on day three. I was the first to wake that morning. As the others slept off their hangovers I crept out of the apartment and sat by the pool overlooking the horizon. I thought about the moment the day before when the four of us had taken a walk down the beach. Anthony and I were having a chat about Jackson when I looked up and saw a woman strolling along the shore with her teenage son. They looked casually contented – a look that I imagine I used to radiate when I took happiness for granted. I felt my chest ache as I thought about the close relationship that I, at thirty-three, still had with my mum and then about how much my son would miss out on that kind of relationship with Desreen. I sat alone for a while and listened to a couple of songs that were played at our wedding and then at my wife's funeral: 'No One' by Alicia Keys and 'Finally' by Kings of Tomorrow. I don't remember crying at all, I just stared out at the sea and felt empty, deflated and lonely.

When the lads woke up they joined me at the pool. They each gave me a hug and then Lee held back and said something that made me smile. 'Happy anniversary, mate.' He was the only person who said that to me that day. Lots of people sent me messages to say that they were thinking about me, but no one else wished me a happy anniversary. I thought about it for ages after and realised that it took real balls to say it; I might have responded with something like '*What the fuck's happy about it?*' But he knows me better than that. He knows how happy I was to marry Desreen, what an incredible time we had that day, how much we had planned for our future together, and that I would do it all over again even if I were able to foresee our eventual fate. I was devastated that I was spending my second anniversary with my best men and without my bride, but I was happy that, for the rest of my life, I would have a special date when I could remember how proud I was to have married the woman I love.

That night the four of us went for dinner at a restaurant that Desreen loved. I didn't want to turn the whole night into a sad exchange but there was a question that I needed to ask them. I wanted to know how long it took for people around them to stop talking or asking about their loss. To my surprise they all gave the same response; about a year was just enough for most people to imagine that my friends should have been something like fine. But it was no surprise to me that none of them really were. Like me, they had just got more used to their loved ones being gone, and better at hiding the pain their loss had caused.

Flying home the next morning, I cried all the tears that I hadn't realised I'd held inside for the past four days. Being on a plane without Desreen anxiously squeezing my arm, blubbing hysterically or throwing up into a little paper bag through fear of flying made me feel her absence even more than usual. By now I just wanted to be back with Jackson. I knew he would help bring me back down to earth; I just hadn't banked on him doing it quite so abruptly.

'Daddy!' he squealed as I walked into our house. 'I done a poo!' he continued before I'd even had chance to say hello. And he really had – it was quite something in fact. But somehow it was also the nicest welcome home I had ever received. We were back together and I'd missed him so much – nappies and all.

It was my birthday a few days later and I was pretty clear about what I wanted to do: nothing. Since meeting Desreen, birthdays had always been about the two of us spending time together. We would generally take the day off work, go for lunch, talk, drink and have fun. But she seemed to have taken all my fun with her when she died and I felt I had little to celebrate. Turning thirty-four just made me worry about turning thirty-five and then thirty-six and then, eventually, forty, and seeing myself growing older than my wife could ever be.

Jackson and I had a quiet day and then went for pizza at Marianne and Olly's house. She was just about to return to work after maternity leave but had reduced her working week from five days to four. She was going to take Mondays off and suggested that Jackson and I should go for dinner as often as possible on her day off. She and I could pick up the kids early from nursery, have a play and a bite to eat and then bathe them at their house so that Jackson was all ready for bed by the time Olly drove us home. I see how much their love for Desreen carries on in how much they still care for her husband and son.

As 'firsts' go, I don't suppose they were too bad. But it was Desreen's birthday that I was really dreading. Somehow the anniversary of the day she was born made the fact of her death feel even more pronounced. Desreen loved her birthday. One of the many things that makes me so exceptionally sad about her dying at thirty-three is that she spent so much time talking about what she wanted to do for her fortieth. There was no doubt in her mind that we would be flying high financially by then. She knew what handbag she wanted me to buy and what jewellery she expected gift-wrapped, and she had plans for both the holiday and the party she expected to be thrown. As her husband, the wonderful thing was that she was impossible to disappoint because she took things into her own hands: invites to friends months in advance; her birthday outfit (or outfits) planned and purchased; and links to all of the gifts she wanted emailed straight to my inbox.

As the day crept closer, I realised that I really wanted to mark the occasion somehow. The trouble was that I equally wanted to lock myself away and cry alone in a dark room. The conflict of grief revealed its ugly head once again. Even up until the day before the gathering I eventually arranged I would have done almost anything I could to call it off. But I understood that it had become just as important to others as it must have been to me when I first had the idea. A large number of people had only seen Jackson and me once since Desreen died – at her funeral – and some hadn't seen us at all. For many, the two of us were all they had left of the girl they loved. Desreen's birthday gave everyone the opportunity to get together in one place, on one occasion and before the first anniversary of her death. I suspected that any so-called progress that I'd made up until that time would probably go into reverse as 10 November came back around.

Later I noticed a pattern in how I feel about significant calendar dates since Desreen's death. If it's Jackson's day or my day it's not so bad; if it's Desreen's, it's horrendous. Father's Day was nice, my birthday was okay and it turned out to be a joy to see Jackson happy on his. Mother's Day and Desreen's birthday were awful, as were the days leading up to both. I put this down to the fact that days dedicated to the living make me grateful that they are still alive. Those that focus on the dead just seem to accentuate their death.

During the month of September I put myself back through the detox that Desreen and I had undertaken the year before. Every inch of my being felt terrible. I had been eating all the wrong things, drinking too often and I wasn't sleeping enough. As a result I never seemed to have the energy to exercise and not training made my insomnia worse still. So out went the wheat, gluten, dairy, alcohol, caffeine and refined sugars once again and in came the personal trainer, hot yoga and a diet that made it almost impossible to socialise for a month.

I felt the closest thing to great that I'd felt in ten months. Taking the pressure off my system lightened the heaviness in my head. Friends remarked on the positivity they could hear in my voice and I found that it became easier to live with myself. I was less tortured, less controlled by grief and more inclined to focus on the good things that life might still have in store.

But I knew it couldn't last uninterrupted forever. As the countdown to Desreen's birthday ticked away I regressed. In the week before 4 October my mood grew dark again: when I got into bed at night, I couldn't stop thinking about the crash; I pictured Desreen dead and I couldn't sleep without chemical assistance; I wanted to be alone and I felt my energy fading. Having thrown myself into a fitness regime that had made me feel so good for weeks, I suddenly felt the need to rest. I realised for the first time in my life how much more exhausting emotional pressures can be for the body than physical exertion. The mental anticipation of being without my wife on her own birthday sapped me of any drive to do anything. Sometimes I would crawl into my bed in the afternoon, fall asleep immediately and not wake for an hour or two. I began to suspect I was going through a period of depression.

I struggled to find a way to make Jackson understand that it was a special day for his mummy but that she wouldn't be around to celebrate. So, for the first time, I more or less let an occasion pass by unmentioned to him. *Next year,* I told myself, *it's just too soon to start making cakes for someone whose candle has already blown out.*

The night before her birthday I went out for dinner with the Spice Girls and Lee, 'Sporty' Caroline's fiancé. Almost a year on and still none of us could get used to the space left empty at the table after Desreen's death. On her birthday itself I went for lunch with Jackson and my in-laws. It felt only fitting that I should spend time with the people who had given her life and also helped keep mine on track after her death. Afterwards I met Olly in the pub for a few drinks before calling time and having an early night.

The next day I'd arranged for dozens of friends and family members to meet in a pub near to our home. By this time it was something I was dreading rather than looking forward to. This was different from those pre-event jitters people get before their own birthday parties. I wasn't worried about who came and who didn't; popularity contests were now way down my list of concerns. But I felt that I was on show, that I would have to go over things that I'd gone over a thousand times before and that, worst of all, I was likely to fall into the grief trap of trying to end all of my conversations positively lest I appeared broken, miserable or just a total bore. 'But at least we've had nice weather this summer,' I might say, or 'But we should be thankful that we have a roof over our heads.' Sometimes it wasn't the company of others I needed to avoid, rather the sound of my own voice in company. Often, when I blurt out some vacuous platitude, as much to myself as to others, all I really want to say is '*I'm totally fucked off, I can't believe that this fucking bullshit has happened to my wife and I can't fucking believe how bad it's going to make me feel for the rest of my fucking life.*' For some reason I never say it though. The only time I ever really remember speaking that way was the night I spent with Lee and Woody on the first anniversary of Woody's mum's death – just five weeks after Desreen was killed – and I remember hating the sound of my own voice.

The day after Desreen's birthday gathering I woke up feeling worse than I did the day before – hungover and upset. It had overwhelmed me. The pressure of trying to speak to everyone and make sure Jackson was comfortable in so much company – both familiar and less so – was too much to cope with. I was glad I'd marked the occasion and I suspect I'll do it again, but I felt bad that I got so little time to talk to most of the people who had taken the time to come. Perhaps, also, the occasion had reminded me of how I had reacted to Desreen's death; how I often spent more energy worrying about other people's feelings than I did my own. I had wanted to arrange something public but what mattered to me most was private.

I felt I wanted to do something intimate and lasting to mark both Desreen's and Jackson's birthdays but I didn't know what. It's a real challenge to buy a gift for someone who's already dead and it's almost as hard to find something fitting for a child's third birthday that won't be discarded by their fourth. But after giving it a lot of consideration I thought of something that would enable me to do both.

When Desreen and I got married she didn't have a wedding ring as such. She took off her engagement ring and had the vicar bless that along with the ring she'd had made for me for my thirtieth birthday. The setting of her ring was such that it was tricky to find a wedding band that worked with it. She told me that it was being married to me that mattered to her most, not decorating herself with another piece of jewellery. In her typical style her position on this didn't last too long, though. As her thirty-third birthday approached she reminded herself that her left hand wasn't as fully adorned as it might be. And not long after, she reminded me. In the end she found a ring she loved in Liberty – a simple thin white gold band encrusted with tiny white diamonds. She wore it for just five weeks before she died. Having bought it gift-wrapped in a stylish gold and black box from a friendly sales assistant just a month earlier, it was handed back to me in a clear plastic bag by a grave police officer the night she was killed. I slipped it onto my little finger next to my wedding band where it remains to this day.

Desreen was a smart woman. She opted for something simple that she wore on the middle finger of her left hand not just because nothing she liked worked with her engagement ring, but also because the ring she eventually found was designed to be stacked with others by the same designer. This ring was the start of a fledgling collection, for which she fully intended me to pick up the tab. So as I wondered what birthday gestures I could make in a nod to my late wife's past and my son's future, I went back to Liberty and fulfilled her expectations. I bought exactly the same ring in the same size but this time with black diamonds instead of white. And when the time comes to tell my son what I bought his mum for the thirty-fourth birthday she never had, the gift will be for him. I'll keep her white wedding band and he'll have an exact match in black – gifts both to and from Desreen, which Jackson and I can treasure for the rest of our lives.

Although I had made myself a promise not to attempt to make life perfect for Jackson earlier on in the year, I did want to make a special effort on his birthday, just not through grand gestures, which don't much interest toddlers. 'You like to play trains?' are the words Jackson uses most often, so on his birthday my only answer would be *yes*. I listened carefully for weeks to ensure that I could supplement his already enormous collection with the missing characters he appeared to pine for most. I made cakes, blew up balloons and wrapped his presents the night before, and when he awoke on his birthday he filled his face with birthday treats and reached dizzy new heights of locomotive bliss. We played and he was happy.

He taught me something that day. He made me understand that when a child is content they are best left to enjoy the moment rather than being pushed into doing things that only serve to make adults feel better about themselves. I had it all planned out: we would wake up and open presents, then hastily make a dash to visit the dinosaur sculptures at Crystal Palace Park and end the day with more cake and his favourite dinner. But as I watched him play and asked him when he would like to leave, he said he didn't want to go. He just wanted to play with his trains. When I asked him the day before what he wanted for his birthday dinner his answer was 'chicken and rice'. And the day before that when I mentioned it was his birthday in two days, he told me that he'd already had it the day before. His nursery must have put on a show for my little boy, and he was fulfilled. He reminded me that showering a child with material things and overblown gestures wasn't what mattered at all if that child would rather just have his daddy there to play.

I felt so touched by his generosity of spirit. In the end all he wanted to do was take a walk to the park at the end of our road with a few balloons tied to a ribbon and then take a ride back home on my shoulders. He was a joy and seemed unaffected by the fact that I was a mess that day. I realised I had been building up the dread for all of my 'firsts' and this would be my last until the first anniversary of Desreen's death on 10 November.

Any energy that I had mustered for Jackson's birthday was spent. So much so that at one point I collapsed on my bed and had to sleep off the emotional turmoil that the day had brought. This was becoming increasingly common and of growing concern to me. Perhaps I would have to face up to the idea that I was depressed. *After all*, I thought, *wouldn't it be weirder if I weren't?* I chose not to speak to my doctor about it. I would keep an eye on myself and explain my feelings to my friends and family so that they could keep an eye on me too, but it felt more fleeting than it did chronic.

If I could feel good for just one day out of the year after Desreen's death, Jackson's birthday probably should have been it. In find grief has a tendency to permit just a temporary sense of buoyancy before eventually bringing you plummeting back to earth – a bit like a birthday balloon, you could say. And it was a birthday balloon that brought me crashing back down. In fact it was two. Two innocent looking birthday balloons reinforced the lesson I had learned from Desreen's sudden death: that life's harmony can be shattered in an instant under the most unexpected of circumstances. Thankfully, the fallout this time was distressing but nowhere near as tragic.

Lee, Olive and Albie sent Jackson a beautiful transparent balloon, filled with helium and colourful strips of tissue paper and attached to a tail made from ribbons and multicoloured paper sequins. As we opened the box it was delivered in, it gently floated around our kitchen and brought with it a touch of our friends' love. Just a few minutes later, as Jackson and I made our way from the kitchen to the living room, the balloon followed silently.

We were playing with trains in one corner of the room when we heard an almighty crash right behind us in another. The balloon had breezed into the middle of the ceiling, knocking the lampshade from its fixture, which in turn sent the light bulb crashing and smashing to the ground. There was glass everywhere. I swept Jackson up, took him out of the room and reached for his slippers to keep his feet safe, just in case. Typically he was entirely unfazed and I could hardly wait to tell my friends about the damage their once harmless gift had caused since its arrival in our home. I suppose I thought it was quite funny at the time.

The next day, Lee turned up at our front door. It was a flying visit but not without drama. My son, who adores Lee, grew a little frenzied. I had decorated the house for the small gathering I had organised for later in the day with yet more balloons, and as Jackson rushed excitedly round the room he tripped over one and landed on his chin. We weren't sure what had happened at first but there was a loud thud and a stream of blood. It turned out that his razor-sharp front teeth had bitten into his tongue, creating what looked like a vampire attack to the mouth.

It was beyond stressful: he was covered in blood, I was covered in blood, the off-white kitchen floor tiles were covered in blood and the blood gushing from his tongue showed no sign of abating. He had been eating rice cakes too, so when he opened his mouth to show me it looked as though it was filled with smashed-up bits of teeth. And I couldn't actually see his teeth for the blood to know if they were still intact. He had never tasted blood before so he was spitting with a combination of disgust, distaste and rage.

My memory of the accident lasted much longer than his injury. Five minutes after he'd swallowed down a dose of Nurofen, he enthusiastically devoured a fairy cake and a tongue-cooling ice cream, which suggested he was going to be okay. By the next day, save the painful looking hole in his tongue, you wouldn't even have known it had happened. When I asked him to open up his mouth so that I could inspect the damage again, he looked at me like I was mad. He had all but forgotten both the incident that left him wounded and the other that might have done if we hadn't been in the same room together. But neither balloon episode had left my mind for a moment because of the parallels that each made me draw: beauty and light brought crashing down; happiness one moment followed by pain the next; wrong time, wrong place; a life once buoyant so suddenly deflated.

BIRTHDAY BOY

Jackson, my boy, as you're three today,
There are two or three things that I'd like say.
There are one or two things you might never have known,
And there are some things I'll remind you of when you are grown.
One lovely thing that I'd first like to say,
Is that we found out you were coming on Valentine's Day.
We waited a long time for you to come,
Then finally you were there in your mummy's tum.
And you slept best in there during the day,
When you'd never wriggle nor ever play.
At night, however, your limbs grew twitchy,
You'd stop Mummy sleeping and that made her witchy.
So she ate strange things to ease her troubles,
Like fistfuls of soap and Fairy Liquid bubbles.
Did you know you like fish fingers because of your mummy?
She ate millions of them when you were in her tummy.
Did you also know she nearly called you Sonny?
Or that we named you Jackson after my mummy's mummy?
It was Great-Grandma's last name when she was a baby,
Do you remember her, Jackson? She was a lovely lady.
And there's still so much that I'd like to say,
About my boy born on a Sunday.
And that's the day that Daddy came too,
But I don't think I held out as long as you.
You took four days and Daddy grew drowsy,
I shouldn't have told Mummy though, she thought that was lousy.
You were perfect that day, your skin soft as peaches,
You wouldn't come naturally but that spared your features.

And the emergency delivery room was so chilly,
That Mummy didn't even notice your willy.
You had big brown eyes and hair that looked styled,
And everyone said that you'd drive the girls wild.
You drove our hearts crazy, that's for sure,
You changed our lives forever more.
And the next two years were our happiest ever,
And I won't forget them, son, I promise I'll never.
And I want you to know more about Mummy and you:
Little things like your trip to the zoo,
Small things like how you'd share a bath,
And all the things she did to make you laugh.
No one made you laugh more than she,
And everything she did was for you and for me.
And you made her the happiest that she'd ever been,
The most devoted mummy that I'd ever seen.
And it's a small thing, I know, but your mummy cried,
At something you did the day that she died.
You sat on our bed and sang Happy Birthday at last,
You'd learned the words after her birthday had passed.
And the pride in her eyes was something to treasure,
And the love in her heart for you beyond measure.
And her love and pride for you were her last words spoken,
And her love and pride for you can never be broken.
And I'd like to say thank you for helping me through,
And I want you to know how much I love you.

ONE YEAR

Living through a year's worth of anniversaries and birthdays without Desreen by my side left me feeling, in some ways, unexpectedly indifferent towards the first anniversary of her death. I had realised that preempting all of our significant dates with dread and fear actually served to prepare me for them once they came around. Every date that meant something to me before Desreen died only hurt so much because it had once made me so happy.

10 November, on the other hand, held no happy memories. That date was of no consequence before she was killed and it surprised me that it felt rather meaningless and irrelevant a year after the event. The fact that 365 days had passed since her death was of no more significance to me than if she had died 364 or 366 days before; it neither made her any more dead nor me feel any more alive than the day before or the day after. If I were to quantify the year by depth of feeling rather than the passage of time, then the twelve months that followed Desreen's death would have been the longest (or perhaps deepest) I had ever lived. And yet, in the terms I previously used to gauge time, it felt no longer than six weeks since she died. Perhaps the fact that the season that took my wife had now returned made me forget the other three that had passed in between. But whether dread and fear made the day easier to bear than I expected was

of little consequence – everything's relative, after all, and getting there still felt awful.

Fittingly, the first anniversary of her death fell on Remembrance Sunday, which meant that people would inevitably take a moment out of their day to remember the dead. But for me it was more than just a day. I now know that every day is a day of remembrance: of the good times we spent together, of the many wonderful gifts my wife gave me including our son, of the things we hoped to achieve together, of the love we shared, of the night she was killed, of going to sleep every night since in a half-empty bed, of being the person I once was. Whatever the day, I found myself considering how grief felt on its first anniversary – how it felt to me. And so I captured my feelings in the same format I had immediately after Desreen died and then again six months later.

ONE YEAR

It feels different. Different because the shock has worn off and reality is slowly appearing in its place. Different because in some ways it's getting easier and in others it's getting harder.

It feels cyclical. Cyclical because the return of the season that took my wife has brought back many of the feelings I felt immediately after her death. Cyclical because as I look towards the winter ahead my heart sinks at the repeated sorrow it may bring.

It feels disappointing. Disappointing because so many of the things we had planned will never transpire. Disappointing because the house my son and I now live in doesn't feel like a home. Disappointing because if things had gone to plan we would have had a second child on the way by now. Disappointing because I know my wife would have had a wonderful life. Disappointing because I know we would have had a wonderful life together. Disappointing because my son will have to miss out on sharing that wonderful life with her.

It feels imprisoning. Imprisoning because I can never escape grief's grasp. Imprisoning because it will never let me fully feel any other emotion without trying to overshadow it with sorrow and sadness.

It feels schizophrenic. Schizophrenic because one moment I'll convince myself that I'm happy, then the next I'll feel as low as I've ever felt.

It feels volatile. Volatile because I think grief has made me a softer, kinder and less fiery person, but then something stupid like not being able to locate a particular tube station on the London Underground map can make me feel as if I'm going to explode with rage.

It feels as if I have an open wound. An open wound because society would have me believe that I would get back to normal twelve months after Desreen's death but I feel none of the closure that I was promised. An open wound because I've realised that, regardless of the pain it will cause, I would rather open up my heart to the love I still feel for my wife than close if off for the sake of a resolution that I do not seek.

It feels enduring. Enduring because I've come to terms with the fact that grief will live with me for life. Enduring because I've realised that I'm not in battle with it, I'm just living with a war wound that will never fully heal.

It feels inconclusive. Inconclusive because I've realised that grief doesn't come with an off switch.

It feels like pressure. Pressure because I can feel people willing me to recover when I can't. Pressure because the so-called milestone of a year suggests that I should feel better than I actually do. Pressure because I have a child who still deserves to enjoy Christmas when I don't think I want to face it. Pressure because I know that I'm so damn hard on myself.

It feels like carrying on. Carrying on and not moving on because 'moving on' comes with a barrage of connotations that speak more to the pressures of what people may expect from a young widower than what I want for myself: to stop grieving, to stop being outwardly upset, to find someone else, to do what some might call 'getting on with your life'.

It feels sensorial. Sensorial because when I hear fireworks I'm transported back to the time when Desreeen died. Sensorial because sirens have the same effect. Sensorial because the touch of my son's hair on my face reminds me of my wife. Sensorial because seeing happy couples together can make me sad. Sensorial because seeing unhappy couples together can make me mad.

It feels like boredom. Boredom because I knew how it felt to have a fun life. Boredom because my ability to have pure unadulterated fun has gone. Boredom because I'd met the person who made me laugh the most and life's just not as exciting or funny without her.

It feels like loneliness. Loneliness because no matter how much I fill my days with the company of family and friends I always go to sleep on my own. Loneliness because I know what it felt like to have a wife who was always there for me and now she's not. Loneliness because the one person who would always be there to make me smile when I'm down can't be there at all.

It feels like gratitude. Gratitude because of the incredible times we spent together. Gratitude for the memories we made. Gratitude for the son my wife gave me. Gratitude for the fact that I still have my life and he still has his.

It feels like sorrow. Sorrow for Jackson that he won't have his mummy there to support him through life. Sorrow that, of all of us, he spent the least time with her. Sorrow for Desreen's friends and family who miss her so much. Sorrow for myself that she's gone.

It feels like hope. Hope because the intensity of the shock and pain has worn off. Hope because I've realised that I want to try to live a full life. Hope because I understand that may still be possible even though everything has changed. Hope because I'm not as scared about the future as I was a year ago. Hope because I understand that feeling some sense of happiness again in the future must start with wanting to, which I do.

It feels like despair. Despair because sometimes it feels like there's no hope. Despair because some days I don't even feel fully alive. Despair because I can't ever get back what I once had.

It feels motivating. Motivating because wanting to honour Desreen's memory gives me drive. Motivating because wanting to do right by my son gives me energy to succeed. Motivating because I feel compelled to do something good with my life. Motivating because I've decided to let myself become my own boss when it comes to the plan for the rest of my life. Motivating because I realise that if that plan takes another year, or even two or three, then that's fine because I know that putting more pressure on myself just makes me feel worse than I already do.

It feels demotivating. Demotivating because it's hard to feel good about myself no matter what I do. Demotivating because I feel no sense of achievement from any activities I complete.

It feels rebellious. Rebellious because I care so much less than I once did about what people think of me. Rebellious because I feel entitled to do what I want and not what people expect of me. Rebellious because I'm willing to reject conventions and do what I believe is right for my son and me. Rebellious because I'm going to be the one who decides whether my life has been a success, and that decision will be based on emotional fulfilment and not on money or material trappings.

It feels conflicting. Conflicting because so many of my feelings are contradictory. Conflicting because I can be happy and sad at the same time. Conflicting because I want to live a good life again but I know that I'm wasting my time trying to live the life I had before.

It feels like love. Love because otherwise I couldn't feel this bad now that she's gone. Love because I feel an ache in my chest when I think about her at night. Love because I still want to do nice things for my wife even though she's no longer here. Love because I feel no less for her than I did when she was still alive.

And it feels unreal. Unreal because it won't quite sink in. Unreal because sometimes I still expect her to walk through the door. Unreal because I can't believe she never will. Unreal because I can't bring myself to accept that this is the end.

BIG BOY

Dear Dad,

I know you hate it that I already call you *Dad* but I'm three now and that means I'm a big boy. When I first caught myself doing it, just after my third birthday, it occurred to me that Mummy will always be *Mummy*. I'll never know her as anything else because I never got the chance. She won't suddenly become *Mum* because the me who knew her will always be two years old. *Mummy* will never fade into the past because *Mum* was never part of my present.

And that's a bit like love. Now, I might not have started school yet – and even when I do they'll probably teach me nothing about grammar – but my *love* for Mummy can't suddenly become *loved*, because I never stopped loving her. If I've got this right, Dad, *loved* is the past tense of love and so *loved* would suggest that my love is in the past. But I still love my mummy. She might have passed but my love for her is still present and I can tell yours is too by the sadness in your eyes now that she's gone.

And I worry about your sadness, Dad. I know that you try to hide it sometimes, but you've started to look a bit like the bread that we feed to the ducks in the park. You tell me not to eat it because it's not as happy as it used to be and it's got grey hair like you. Does that mean that you're not happy anymore? Have you gone off too, Dad? I do hope that you're not past your best. What will I do if we have to throw you into the pond next? Now that Mummy's gone I need you more than ever. I don't want to lose you too.

So I've decided that we need a plan to stop you going off and I've got it all worked out. Just hang out with me! I'll try my best to keep you fresh: I'll stop you from getting old and crusty too soon; I'll help make life fun again; I'll share my sweets with you, I'll give you a squeeze when you wake up in the morning and if I ever see anyone try to lay a finger on you, I'll give them hell. I'll give you a bloody hard time too, don't you worry about that, but I'll also love you as much as I know you love me. And I'll do that because I love Mummy so much and if Mummy loved you so much then I love you so much, too.

It's not the same without her, Dad. I miss her more than I even know how to show. I'm confused by why she's gone and I don't really know where she's gone either. I thought you would be so happy when I told you that I was going to go up to the sky to rescue her today, but I don't think you were. I don't know why I can't. Why won't you let me try, Dad? I just want to get her back but you keep telling me that I can't. So if I can't have my mummy back then I want my daddy back instead. It's not raining today, Dad, so let's go out and play. If we're lucky maybe we can find Daddy, too. I'd be so happy to see him again.

I love you, Dad.
Jackson x

ACKNOWLEDGEMENTS

My aim in writing this book was twofold: to create a legacy for my wife on behalf of our son; and to capture raw and live grief, as it happened, in the hope of helping others suffering the pain of loss. I could never have achieved this without the kindness, love and support of my family and friends, old and new.

I would like to thank everyone at Hodder & Stoughton for believing in the potential of this story and for helping me turn the torturous words in my head into a beautiful book that my son can read when the time is right. I am particularly indebted to my editor, Hannah Black, whose gentle but never overly cautious approach helped me find the confidence and courage to tackle elements of my grief that I was often too afraid to confront. More specifically I thank her for helping persuade me to make Desreen's life play such a big part of the story of her death. This wouldn't be half the book I wanted it to be without Hannah's guidance; she deserves so much credit. I'm also very grateful to Helen Coyle for her copyediting skills. She did a wonderful job at helping keep the story on track.

It would be a great disservice to thank Ajda Vucicevic at Luigi Bonomi Associates for being my agent without also acknowledging her as a friend. I made a request to everyone who worked with me on this book that I didn't want to be handled too sensitively; few could have responded to this wish better than she. It's really quite hard to believe that we were able to share quite so many laughs along the way.

The stunning jacket Alice Laurent designed for this book will forever move me. I'm grateful that she shared her talents and turned a fleeting iPhone snap into an extraordinary book cover that now means so much to me.

I owe so much to my mother-in-law, Bev Brooks, for giving up everything to support my son and me. There is little I could have done without her in the aftermath of Desreen's death, not least write a book. Praise and gratitude is also owed to all of my family: my mum and dad for their boundless love, support and patience; to my grandma for wise words, fun times and for being so damn lovely; to my brothers, Mat and Nick, and their families for always being there; to my father-in-law and brother-in-law, Kelson and Anthony, for continuing to treat me as nothing less than a son and a brother; and to everyone else on both sides of mine and Desreen's family for always being there.

Continued thanks and love go out to every single one of our friends too. I'm so fortunate to have met so many wonderfully supportive, loyal, caring and entertaining people throughout the best times of my life. I can't bear to think what it would have been like to face the worst times without them all, either.

Special thanks to: Woody, who couldn't have been any more supportive if he had tried (and who probably wouldn't have been able to had he not had his incredible fiancée Katy behind him); Lee and Olive – it breaks my heart to think of the four of us not being together again, but it also lifts it to know that we will have good times again in future, and that our little lads will bring so much happiness back to our lives; Michael and Vikki (and Dave) for endless love, laughs and friendship, for making me godfather to the very gorgeous Jemima and for giving me a copy of a book that made me approach things differently; Marianne and Olly for unfaltering support and for giving Jackson such a special little friend in Annalise; Dan for giving me the confidence to do what I felt was right; Paul for composing a song that Jackson and I can cherish forever; Mitch for supporting me through work and beyond; all the boys for the weekend away in the Witterings; Lee and Big and Little Woody for Ibiza; and Zac and Laura for picking me up off the floor that night and for never letting go since.

The already incredibly difficult year that I tackle in this book would have been harder still without the support of child bereavement charities including Grief Encounter, Winston's Wish and Child Bereavement UK. A collective thank you for all of the time and advice they have given me since my son lost his mum. Shelley Gilbert and Vicky Baruch from Grief Encounter deserve particular credit for the special attention they have given both Jackson and me. I'm proud to be able to call them friends.

Other charities I would like to commend are Care for the Family for the guidance and inspiration offered to me so soon after my wife was killed, and the WAY Foundation for the incredible support they provide to young widowed people who can find it so hard to know where to turn for help.

I'll forever be humbled by all of the care and affection shown to my son and me through my blog, *Life as a Widower.* I have learned invaluable lessons along the way for which I will be eternally grateful. I have also encountered the most encouraging and compassionate people I could have wished for and it touches me that we have been able to help one another through such difficult times. I have much admiration for all of the guest writers who contributed honest and open stories about how grief has affected their own lives with a shared goal of helping others in mind. I would like to thank them all.

Emma Latchem is thanked for teaching me ways to hear my son through play. She has assisted in his development without even knowing it and I wouldn't want this to go unspoken simply because we have never met. I am also indebted to Rob Savage for his financial guidance, which enabled me to take time out with Jackson when I felt he needed it most.

I thank all the media outlets that helped bring the issue of child bereavement into the spotlight so sensitively: the *Guardian, Sunday Times Style,* the *Sun,* the *Sunday People, This Morning, BBC Breakfast* and countless others who covered our story and supported my blog. Thanks to BritMums too for the vote of confidence shown through the BiBs 2013 blog awards. I am also grateful to all of the people who spread the word and helped my blog reach the people it was designed for.

And, of course, heartfelt love, friendship and gratitude go out to the skirmish of widowers in our own private little fight club. They say that if you build it they will come. Well thank God we did because what once felt impossible was made a little less so because of the empathy, support and honesty we have been able to offer one another. We may be friends from afar but we are friends nonetheless and I'm glad we all found each other.

Finally I want to give my endless love and thanks to Desreen and Jackson. I have found words to be more powerful than I ever knew but none can express quite the depth of the love I have in my heart for my much missed wife and lifesaving son.

APPENDIX

HOW YOU CAN HELP THOSE WIDOWED YOUNG

- things I'd like you to know

Tel: 029 2081 0800
www.careforthefamily.org.uk/wys

Do talk to me – even if you don't know what to say. Knowing you are sorry is a good start.

Don't avoid me – it hurts so much when you cross the road when you see me coming rather than be willing to face me.

Do keep in touch; keep phoning especially as weeks turn into months and years. Be available.

Don't phone and just say *'Let me know if I can help'* and leave it at that.

Do talk about my partner. I love to hear your memories of him/her.

Don't worry about feeling 'awkward' – be normal, yourself, my friend – I am still the same person.

Do think carefully before you speak – I'm feeling vulnerable at the moment and insensitivity could pull me down very low.

Don't come out with platitudes, trite answers or comments. Right now, all I want is to have him/her back.

Do listen – it can be more important than what you say. Sometimes I need to know that I am heard.

Don't say things like – *'You can always marry again, you're still young.'*

Do give practical support. I'm not able to cope with routines at the moment so providing meals, or help at home and with my children is vital.

Don't wait to be asked for help – initially there is so much help I need with just about everything.

Do offer specific help – *'I'll pick the children up on Friday, take them out, give them tea and bring them back at 6.'*

Don't overload me with responsibilities – for a while it will be all I can cope with to get out of bed and get dressed.

Do still talk about everyday things *that matter* as well. I'm still interested in you and what is going on around me, but 'small talk' can seem very trivial.

If you have a faith, **don't** be super-spiritual and feel you have to defend God's case.

Do understand that it will take time for me even to begin to adjust to life as is has to be for me from now on.

Do give me space to be as I am, tears and all. Don't try to discourage my tears and please be willing to cry with me too.

Do be sensitive and aware e.g. Christmas cards – a mention of my partner will let me know that you miss him/her at this time too.

Do remember my children! They can sometimes be neglected as they may not be so willing to talk.

Do invite me out to coffee or lunch – just to change the scene for a while.

Do make allowances for my children's behaviour. It may be very disruptive and difficult. They need lots of patience and love.

Do still invite me to events and parties, but understand if sometimes I feel unable to go or have to leave early.

Do remember that appearances can be deceptive – I may look as if I'm coping okay, but inside I may be falling apart.

Do remember that there is no time limit on grief – it will go on long after others expect. Please walk that road with me.

Do find ways to remember the anniversaries that the family will appreciate – be creative, I appreciate others' ideas.

Don't feel you have to do something – just be there.

Don't ignore the loss, or avoid asking questions about the person who has died.

Don't expect me to be over it – I will never get over it, but I may find a 'new normal' in time.

Don't say '*Be strong*' – it means '*Don't share your pain, keep it to yourself*'.

Don't avoid the issue publicly – in schools, churches, etc.

Don't forget to give time and attention to my children – I may be struggling with my feelings towards them.

Don't tell me that you've been too busy to phone or get in touch. Better to say '*I didn't know what to say.*'

Don't ask me how I am if you only want to hear '*I'm okay thank you.*' Be prepared for the truth.

If you have a faith, **don't** just say '*I'm praying for you.*' Be prepared to be part of the answer by getting involved.

Don't be afraid to show your emotions, cry with me, and tell me how you feel.

Do be ready to listen to all the jumble of emotions I may be feeling without trying to give answers or being judgmental.

Don't judge me for my behaviour, words, actions or attitudes – they will find a proper level in time.

Do be aware that my children may react in ways that seem out of character – they have gone through the worst experience imaginable and may be very frightened and insecure.

Don't try and give me answers – it is unlikely that you will have any that will satisfy me – just allow me to express all my fears, questions and doubts.

Do show sensitivity – ring first – don't just show up at the door. Although sometimes it may be just the break I need – be prepared for me to say that I can't cope with company just now.

Don't measure the way I react and the emotions I express by your own expectations or experience. My grief is unique to me.

Do be aware that there will be times when I don't feel able to talk – but this doesn't mean I won't want to talk at another time.

Don't say that you understand how I feel – whatever your loss it will be different to mine as each grief is individual.

Do let me know that you share my sense of loss and that you miss my partner too. This can take away isolation and be a great support.

Don't think that *'he/she has still got many years of life ahead of him/her'*. The life I was living and planning for is over. I just need to adjust to that first before thinking about the future.

Do encourage me to be kind to myself and not to push myself to meet other people's expectations of how I should be.

Don't try to find something positive in my partner's death.

Do help with planning and suggestions for the funeral – you could spend months thinking of a wedding and just a few days for a funeral. The details are very important.

Don't think that death puts a ban on laughter. Remembering and enjoying the good times we had together is important and helps me to heal.

Ben's blog can be found at www.lifeasawidower.com, he tweets from @lifeasawidower and can be found on Facebook at www.facebook.com/lifeasawidower

An invitation from the publisher

Join us at www.hodder.co.uk, or follow us on Twitter @hodderbooks to be a part of our community of people who love the very best in books and reading.

Whether you want to discover more about a book or an author, watch trailers and interviews, have the chance to win early limited editions, or simply browse our expert readers' selection of the very best books, we think you'll find what you're looking for.

And if you don't, that's the place to tell us what's missing.

We love what we do, and we'd love you to be a part of it.

www.hodder.co.uk

@hodderbooks

HodderBooks

HodderBooks